REVIEWS

Manijeh's teachings have helped increase further insight and accountability with myself, in habits/actions regarding our planet, as well as my professional practice. I have increasingly become a better clinician for it. Her Life Optimization method and approach exceed the training and education we've received to become therapists. It incorporates more depth into treatment, regardless of diagnosis. It helps achieve a healthy, happy lifestyle rather than just coping strategies/tools.

— Mary Aroyan, Psychotherapist

*   *   *

Dr. Manijeh Motaghy's It's Not Easy to Be Human is a compassionate and insightful guide that has profoundly impacted me. Her blend of real stories and research-based wisdom offers not only clarity but actionable tools to navigate the complexities of life with kindness and purpose.

What I found most powerful is how she connects personal growth with systemic and ecological well-being. Her writing is a gentle reminder of our interconnectedness and the importance of showing up with authenticity and care — not just for others but for ourselves.

As if the stories and insights weren't enough, Dr. Motaghy weaves in so much history and research, along with intersectional perspectives, that my curiosity feels stimulated for the foreseeable future. This book also serves as a practical guide worth keeping within arm's reach for those moments when life feels like the descent of a roller coaster — reminding us of the tools we have to stabilize, reflect, and move forward with intention. This book is a gift to the world. I can't recommend it highly enough to anyone seeking deeper fulfillment, clarity, and a path to make meaningful change in his or her life and community.

— Vincent Mc Neeley, global inclusion, AI, innovation, and human rights strategist and speaker

*   *   *

It's Not Easy to Be Human is a guide for modern life, focusing on transforming our human experiences, both positive and negative, into a sustainable and happy life for individuals and the general health of the planet. The practical strategies and insights included here can help anyone examine his or her life and improve his or her well-being.

— Elizabeth Rothman, attorney and adviser in
intellectual property, AI ethics, and tech policies

*   *   *

Manijeh has a rich and distinct background rooted in Buddhist traditions and a solid grasp of organizational psychology (Psy D, Doctor of Psychology), conscious leadership, and training adult ADHD. As a teacher, she has an incredible ability to connect with groups and individuals, fostering meaningful human connections. Her extensive life experiences enrich her teaching, making her insights deeply impactful. The Mindful Life Optimization (MLO) lessons included in this book provide actionable strategies for integrating personal development with broader societal and environmental goals, emphasizing how we can nourish and flourish as a community.

Manijeh is actively involved in various conferences, podcasts, and speaking engagements, striving to share her ambitious and inspiring vision: to bring MLO to more than one billion people worldwide. Her methods promote personal well-being and advocate for planetary health, making her contributions essential in our quest for a more harmonious world. I highly recommend this book for its methodology in transforming inner and outer systems.

— Matthew Law, leader in sustainability,
operational excellence, and change management

IT'S NOT EASY TO BE HUMAN

A Compassionate Journey and Guide to Optimize Human Potential and Achieve Fulfillment, Systemic, and Ecological Well-Being.

DR. MANIJEH MOTAGHY

Organizational Psychologist

UCLA Mindful Teacher

JOIN THE MAKING IT EASY TO BE HUMAN COMMUNITY

Scan to Register Your Book to Meet the Author.
Get Support on Your Transformation Journey.

A HUMAN OPTIMIZATION ONTOLOGY

Published and printed by AHOO Press LLC through sustainable on-demand practices.

ISBN: 979-8-9939287-0-8 (audio)
ISBN: 979-8-9939287-1-5 (sc)
ISBN: 979-8-9939287-2-2 (e)

Library of Congress Control Number: 2026906998

First Published by Balboa Press: 06/30/2025

AHOO Press Edition
AHOO Press Publication Date: 01/26/2026

CONTENT

PART I: FROM LOSING LIFE
INTELLIGENCE TO BECOMING THE HERO

PART II: MINDFUL LIFE OPTIMIZATION (MLO)

- *MLOL 8: Mindful of Systems That Favor Those in Power*
- *MLOL 9: Mindful of Invisible Systems*
- *MLOL 10: Mindful of One-Dimensional Capitalism*
- *MLOL 11: Mindful of Issues with Maintaining Competitive Edge*
- *MLOL 12: Mindful of Consumerism and Circular Anxiety Economy*
- *MLOL 13: Mindfully Abandoning Stress-Producing Activities*
- *MLOL 14: Mindful Solutions to Wicked Problems*
- *MLOL 15: Building Systems as a Force for Good*

- *MLOL 16: Mindful of the Falsehood of Ownership*
- *MLOL 17: Mindfully Flowing to Relieve Death Anxiety*
- *MLOL 18: Mindful of Evolution: Humans Are Not Better Evolved*
- *MLOL 19: Mindfully Transforming Learned Nature Anxieties*
- *MLOL 20: Mindfully Transforming Resource Narcissism and Climate Anxiety*
- *MLOL 21: Mindful of Life Source Intelligence: A Regenerative Generosity*
- *MLOL 22: Mindful of Oneness: The Antidote to Separation and Loneliness Anxiety*

- *MLOL 23: Mindful of the Boundaries and Limitations of Earth's*
- *Resilience*
- *MLOL 24: Mindfully Stewarding Earth Through Conscious Action*
- *MLOL 25: Being Mindful Ancestors*
- *MLOL 26: Mindful Manufacturing: Regenerative Integration Management System (RIMS)*

PART IV: THE THIRD DOMAIN: HUMAN EXPERIENCE, CONDUCT, AND HAPPINESS

I dedicate

the goodness of my life and this book to you, my beloved reader, in the hope that you will apply these lessons and carry forward its message imbued with compassion and urgency.

To our most beloved king, Cyrus the Great, the father of all humanity, whose tales of courage, kindness, generosity, wisdom, compassion, discipline, tireless guidance toward ethical living, and humility have touched me so deeply.

To my teachers and students, without whom I could not have realized the tricks and delusions of this mind to continue to become free from them.

To our ancestors and our future generations. To my grandmother, whose hard-earned inner guidance was my foundation. Tomy mother, whose flesh and growing love lifted me this round of life. To my father, who taught me empathy, logic, love, and culture.

Tomy beloved sons, whose genius, spirit, and unceasing love are the life source of my continuance. To my amazing brother and sisters, their families, and my partners and friends.

And to my niece, Sofia, whose curiosity and adaptability are my hope for humanity.

To every pebble on my path, to the sunshine on our land, to every speck of dust and breath, and to every creature that will ever live.

May these essential lessons increase skillfulness, harmony, and joy for all humanity.

FOREWORD

It's Not Easy to Be Human is the culmination of many years of contemplation and reflection by Manijeh Motaghy. She is someone who has dedicated much time and energy in her life these past years toward her spiritual practice and training. She has also been sharing her experience with people now for many years. This has resulted in her developing the communication skills needed to pass on her experience to others. Manijeh has been coming to our monastery in Northern California regularly now for well over ten years, and she has always impressed me with her sincerity and enthusiasm.

This same spirit of sincerity and enthusiasm infuses this whole book. She has explored how her background knowledge of science and psychology intersects with the traditional teachings and practices of Buddhism. The book tries to use a modern framework of concepts, investigation of systems, and more global awareness in a search into the age-old questions of how to live with freedom from dissatisfaction and to live with happiness as our foundation.

These are worthy topics of exploration, and hopefully, the reader will find attitudes, perspectives, tools, and models of lifestyle that will be relevant and useful. Manijeh's wish for transformation is important to recognize as possible for anyone who puts his or her attention into reflection and training. May the spirit of sincerity and enthusiasm in which Manijeh has written this book allow it to be a source of inspiration for seekers and help to motivate a curiosity about how we can live more skillfully in this world.

All good wishes,
Pasanno Bhikkhu

PREFACE

MY STORY

From the beginning of time, there have come legions of teachers to guide humanity on how to be human. Some have even been worshipped as gods or seen as prophets, and many have been revered as masters. I have been on an ever-curious quest to know the truths of life so that I can live passionately, lovingly, authentically, and happily and fulfill a significant but doable vision: to engage and help humanity reach its full potential.

Welcome to a compassionate journey of understanding why it's not easy to be human, why we get stuck and suffer in many ways, and how to fix it. I can't wait to share this transformational experience filled with stories, life lessons, guidance, science, and practical tools and applications to make your life easier and much more meaningful.

Each of us has a personal story, plus a cultural or societal story, to tell. Our stories are filled with joy, pain, and conquest. They include the imprint of our heritage and paint the picture of our programming as we grow up and as we become adults. My personal story is interwoven with pride, responsibility, compassion, generosity, humility, and gratitude, as well as chaos caused by family addiction and cultural restrictions and shock from experiencing a foreign land.

I was born in 1963 in Tehran, Iran, on one of the most celebrated national holidays, which began the very day I was born. It was the day the White Revolution, a.k.a. the Shah and People Revolution, took off to accomplish great things. The term white refers to peaceful revolution.

It was a nonviolent movement to modernize the country

by providing many resources and privileges to its impoverished and marginalized citizens. Along with his queen and designated experts and corps, the Shah further emancipated women to be able to attend college, drive, vote, and live free of forced attire, as well as empowering industrialization and creating a booming economy.

The White Revolution made a substantial positive impact. It was also met with some expected challenges and resistance. It consisted of nineteen elements introduced over a period of sixteen years. Wikipedia lists the elements as follows:

1. Land reforms program and abolishing feudalism
2. Nationalization of forests and pasturelands
3. Privatization of the government-owned enterprises
4. Profit sharing
5. Extending the right to vote to women
6. Formation of the Literacy Corps
7. Formation of the Health Corps
8. Reconstruction and Development Corps
9. Formation of the Houses of Equity
10. Nationalization of all water resources
11. Urban and rural modernization and reconstruction
12. Didactic reforms
13. Workers' right to own shares in the industrial complexes
14. Price stabilization
15. Free and compulsory education
16. Free food for needy mothers
17. Introduction of Social Security and national insurance for all Iranians
18. Stable and reasonable cost of renting or buying residential properties
19. Introduction of measures to fight against corruption

I lived on the poorer side of Tehran and personally benefited from the reform and heard news of the positive changes that took place across the country. My mom told me she had given birth to me for free at the queen's hospital, where the queen had delivered her own children. She felt happy and fortunate. Doctor visits and medicine were as cheap as a loaf of bread. Streets were safer, and essential foods, such as meat and milk, were more accessible to the needy. Owning a house was very affordable. With some money my uncle had sent from the United States, my parents had bought a little house of our own. As school children, we got a nutritious breakfast and snacks before going home for lunch. I heard the evening news regularly report on the progress of the White Revolution corps, which were made up of teachers, doctors, nurses, engineers, scientists, and other experts bringing education, health care, safe drinking water, electricity, and better farming practices and urbanizing remote villages. Interestingly, I do not remember the Shah raising taxes on any ordinary people to implement these national projects. In fact, I never heard my family or anyone else talk about paying taxes.

I assume the cost of this massive undertaking was covered by the sales of our natural resources and oil, which had been nationalized during the term of the previous Iranian prime minister, Mosaddegh. Mosaddegh, among many other democratic influencers, had taken back the right to our oil resources from British dominance. You may wonder, If people were happy, why did the Islamic Revolution happen? Well, I cannot tell you, because I am not an expert in the complex matters, and given that we humans suffer from inherent truth and confirmation biases, I find it difficult to know the truth behind any news or political views anyway. As I root for the well-being and happiness of humanity and our planet, I have decided the best way for me to help is to focus my efforts on understanding and optimizing the human mind.

Hence, I continually learn about the causes of human suffering, both specifically and in general, especially from many who understood the causes of suffering and did something about it. Nelson Mandela, Gandhi, Jesus, Mother Teresa, the Buddha, Martin Luther King Jr., and countless others rose in their own ways to end the sufferings of the masses. These leaders and changemakers were sharp and used clear and compassionate strategies; they were humble and had one goal in mind — the good of the people — and left remarkable lessons for us. We can take these lessons with earnestness and gratitude to avoid grave mistakes and achieve our great visions.

Recently, I read *Cyrus the Great: The Arts of Leadership and War* by Xenophon, who himself was a renowned ancient Athenian warrior and a highly trusted, compassionate, and wise leader. Xenophon, who was in awe of the magnificence of Cyrus, the king of Persia, explained in detail why Cyrus the Great was the most noteworthy and revered leader in the ancient world. Cyrus issued the first known proclamation of human rights (The Cyrus Cylinder), and his strategies, policies, and rules were aligned with and supported his declaration. Whatever territory he conquered, he used tactics that ensured his victory while making sure that people on all sides suffered the least and gained better lives. He ordered that all people who were under his rule and protection, which spanned half the ancient world, be treated with dignity and have freedom of thought, religion, and culture. He abolished slavery and provided his subjects with comfort, education, and the means to become skilled at living happy and content lives.

As I read the details of Cyrus's thoughts, choices, actions, and plans, I could see what this contemporary Shah of Iran, Mohammad Reza Pahlavi, was trying to accomplish through his *White Revolution*. A child then, I hadn't paid much attention. He aimed to follow the example of his Persian roots to bring comfort, justice, and advancement and uplift Iranian citizens with pride, compassion, and service in the international community. By implementing Cyrus's strategic tactics, he formed alliances to benefit larger regions outside of Iran without having to conquer them. Aside from administering reform in his own country, he protected oil countries, many of which lived in poverty. As the head of OPEC (Organization of the Petroleum Exporting Countries), he had great influence on adjusting and raising prices on oil for the region. This price adjustment created an oil crisis for the Western countries that depend heavily on these oil and gas sources.

Within sixteen years, the Shah had accomplished his vision of bringing Iran into the twenty-first century, implementing the nineteen elements of the White Revolution. It was time to revive Cyrus the Great's greatness and honor by celebrating the 2,500-year Persian Empire. He recreated massive celebrations, something like what Cyrus the Great had done after conquering half the world. Aiming to acknowledge the work of his national corps and the international standing of his country, the Shah invited heads of state from all over the world to what were monumental displays of power and pride, while he and his queen led the chariots of victory.

Some historians say these massively costly and extravagant displays, along with ignoring or punishing the voices of opposition to his White Revolution, were probably his biggest mistakes, which led to his fall. He had missed how Cyrus had constantly mastered his ego and the temptations of pride. Cyrus hadn't worn more luxurious attire than his generals. He never had taken all the credit for himself. He never had indulged and always had discouraged his armies and people from overconsumption and wasteful living. Even on his deathbed, he'd ordered that his body be buried with no coverings and no jewelry when put into the bosom of Mother Earth, where he had come from. The Shah did the opposite, trying to impress the world with the most extravagant events. The celebration of the 2,500th anniversary of the founding of the Persian Empire is in Guinness World Records as "the longest and most lavish official banquet in modern history."

With all these alliances, he gained more and more power in the region. Other historians claim his fall was due to this accelerated gain of power in one of the most important regions of the world. That was when the Westerners thought he needed to be stopped — otherwise, who knew how far his influence and ambition might reach? We Iranians, though, were joyous and proud of our heritage signifying peace, humanitarianism, art and culture, poetry, generosity, open doors, and hospitality.

But as you'll learn in the chapters to come, nothing is ever permanent. The Buddha taught the four worldly winds: with gain comes loss, with success comes failure, with happiness comes unhappiness, and with fame comes ill repute. So did he lose his gain, success, happiness, and fame.

In 1979, right after I came to the United States at fifteen, I saw horrible, shaming news on the television about my beloved country holding American hostages. I was in a fog and couldn't understand how we got there. Overnight, Iranians went from not needing to obtain a visa to visit America to being known as terrorists.

Being put into tenth grade with no ability to speak English, feeling lost when going from classroom to classroom, and being laughed at for my accent or clothes by other girls in the locker room during physical education were challenges I had to endure. I went through each day feeling sad, lonely, and disconnected and not fitting in. Having to find my way around education with language barriers, create new friendships, and find love while being completely sheltered by a family dynamic that included double standards, I became a deeply reflective teenager. As time passed and I learned about American history, slavery, and injustices that still went on in the so-called free world, feeling their pain, I felt even more horrified — traumatized, really. I expressed my deepest pains, insights, and desires through more than one hundred poems about the pain that comes from a lack of humanity, equality, and justice, but I always found some degree of healing in nature.

Reflecting back on my teen years, as an American citizen for the past forty-five years, I deeply resonate with the dilemma our youth have been facing with our political system in the United States. There is pride in being an American, as America is a leading humanitarian nation of the world, and there are shame and dismay at the controversies related to corruption, lies, deceitfulness, and conspiracies involving the government. Mixed feelings wave through the country. While some are hopeful, others feel helpless, fearful, and confused about their futures. I get it because that was exactly how I felt as a teenage girl newly arrived here. Even though I felt confused and helpless, my sense of self was sustained by my pride — and I am still prouder today — to bear the legacy of an incomparable emperor, Cyrus the Great, who, more than two millennia ago, became the father of all humanity by laying out the foundations of human rights, which have been used by nations across the world.

According to the Ingenia history blog,

> The Cyrus Cylinder inspired many government policies around the world, such as The English Magna Carta (1215), The Petition of Right (1628), The United States Declaration of Independence (1776), The Constitution of the United States (1787), The French Declaration of the Rights of Man and of the Citizen (1789), as well as The Birth of the United Nations (1945).

I wholeheartedly believe that you and I and all people of the world are daughters and sons and children of Cyrus the Great—if not by blood, then by intention—and we can benefit from his benevolence through developing our own.

I realized pride and leaving our happiness to human rights are not guarantee of enjoying a fulfilling life. Hence, Took matters into my own hands and took actions that led me to better results. At the age of nineteen, feeling lost and disconnected, I paused my college education and went back to Iran without telling anyone. I basically ran away to marry a man I thought could give me some sense of stability and love. I soon came back to the United States, pregnant with my first son, and my husband followed. That life included twenty-five years of ups and downs, chaos, fear, anxiety, codependency, luxury, love, joy, and raising two incredible sons. Through all of it, I never quite knew how to best manage my own inner doubts, emotional pains, unfulfilled expectations, and reactions—until that fateful day on which it became clear that nothing was ever going to be different unless I stopped. I had to stop fixing and trying to save my marriage.

Before that, divorce felt terrifying and unknown, as if I were diving off a cliff into darkness. But in that moment of clarity, I knew that what I was going to experience was another cycle of suffering, and I refused to go through with it. I plugged a powerful intention into the universe and began a new journey, which I'm about to take you on. All the pain and suffering gradually shifted and re-formed, and I became whole and integrated, optimized, and fully content.

As an ordinary citizen of this planet, like billions of others, I tried to figure out how to live a human life with all the challenges that arise from cultural, political, religious, and other systemic restrictions, and limitations. But there was a deeper desire in me: the desire to know for myself what science, philosophy, and psychology had to say about life and solutions to pain and suffering. My journey of personal healing, transformation, and optimization and my creation of the Mindful Life Optimization programs were shaped over the next two decades with countless resources. My path was a multifaceted learning process from varied sources ranging from meetings of Co-Dependents Anonymous (a twelve-step program) to a doctorate in psychology of management consulting, two mindfulness and other certifications. I continued reading and researching scientific perspectives and applying psychological and spiritual models and paradigms that helped me understand the human mind (conscious and unconscious), emotions, and actions.

I was driven to learn from biographies of geniuses and highly accomplished people from all walks of life, including writers, poets, filmmakers, fashion designers (I have a degree in fashion design), mathematicians, landscapers, lawmakers, humanitarians, innovators, singers, artists, leaders of the world, and many others who suffered extensively and triumphed by persevering and sticking to their ethical principles of nonharming and kindness. I saw a piece of myself in all of them, and their hero's journeys were to become mine.

When I came across success stories, I was eager to know the features and programming in their human software that made them successful and happy. I was deeply curious about their character, their inner strengths, and how they had become content and efficient, and I sought to discover effective qualities I needed to gain. I realized the human psyche might be one of the most complex conundrums to figure out, because no two people have the exact same experiences and conditions that design their neuropathways and life templates. A person, like me, can come from a proud background, be good-looking, creative, lovable, and smart but have little self-worth and self-love. Lacking self-love creates fertile ground for falling into narcissistic relationships. The funny thing is, those who lack self-love might not even know they have no love for themselves. I didn't. Hidden traumas, unlabeled abandonments, and unexplained painful events can make a person feel obligated to suffer.

Well, I could no longer endure those assumed obligations to suffer, and being free of the underlying emotional pains motivated me to continue. I dissected every story, model, and approach I found; I reflected on them, put them to the test, and practiced to become skilled at them. Deeper understanding and healing were upon me. Eventually, out of this sea of data points and embodiment, a model began to emerge. I began to organize the common threads of excellent, timeless, boundless qualities and characteristics into a collection of fundamental Mindful Life Optimization lessons (MLOLs). These lessons became the manual of my own optimized life, and I found they could also optimize the lives of many of my students, clients, and mentees. There were key sources that helped shape these foundations.

I learned about the nature of life and suffering through the Buddha's core teachings. Looking for answers in the thick forests of New Zealand, Thailand, England, and California monasteries, I had sobbed intensely for the painful losses and lack of fulfillment in my life and for the pains of humanity. During silent retreat after silent retreat, I studied and dove into the Buddha's Four Noble Truths about suffering, the causes of suffering, and the path to ending it. I took on the Noble Eightfold Path and his numerous other teachings as the way to end the big and small incorrect notions about myself and the web of misconceptions I had learned about life and replaced them with beautiful truths and immutable principles.

Going through UCLA's mindfulness facilitation training was a meaningful experience. Not only did I learn how to translate those spiritual teachings into a secular, every day, practical language, but also, the training played an equally important part in my own continued growth and development. Other sources that had a noteworthy impact on my transformation were two books on the brain and emotions by neuropsychologist Dr. Lisa Feldman Barrett. The understanding she offers about emotions as not innate but learned, along with Dr. Gabor Maté's findings that interpretations can cause trauma and that emotions act as our immune system, had revolutionary effects on my achieving emotional health and well-being. Other neuroscience discoveries about our brains' inherent biases, such as the truth bias, took my progress to another level. The theory of the selfish gene revealed the trap that keeps people stuck with unhealthy attachments and clinging. Another fascinating model that was instrumental in my growth and transformation was the book Human Magnet Syndrome by Ross Rosenberg. His reframing of codependency as self-love deficit disorder (SLDD) and his laying out its causes and conditions were eye-opening. I finally understood why I couldn't be free of narcissistic relationships. I became empowered and motivated to increase my self-love and self- compassion so I could release myself from these painful cycles. Teaching self-love and self-compassion to others has been more rewarding than I can say.

I took many personality tests, but Strengths Finder 2.0 by Tom Rath was most effective for recognizing my natural talents, developing them into strengths, and living through them. Infusing mindfulness into this model, I trained many departments at corporations, such as the fortune 500, Health Net insurance company, to help them become more cohesive and supportive teams and build stronger, more functional interdepartmental relationships.

Dr. William Dodson's IBNS model, which reframes adult ADHD as an "interest-based nervous system," was vital to recognizing my brain as diverse, brilliant, and capable, not defective and disordered. Up until then, I had always felt different and had a hard time fitting in. With this perspective, I learned to lead my life by using the ways my brain naturally works, and hundreds of others have immensely benefited from my mindfulness-based IBNS ADHD courses. My students' comments about how free they feel always give me goose bumps. One fifty-five- year-old woman said, "I realize that contrary to all the ways that I judge myself, I actually am responsible, productive, and competent. It's like coming out. I am more present and joyous than Have ever been before."

Other learning opportunities, such as the Inner MBA program by Sounds True, Mindful NYU, and Linked In, amplified my prior knowledge of conscious business and leadership and reopened my mind to look at natural and human generated systems that influence us.

I found my way to discussions about the ethics and imperatives of AI through a thoughtful organization called Morality and Knowledge of Artificial Intelligence (MKAI), based in the United Kingdom. These discussions have been phenomenally enlightening about the increasing impacts of AI on business, education, culture, and many other aspects of human lives and societies. As important, participating in the monumental creation and editing of the four-hundred-plus- page Planet Positive 2030 project (by the Institute of Electrical and Electronics Engineers [IEEE] under Stanford University) took my knowledge, awareness, love, and sense of responsibility toward our planet to a whole new level and degree, for which I am eternally grateful. (See the bibliography's "Environmental Information" section for a link to my contributions.)

There were countless other resources I drew from, whose positive impact on my transformation and increase in life intelligence could never be properly evaluated or thanked. However, I know that putting my own healing, growth, and curiosity to find the missing links to happiness above any other priority resulted in great benefits for myself and others through my Mindful Life Optimization (MLO) methodology.

My beloved Buddhist teacher Ajahn Pasanno was asked once, "In your fifty years of being a Buddhist monk, what have you gained?"
He simply said, "At the least, I know I have harmed less." Yet he has brought unparalleled goodness into the world.

Having many years of learning and inner growth, I share this same aspiration — to at least now I have harmed less; therefore I have suffered less. But beyond this, I also aspire to achieve a lofty, still-meaningful vision.

My vision is to provide training resources and optimize one billion people by 2042 — that's really only 12.5 percent of the world population today. Generation Z alone makes up two billion people, the largest generational population, and they are the most open to and curious about the truths of life, as opposed to accepting things blindly. My mission is to train ten thousand MLO PCs (Mindful Life Optimization professional counselors) around the world and equip them with the essential life intelligence and inner qualities and skills they need to assist in accomplishing this vision.

My non-profit organization, Perfectly Here, is not alone in providing such life intelligence lessons. We have been and are open to forming alliances with others who offer bits and pieces of these lessons in their own domains (e.g., leadership, business, regenerative living, farming, and conscious purchasing and consumption). My friends in AI assure me this is possible. I am optimistic that the optimized one billion people will assist the remaining seven billion. As I see it, it is every human's right to be able to enjoy an optimized life. You, my reader, are part of this vision and one of the one billion who can benefit from fully developed and upgraded inner capabilities.

I also envision allocating an aspect of our efforts to teaching orphaned children to become a whole new generation of mindful, conscious, and compassionate humans and leaders. With support, we will provide entire MLO programs for children as we do for adults, expand our online courses to reach broader audiences, and incorporate games—digital as well as manual—to help grow mindful life intelligence where it's needed. Many people and organizations are already supporting this vision with their own efforts and similar missions. For your contributions, even including purchasing this book and improving your own life, I thank you wholeheartedly for supporting humanity to reach its potential.

BEHIND MLO, MINDFUL LIFE OPTIMIZATION

When people are upset that something didn't go their way or complain that someone else didn't do the right thing, I say, "It's not easy to be human." Hearing this, people often pause and look down at the floor or up into space to digest it. There is a moment of doubt and then a quick sense of relief. I can almost see it in their eyes: Thank God someone is acknowledging this. Most people quickly confirm. Others say nothing at first, perhaps because if they agreed with it, they'd be betraying all the ways they felt justified in judging themselves and others. They have to think about it and come to grasp the depth of this reality. And as they hear me repeat this on various occasions, they begin to feel comfortable enough with the idea to say it to others as well. Thankfully, I have developed a powerful model to help fix this. Let me explain.

The last sixteen years of my twenty-five-year journey to evolve myself included teaching secular mindfulness courses for UCLA Mindful, plus advanced curricula for continuing development, drawing from science, psychology, and the wisdom of the Buddha's teachings. So far, I have organized and taught more than 122 daylong retreats, designed hundreds of courses, and trained thousands of people. My teachings evolved as I did, and I began to recognize a natural dynamic methodology. I realized over and over through unresolved internal issues (anger, clinging, confusion, restlessness, and lethargy) how hard it is to be happy. These are inner obstacles to happiness.

I spent thousands of hours teaching, presenting, leading workshops and retreats, and coaching clients privately. I helped them examine these inner entanglements, guiding them and transforming their minds, emotions, and behaviors. I raised their bar for happiness and taught them how to decrease their grief, dissatisfaction, confusion, and stuck feelings. As the lessons that had transformed my life became practical lessons that were applicable to the lives of others, I saw them not only as tools but also as pieces of core life intelligence lessons that needed to be intentionally developed to heal people from trauma and unhappiness. I realized that the deeper applications of these lessons could lead to experiencing the oneness that the human race needs, craves, and looks for in all the wrong places, such as alcohol, drugs, and blind beliefs.

As I continued to work with people to help them become more successful and better manage their jobs, relationships, and lives, I noticed that no matter how skilled they became in demonstrating self-awareness, self-love, mindfulness, and compassion; soothing and regulating their emotions; communicating with kindness and effectivity; and improving their happiness, they generally still were afraid of death and would agonize over loss; stress over politics; and be disgusted by any spiders, mosquitoes, flies, or cockroaches that crossed their path. They still complained about the gopher that ate the roots of their plants, with hatred and an intention to kill it, oblivious to the fact that life mattered to the gopher. All this agitation seemed justified to them; nonetheless, it was agitation. It was biased. There was still unhappiness left to be decoded and replaced with ease and well-being. I realized that when people don't understand how the natural systems work, their grief over the loss of a loved one will not resolve. Without seeing that life matters in all its forms and without understanding that Earth's ecosystems support our lives, people continue to fear and complain about bugs and other things they consider undesirable. People need to learn how our very lives depend upon not just bees but all creatures, such as flies, ants, cockroaches, lizards, and crickets. We need wolves, birds, sharks, whales, and coral reefs to maintain the delicate balance of nature that supports life as we know it on our planet.

A recent study from the University Medical Center Hamburg Eppendorf in Germany found that disconnection with nature meaning not only distance from trees, rocks, flowers, and rivers but also a lack of knowledge of and connection to the ecosystems and important processes that keep life going—can result in feelings of eco-anxiety, helplessness, social isolation, and loneliness. No child or adult deserves to experience these painful experiences. We can and should do something about this.

Furthermore, climate change, whether you believe in it or not, has already ruined cities and countless lives and caused tremendous physical, psychological, emotional, and economic hardships for families and children across the world, even in developed and advanced countries, such as the United States. Our conscious and unconscious lives have great impact and can work against the vibrancy and productivity of life and cause tremendous hardships around the world. This is why I felt it was necessary to add the planet and sustainable living to mindfulness training as the second domain of life intelligence. The third domain includes pertinent lessons about the being of a human.

Maybe you are reading this fifty years after its publication, and climate concerns are no longer an issue; I hope so. But war, hatred, fear, worry, discrimination, anxiety, and unhappiness might still be going on. So I implore you to read on and embody the lessons in this book until we optimize the entire human species.

What took me twenty-five years to discover and internalize — a lifetime, really — I offer here as a compilation of an overarching model I teach: Mindful Life Optimization, or MLO. This modality includes lessons from my suggested three domains of life intelligence, which I will explain in detail, along with a five-stage model that makes humans stuck in suffering called SMADE life stuck and a five-stage process I call Human Software Optimization (HSO) to get you unstuck. Together they provide the reason behind personality issues and the means for transforming misconceptions and unhealthy biases to enable healing and optimization of your life or your clients' lives systematically and organically. Mindful Life Optimization lessons are referred to as MLOLs.

Throughout the book, I have tried to make topics relatable by including stories from my own journey and the journeys of some of my students and clients. In each story, there are lessons of hardship and how we've overcome them. Some unintended lessons may reveal themselves to you as you put two and two together. My hope is to elicit reflection that inspires insight, or to plant the seed for insights to come, while nourishing and strengthening the growth and development you already have.

INTRODUCTION

MINDFULNESS IS NOT ENOUGH

When I first began to write this book in 2020, my title was going to be Mindfulness Is Not Enough because I saw how separating mindfulness from the rest of the teachings it came from and focusing it on stress reduction had reduced its full benefits and led to disappointment for some. Many people have gained great benefit from taking up meditation and mindfulness to regulate their emotions, reduce their anxiety and stress, and make better decisions. But they could hit a wall because that limited use of mindfulness might not resolve all their everyday issues. I believe those issues can be resolved if they have the opportunity to learn and develop the full path.

In the process of making my point about the necessity of learning the full Buddhist path, I learned that for some, practicing mindfulness meditation causes disturbances. Going deeper within, they face the dark emotions of their past traumas and depressions and are unable to reach a state of joyful peace. This might be the case even if they practice to develop the whole path, even though it clearly lays out how to end the suffering that is created and exists in the mind and to reach enlightenment.

Hence, I found that the effort to cultivate the full path is not enough on its own. Other aspects need tending to. For example, if you suffer from depression or painful traumas that might be exacerbated by meditation or deep reflections, please cut down on meditating and seek medical help. Often, the right medication can help with balancing the chemicals in the brain and support your journey to growth and refinement. I will cover some key aspects of trauma and how to resolve some of it on your own. There are other factors to consider and learn about to help the process of ending suffering.

Luckily we have access to much understanding about how the universe works, how our brains and emotions work, and how to hone our choices and actions for greater results. I saw how combining the wisdom and methodology of Buddhist psychology with insights drawn from other scientific, psychological, and environmental resources and practices could result in the balanced development of essential inner qualities and capabilities that make up a powerful inner navigation system. This mindful inner system can guide you, my dear readers, as it did me, in living not only peacefully and productively but also with fulfillment and freedom from suffering.

Some of these qualities need full development, while others can be polished. To clarify which essential qualities and capabilities need development or polishing I have organized them under three domains. The three domains we need to understand and align with are the following:

1. Natural laws and constructed systems
2. Our planet and sustainable living
3. Human experience, conduct, and happiness

These domains overlap, interact, and influence one another, so the order is not set in stone. However, I believe the domain of natural laws and constructed systems should be learned first, since it is about how universal principles override us in governing our lives.

Of course, you already know some of these lessons and principles, but knowing and internalizing them all is necessary to avoid conflict, grief, and unhappiness. Having full knowledge and skill in fundamental principles and essential qualities under these three domains can shift individuals, groups, and societies away from dominating, exploiting, acting unjustly, and promoting inequality and discrimination and reduce trauma, anxiety, and poor mental health. This book and associated programs seek to optimize humanity's potential and change this widespread challenge.

When you have learned and internalized the three domains of mindful life intelligence, you'll be more emotionally, mentally, and spiritually mature and balanced. You will become better at conducting your relationships and enjoy them more consistently. You'll be more skilled at responding to challenging events appropriately and effortlessly, with the greater good of all in mind. And with collective transformation, we can have a more compassionate, equitable, and mentally healthy world. Furthermore, these Mindful Life Optimization lessons, or MLOLs, are pertinent to our health and well-being, both personally and relationally, as well as to the health and well-being of all ecosystems and our planet.

A FIVE STAGE METHOD TO MAKE YOUR INNER NAVIGATION SYSTEM YOUR MOST VALUED ASSET

To develop yourself in the three domains of mindful life intelligence, you need a methodology, which I have discovered and organized the five stages to optimize your human software. With this methodology, you can test and gain insight into any of the inner qualities offered in this book or any other fine quality you want to test and develop. A summary is below, and the full descriptions and how to use them are found in chapters 5 to 10.

THE FIVE-STAGE HUMAN SOFTWARE OPTIMIZATION METHOD

Stage 1: Mindful Life Optimization Lessons (MLOLs). These are lessons about the principles and necessary inner qualities and skills to be considered and developed. The goal is to take any of the MLOLs listed in chapters 12 through 21 and throughout this book and run them through stages 2 through 5.

Stage 2: Mindful Authentication. In this stage, I encourage and teach you to bring an MLOL into your experience and verify those lessons to reduce the negative impact of inherent truth bias.

Stage 3: Development. Here I provide guidance about relevant skills with exercises, practices, and tools to develop those skills in alignment with your chosen MLOL.

Stage 4: transformation. This is about the changes you'll experience as a result of going through each learning process. It's when the neuropathways in your brain re-form, your inner manual evolves, and you see and do things more wisely. If you are pulled back to old ways by related habits, you'll know how to get to the improved you.

Stage 5: optimization. Transformation in one quality or area is great, but through the optimization stage, you get to assess what else you'd like to improve on to strengthen your inner navigation capabilities and assets. You can continue to choose the next principle, quality, or skill to work on to cover them all. So keep at it, and enjoy the process.

Note: The five stages of HSO and the three domains of mindful life intelligence are both under the umbrella of Mindful Life Optimization (MLO). MLO can be applied to both personal and professional development. Please don't hesitate to reach out by writing to http://drmotaghy.com for further assistance beyond this book.

HOW TO READ THIS BOOK

This book is meant to be inspirational, educational, and, most of all, transformational. For transformation to happen, you may need to dig a bit deeper, and while doing so, you may face resistance and give up before achieving your desired change. Change does not come quickly for most people. So please be kind to yourself while developing the character and ability to embrace something that is difficult. Take as much time as you need—but do cover all the material so that you may gain the full benefits.

Please keep in mind that throughout the history of humanity theories and concepts have been debunked or rejected. Therefore, if any of the concepts presented here were to be disproved through rigorous and honest scrutiny and proof, that we shall humbly abide.

THE ORDER

I have carefully sequenced the lessons in this book for maximum effect, but you can skip around and focus on the lessons that call to you. Some might immediately awaken a new awareness within you, and some will sink in slowly over time. Either way, the intention is for these lessons to help debug false notions or treat mental viruses you may have picked up and to help you rebuild your strength and confidence. As you gain greater awareness, skill, and mindful life intelligence, you will notice your ability to create and maintain reliable happiness increasing. As that continues to develop, your ability to lead and care for others and the planet will also increase, and you will find yourself less a part of the problem and more at ease and skilled at being a part of the solution.

No matter where you are in the book, you can verify and develop any of the principles or lessons. Simply go to chapter 7, which explains stage 2 of Human Software Optimization (mindful authentication), and chapter 8, stage 3 (development), and run the lesson or concept through them as best as you can.

You may find some areas of the book read a bit more like a textbook. That's because I am trying to describe some of the concepts and processes. Other areas of the book include real stories and examples that may feel more like a memoir. These address the experiential part and help you to relate to the content and make it your own. Please take what is useful, and consider the rest.

FACING RESISTANCE

In my experience, sometimes new concepts or teachings take time to reveal their beneficial effects. There are a few reasons for this. One, our brains may not have prior associations to such new concepts yet.

There may be resistance toward change because of real or perceived benefits that come from holding on to old ideas and habits. It may be that when reading some sections, your mind and heart are preoccupied, not fully present. Not to worry — whatever gets in and benefits you, no matter how small, it's great. An important goal of this book is to help you become your own best friend, who is the one you can rely on until your last breath, so that you may confidently manage difficulties with love and care for yourself. Because for you, for me, and for all of us, it's not easy to be human.

ABOUT ABBREVIATIONS

There are five abbreviations: SMADE (senses, meaning, adaptation, default, and engulfed), a faulty programming that makes us stuck in life; HSO (Human Software Optimization); MLO (Mindful Life Optimization methodology); MLOL (Mindful Life Optimization lesson); HQ (heart intelligence); and IDG (inner development goal). Don't worry about remembering them. I make enough reference to them so that you can know what I'm talking about.

TERMS USED INTERCHANGEABLY

The following are terms I use interchangeably to avoid tedious repetition:

- Mindful Life Optimization lessons: MLOLs, truths of life, wisdom, insights
- Human software: life template, programming, codes, brain wiring, inner navigation capabilities, system, asset, outlook on life, life manual, traits
- Life stuck codes: faulty codes, faulty programming, faulty inner manual, false truths, false notions
- Planet: Earth, nature, environment, our shared home

NAMES AND STORIES

The names, circumstances, and identifying details in this book have been altered to protect the privacy and confidentiality of the individuals mentioned. Any resemblance to actual persons, living or deceased, is purely coincidental.

ENCOURAGEMENT FOR YOUR PROCESS

Please enjoy reading, highlighting, making notes, pausing, reflecting, applying, testing, verifying, getting over obstacles, moving away, coming back, and transforming your life—one MLOL at a time. Chances are good that several lessons will create a positive impact simultaneously. Curiosity and openness are key components for growth. If you find any of the topics or exercises difficult or if you find yourself at odds with a lesson or concept, please reach out to http://drmotaghy.com. You can also check out my nonprofit's site, perfectlyhere.org, for learning opportunities and certification programs.

Increase your reward by becoming certified as an MLO professional counselor (MLO PC) and facilitating the MLO methodology in a setting of your choice. We need as many of you as possible to reach our goal of optimizing the lives of one billion people by the end of 2042.

For more information, go to https://perfectlyhere.org/become-a-mindful-life-optimization-professional/.

I hope you will make these lessons and insights an active part of your everyday life, just as they have been a part of mine and hundreds of others.

May your heart and mind shine with joy and clarity.

JOIN THE MAKING IT EASY TO BE
HUMAN CLUB & COMMUNITY

Scan to Register Your Copy of this Book to Meet the Author
and Get Support on Your Journey.

PART I

FROM LOSING LIFE INTELLIGENCE TO BECOMING THE HERO

CHAPTER 1

SUFFERING IS NOT AN OPTION

It is not easy to be human. It's not easy to be a child who must depend on others for everything he or she needs. It's not easy to be a parent who fears his or her child might get hurt or who wonders if he or she is a good parent. It's not easy to be a teenager who is not yet developed, makes a lot of mistakes, and is constantly judged. It's not easy to be a spouse struggling to balance their own needs with the needs of their partner. It's not easy to be a good friend when one is lost in one's own issues. It's not easy to be a supportive sibling if one's experience was different from that of others in the family. It is not easy to be a leader with big dreams who is filled with stress and fear about being blamed or failing. It is not easy to be a doctor, nurse, or mental health professional who can't help being affected by the suffering of others. It's not easy for immigrants who may feel lost and have to assimilate into the new system and culture. Even for the monks who renounce the world, it's not easy to deal with the desirous mind and to see clearly. It's even worse for those with various mental, emotional, and physical illnesses or disabilities or those who are just different from others in their communities.

It's not easy for any of us, no matter the roles we play at various junctures in life or the background, education, or the amount of wealth we possess. We are all bound by the laws of nature, by our programming and conditions, and by not knowing better than we do. And we suffer for it. "Pain is inevitable, but suffering is optional," they say. I, for one, am done with the option of suffering, and I hope you are too.

1

A DESPERATE PARENT WITHOUT A MANUAL

Before I knew how to give up the option of suffering, I was a desperate parent like billions of others. I was desperate to understand how to raise my children properly, especially as they became willful teenagers. So they would be good kids. So they could grow up to achieve success as their society deemed it. So they could be safe in the wilderness of this world.

I went from one educational setting to another and gained little insight into how life really worked. All the information was conceptual, academic, and not relatable. But I persisted, until one day, sitting at a large parenting conference in Los Angeles, I heard something simple and obvious that blew my mind. Dr. Farhang Holakouee, a famous psychologist and speaker in the Iranian community, said, "We do not come with a manual," and he went on to explain why we shouldn't judge ourselves as parents. I realized he was right. Without an operating manual for how to be human, neither we nor our parents are at fault for our dysfunctional lives. We learn as we go, and unfortunately, we make a lot of mistakes. But a lot of these mistakes are mistakes only because of what society makes of them or because of the expectations and the lies society plants in us.

It was 2005, and I had a Bachelor of Arts degree in psychology. Nowhere in any textbook had I read such an acknowledgment of why so many kids and teens are suffering, why so many parents are unskilled at parenting, and how painful and confusing this is for humans. In my psych classes, I was taught that the roots of mental, emotional, and behavioral issues go back to how an infant or child is treated, but the material did not emphasize much that those who raise a child also have to learn as they go, using others' old, insufficient manuals. Parents do not necessarily have perfectly programmed brains to transfer to the child. So not only do we not have a set design and proper manual, but also, when we don't get it right, we're blamed and end up feeling guilty and isolated and responsible for our children's unskillfulness, disobedience, or mental illness.

Stigmas around mental illness have made it hard for a lot of people to seek help and change. In many places, people still resist seeking professional help for mental and emotional issues. Seeking psychological help may be considered an admission of craziness, which can trigger shame and blame. Older generations often saw mental disturbance as a sign of weakness and would avoid addressing it at all costs. This was especially true for men, who have often felt obligated to keep up with the appearance of strength, no matter how much they may be suffering inside.

In 2015, when my nonprofit organization, Perfectly Here, reached out to first responders, such as police, firefighters, and paramedics, to teach them mindfulness for stress reduction, we learned that even those heroes — who arrive at emergencies and take the brunt of the public's dangerous situations — couldn't admit they had stress and anxiety. If they did, we learned, they'd get put on a desk job or be looked upon as weak and defective by their peers or bosses. It was difficult to convince them that learning mindfulness would help them to be more self-aware and present, give them an instant ability to regulate their emotions — and that this would be beneficial to the people they helped as well. Many first responders suffer from divorces, broken families, and personal traumas due to the extreme stress of their work. But they learn to hide it well, so they won't lose their jobs.

So why don't we know how to regulate ourselves? How to love ourselves and care for our emotional experience? Why haven't these skills been part of child education at home and at school? Why are we blamed for behaving badly, when we haven't been trained to behave properly? That day at the parenting seminar, hearing that we don't come into this world with a human manual ignited a light of hope within me. It wasn't completely my fault that I didn't know how to be a perfect parent. With that burden lifted, I had an easier time learning.

Today I recognize that our upbringing, education, life lessons, and life template can place us somewhere on a spectrum between these two ends:

1. People may have poor inner capabilities, with unhealthy habits and attachment issues, and often find themselves stuck in a loop of unhappiness. These people experience stress and anxiety. They can get caught up in a victim mentality and do not know what to do about it. They might be people pleasers, to their own detriment, or selfishly ignore others' complaints and carry on with their behaviors. They may frequently experience unhappiness and cause problems for others. They can be unfair, unjust, and judgmental. They may have become good at deception out of necessity or due to undeveloped boundaries. The list goes on.

2. People may have optimized inner qualities, a navigation system and capabilities with a good amount of development in logic; integrity; understand how life works; and have effective communication. These people are skilled in connection, consideration, and care for others. They are calm, authentic, efficient, and happy. They engage in life with goodwill, are open to change, and follow principles of non-harming.

As I said, there is spectrum. People development falls somewhere in between these two ends, and many people who are well trained and educated can still have qualities that cause them to get stuck in unhappiness. I will talk more about this in chapter 2.

THE BIRTH OF THE HUMAN SOFTWARE

One day, while teaching MAPs (mindful awareness practices) courses for UCLA Mindful, I had an aha moment. I saw the human life manual or programming as coded software with some powerful features, some of which have not been fully developed. When I lectured on how to develop loving-kindness as unconditional love and goodwill for all, some students would question and resist the idea of having unconditional love for someone who "doesn't deserve" it. I used to have similar resistance— but in my case, I had falsely assumed that unconditional goodwill meant I had to be even kinder than I was, which would increase my burden.

4

This part of the course was aimed at helping students to cultivate their emotional capacity, or heart intelligence, to help reduce their stress and increase their sense of wellness. I explained how their unconditional regard first benefited them, but they still were perplexed. That was when I realized the features of heart intelligence are like all the powerful capabilities built into Microsoft's Excel program. I only use or know how to use the most basic features in my daily office work. For those of you who may not know, Excel is a software program designed as a spreadsheet to organize data and perform simple and complex computations and analysis for business, research, accounting, and other projects. It offers mathematical formulas to create statistics and reveal numbers one cannot easily arrive at without the help of such programs. Many users only use a few simple features of Excel and never take advantage of its full potential.

I realized that just as Excel's users may not be fully aware of or may not have utilized its finer, more powerful capabilities, we aren't all experts at operating some of our own human software's greatest features, such as the features and intelligence of the heart. Similarly, I saw how, by not using the more intelligent heart features of our human software (e.g., unconditional goodwill, compassion, generosity, joy for the joy of others, and peacefulness) in optimal ways, we not only miss out on the benefits of these features that empower us to live full lives but also suffer great emotional distresses. The emotional heart can be a source of pain and suffering, but proper usage of the heart's intelligence can release rich, healing qualities that can nourish us and make life fulfilling.

The difference—and difficulty—is that while most technological program features are set and standard no matter who uses them, our human software and programming are anything but standard. This is partly because different cultures or even different family systems experience and express love and other heart qualities in unique ways, and there are no set instructions or manuals that help us to understand the heart's benefits or to utilize them, express them, or even access them fully and wisely. For people in some cultures, such as Italians, South Americans, Persians, and Armenians, it's acceptable to be more emotional than it is for people of other cultures. For these cultures,

5

Positive and negative emotions, such as love and hate, can sometimes be intertwined, which makes it hard to communicate or sort out feelings and needs. Some people may use heart qualities, such as generosity and compassion, excessively, whereas others may use them sparingly or not enough.

Unfortunately, in modern times, many people are detached from the heart and more concerned about reasoning through life, which could be from their own perspectives and done egotistically and not skillfully. Nonetheless, from my own remarkable healing journey, which I heavily credit to the development of my heart's intelligence, I knew how important it was to help my students develop the understanding and skills to access and benefit their hearts fully.

I noticed that the heart feature was coded slightly differently in each of my students and clients. They were sometimes contaminated with toxic negativity and biases. Other times, they were bound to personal agendas. Some people had an overwhelming connection to their hearts but didn't have good boundaries that would curtail the intensity and flow of their emotional expressions. They suffered for being overly empathic. Others had built barricades against love and friendliness to protect their hearts against fear of rejection, abuse, neglect, or abandonment.

Most others were biased toward specific people they loved; some could tap into feelings of compassion and love but could only feel the joy of others under certain circumstances. Some needed cleansing of specific mental viruses that impacted their perceptions and sickened their hearts. Others needed to deal with a constantly analytical mind. Almost every person in every class had his or her own unique process and area they needed to develop.

For others, like me, just hearing wisdom around the benefits of an open heart had great effects. Most of these human programs seemed to be missing some other necessary codes, such as self-awareness, self- love, and a routine for mental hygiene. They also had picked up some unhealthy, aversive codes, such as self-judgment, judgmental attitudes about others, and hate for situations that didn't go their way. Unhealthy attachment codes were also common, such as clinging to their ideas, wanting everything to go their way, and seeing only their side of things. Hence, the metaphor of human software, with its programming, coding, decoding, and recoding, was born in my mind.

I became attuned and sensitive to what was missing for each student and incorporated a mix of realistic views with practices that elevated their hearts to their full potential. Eventually, those who stayed with their growth and continued classes became skilled enough to fully utilize the heart feature of their human software and enjoyed great benefits. I will cover heart intelligence, or HQ, in more depth and detail in chapter 19.

HOW IS OUR HUMAN SOFTWARE CODED?

In looking at how our human software is coded, let's put aside genetic effects on temper and disposition and the minimal learning that might happen in the womb. The vast majority of learning how to be a human comes after one enters the world as a human. Human babies are completely dependent on others. For example, a baby we'll call Rose, upon entering this world, gets gradually exposed to all kinds of unfamiliar cues, sounds, movements, and shapes, including parents, toys, and other objects. She starts experiencing her senses — for example, with the sense of touch and the pleasure of affection when she's warmly held. Rose has to learn to make sense of these experiences, as her little brain has no built-in knowledge or principles about anything. The brain's predictive function produces feelings and emotions when necessary to alert Rose that she needs food, water, a diaper change, or attention.

If all her needs are taken care of properly and in a timely manner, she'll feel a pleasant, peaceful feeling. A sense of trust in the world starts to build up when she is consistently cared for and fed and is clean, reasonably cool or warm, safe, and not overwhelmed by the caretaker's stress or anxiety. Psychologists call this stage of development secure attachment. It is a healthy attachment filled with trust and contentment. With continued care, healthy development, and an understanding of how life works, Rose's human software and programming will develop to manifest competence, confidence, and fulfillment.

If, however, Rose is not tended to in a timely manner or not handled with care and kindness or if she gets overwhelmed by the caretaker's anxiety or emotional imbalances, her brain will produce unpleasant emotions to make her reactive so she can get what she needs. With repeated unpleasant emotions, Rose might develop insecure attachment, which means her brain will learn not to trust that she will consistently get what she needs. She might become clingy and unable to feel balanced and confident on her own. Having this experience repeated throughout her life and not learning the MLO lessons she needs will result in her getting stuck in cycles of dissatisfaction or worse.

In chapter 16, under MLOL 27, you will learn that human brains are only partially wired at birth. That means we're not preprogrammed to become optimal members of our species, unlike most other creatures, which are born with an inherent instinct that, with minimal learning, guides them through their lives. One theory is that human brain evolution left our wiring to be completed by other humans and their community and culture. Unfortunately, the problem is that not everyone is raised by a family and community who are fully developed and have emotional maturity, attentiveness, consideration, calmness, and the fundamental knowledge of life intelligence to pass on.

MAKING OUR CHOICES OURS

One of them any other reasons it's not easy to be human is that we are not born with choice. In the Western world, we are often told that we have the power to choose how we feel and how we act and to choose our experiences. However, often, we fail to make the choices that we wish to make or that are beneficial for us, because choice is more illusory and difficult than it may seem. One of my mentees, Sonia (name changed), expressed that as the first child, she had been dictated to behave and look in specific ways, and even her major in college was not her choice. At one point, she felt lost and confused, which was why she sought my guidance to help her figure out who she was and what she wanted to do in life. This is common among my mentee sand clients and among humans in general. The fact is, who we become or hang out with and how we feel are highly dependent upon who raises us and the cultural and other conditions that program us.

From the moment of our birth, people try to tell us who we are or who we should or shouldn't be. We are categorized as male or female and expected to learn about how we should feel and behave as a boy or a girl, and on top of that, not everyone ends up having an internal experience that fits into the boy/girl binary. We learn what to wear and what not to wear. Short hair is for boys, and long hair is for girls. This color is for boys, and that color is for girls. And when someone realizes they don't feel like a boy or a girl but like something different, making a choice to be what they feel they are is NOT EASY.

Social norms and shared concepts are essential for humans to help them collaborate, support one another, take on various functions, and feel secure. The human brain prefers to have social norms because predictability and autopilot allow it to be more efficient. As a matter of necessity, humans have been (unwittingly) writing life manuals or programs for their own species. They've created them in the forms of religious frameworks and traditions, cultural norms, laws of the land, and hierarchical or structural ways of thinking and manners of conduct. Basically, these are the sources that indicate our choices, not us.

For example, in a country with a collective culture, an individual does not have much of a separate identity. In such cultures, you won't be very successful if you don't think of others and if others don't include you in their affairs. It's a shared learned manual that dictates that everyone should engage in the pains and pleasures of the community. No one goes through life alone, and in most cases, this support is valuable. On the other hand, you may not enjoy much privacy either, as people's lives are open to relatives, friends, and neighbors and up for scrutiny, which causes enmeshment, interference, and conflict. Most importantly, individual members of such cultures usually grow to lack a healthy sense of self, which would allow them to enjoy a sense of fulfillment without being enmeshed.

Other societal structures adhere to a more individualistic manual. Traditionally, under these norms, everyone roots for him or herself. Motivation for success is for the advancement of the individual and his or her family. Trying to help or be part of others' life events may be taken as an intrusion, a crossing of boundaries. Though people yearn to be part of a community, group bonding is not as natural as it is for those who are programmed with collective cultural values. From the individualistic view point, you are either in or out. Although these values have been softening in recent years, in this structure, competition is high. Opportunity seems to be plentiful, but many individuals struggle to get ahead in life. Winning has high value, even though it is not possible for everyone to win all the time. People in these cultures tend to avoid uncertainty and may become anxious if they don't know the future or the results of a situation quickly enough.

According to Hofstede Insights, which created the cultural intelligence quotient, America ranks high in individualism:

> Behavior in school, work, and play are based on the shared values that people should "strive to be the best they can be" and that "the winner takes all." As a result, Americans will tend to display and talk freely about their "successes" and achievements in life. Being successful per se is not a great motivator in American society, but being able to show one's success is.

In individualistic societies, such as the United States or the United Kingdom, the promise of financial gain and wealth is very alluring, motivating people to march ahead for their own advancement and leave others behind. Hence, the rates of loneliness and a sense of failure in such cultures are high as well.

You can see why individuals have a hard time making choices that clash with their culture's values. When they do, they may encounter disharmony, shame, and abandonment. Thankfully, people have become more connected across the world and have had opportunities to experience the positive attributes of other cultural styles, they have become more willing to entertain and make alternative life choices.

Many other nuances and practices hinder humans in making independent choices they wish to make. In fact, researchers, economists, and innovators are constantly studying mass response in order to identify motivators that may help people to behave in particular ways.

In chapter 19, MLOL 46, "HQ for Occupation Fulfillment (Wise Livelihood)," I talk about nudging and choice architecture, which will give you another perspective on why and how it is not as easy to make our choices independently. But as you develop better inner resources via these mindful life intelligence qualities and capabilities, you can break through automatic choice-making based on social realities and programming and instead make choices that are authentic, aligned with reality, and certain to make your life easier and happier.

CHAPTER 2

UNDERSTANDING HOW WE GET STUCK IN A REACTIONARY LIFE

IT'S MORE COMMON THAN YOU THINK

One day a client, Bob (name changed), urgently needed to see me to sort out some issues before going on a trip with his family. He described his issues and said he felt stuck, as he kept finding himself in painful conversations. He even described how he was stuck, which showed great awareness on his part. Bob explained that he couldn't stop blaming others, he was too rigid and sensitive, he tried to control everyone, and his family was fed up with it.

"I'm stuck" are words I often hear from people who want to change but feel they are unable to.

A person might feel stuck in different ways, such as being persistently stressed out or easily irritated, having low self-worth, being too reactive or judgmental, feeling ashamed, being a perfectionist and controlling and the list goes on. People feel stuck when they are unable or unwilling to change their reactions or whatever bad habits they may have.

In these situations, life becomes burdensome, and relationship conflicts add up and potentially create new traumas to add to old ones. Experiencing this menu of hardships makes it hard to heal any of those traumas and creates a vicious cycle of feeling stuck in suffering.

I frequently use two remedies for clients who are stuck in some aspect of their lives. First, I begin by cleansing any mind viruses. I do this by including a healthy truth from one of the related mindful life intelligence domains and then injecting emotional vitamin boosts by modeling compassion and kindness. Their journey with me involves practices that clear their hearts and encourage self-love, which prepares them to move toward other lessons that cultivate their capacity for happiness, confidence, and healthy attachments. Like a chiropractor who begins realignment of clients' bone structure to relieve pain and suffering in the moment, I look for an opening to realign my clients' perspectives in ways that can neutralize their pain. I teach them how to stay in the present moment, calm themselves and regulate their emotions when highly triggered, recognize the depth of what they need, and discern how to fulfill their needs. Then I help them cultivate the skills of reflecting on the core reasons they suffer and identifying the ways their misaligned mindsets create their suffering. Their lives gradually transform as they become more conscious of their thoughts and automatic responses. They become kinder to themselves, are better able to be present with others, and act in healthier ways. Their inability to change transforms into openness and willingness to consciously step into their lives—and live them skillfully.

Next, let's look at some of the common causes that make a person stuck. Remember, it's NOT EASY to be human, and we're trying to understand some of the underlying causes objectively and nonjudgmentally. Some of these causes might be common knowledge, but I feel teasing them out is key to the path of growth and transformation.

COMMON CAUSES THAT MAKE YOU STUCK IN LIFE

Although genes can have an impact on how we become stuck in life, and some believe past-life karma dictates one's present life experiences, I'd like to focus on lessons that explore some of our programming issues that hinder us from living happy, healthy lives. As we understand these causes, we can work on reducing their negative impact and work toward rewriting our inner manual. These common causes include trauma, inherent biases, living on autopilot, and mind viruses.

TRAUMATIC EXPERIENCES

Aside from lacking a good manual or access to optimized humans to teach us and having our choices made for us through our societal expectations, we are also affected by traumatic events, which can lock us in emotional instability. The American Psychological Association (APA) defines trauma as "an emotional response to a terrible event like an accident, rape, or natural disaster" and adds, "Immediately after the event, shock and denial are typical. Longer-term reactions include unpredictable emotions, flashbacks, strained relationships, and even physical symptoms like headaches or nausea."

Dr. Jeffrey Rutstein, a clinical psychologist and expert in treating trauma with mindfulness, teaches that one's nervous system stores the impact of a trauma and that even long past the initial traumatic event, the nervous system reacts to associated triggers as if the trauma were happening again in the moment. Since one of the nervous system's jobs is to protect us from experiencing traumatic events, it produces physiological feelings that urge us to act. Hence, without awareness or knowledge of what is happening in the body, we can get caught up in all manner of troubling reactions, ranging from rage to isolation. These involuntary nervous system reactions make it difficult to heal from trauma with just talk therapy or even hypnosis.

Unfortunately, trauma pains can continue long-term due to several factors, some of which include an inability to recognize the source of triggers that result from previous emotional pains and an inability to be kind and patient with one's difficult emotions. With mindfulness, one is encouraged to gradually experience these painful triggers fully with friendliness, warmth, and kindness to oneself. This provides a chance to recognize that there is no real threat happening in the moment, and the person can calm down. In a calmer state, people can see their thoughts more clearly and be open to examining their stories or interpretations of the situation. With mindfulness, one can at least reduce the intensity of the present-moment experiences of past traumas until they are gradually healed. I offer more details about mindfulness in chapter 20, MLOL 50.

FALSE INTERPRETATION CAN CAUSE TRAUMA

Dr. Gabor Maté, a renowned Canadian physician who works with trauma and addiction, discovered that much of what constitutes recorded trauma isa result of one's initial interpretation of the traumatic event, not necessarily the event itself. The nervous system reacts to our perceptions. Perceptions create the stories we believe in, and our brains and bodies react to them. It's like when you find a joke funny and laugh hard, while a friend from another culture can't understand the joke and doesn't laugh. Your friend's perception is different from yours; hence, his or her brain and body don't react like yours.

In my practice, while listening to clients recount their experiences, I often recognize their limitations in knowing the difference between truths that are real and the way they interpret and build up a story they believe is real. Feeling joyful from a joke and becoming traumatized from an event you perceive as horrible both depend on how you interpret them. This is not to say that horrible things don't happen to us. But some people don't end up traumatized by them. The reaction to trauma is a unique and personal thing that also depends on the conditions and how much information is available to one during the experience. That's why children who grew up in the same household often have varying memories or reactions to past events that seemed traumatic to some of them.

Let me explain the impact of interpretation on the formation of trauma by sharing a deeply personal, formative experience of my own. This is to help you see how, when there isn't enough information, explanation, or clarity, self-assigned interpretation takes over and can be the cause of underlying trauma and suffering for as long as this interpretation persists. Further, it's important to recognize how our assumptions and interpretations can shape our sense of self and our place in the human community.

One fateful day, when I had just become a teen, my mom came

15

home from work earlier than she usually did for lunch. She worked at a hair salon, and in Iran, people commonly took time to go home to have lunch and rest. This could take anywhere from two to three hours in the middle of a work day, so it was like working two shifts with a break time in between. As soon as she got home, my mom asked me to go with her but gave me no information about where she was taking me. She was focused and quiet. She put on her chador, a customary long fabric sewn to cover a woman's hair and body. I didn't wear one, as in those days, the country was not super religious, and it was optional. Most people also walked to most places.

I followed her for thirty minutes in the heat, walking on uneven paving through streets and alleys and crossing busy intersections with honking cars and people everywhere, which was a normal scene. She looked straight ahead, avoiding any eye contact with me, and walked fast, like a woman on a serious mission. So I walked as fast. From her body energy, I felt the situation was so bad that we couldn't talk about it. As we continued, I felt more and more anxious because of her silence and tried to make sense of it in my head. Was she getting divorced and taking me to a lawyer's office? Had my school complained? Was she angry at me for something? I couldn't find any sure explanation.

We finally arrived at a medical building and went into a doctor's office, where a female doctor (also without the slightest explanation) asked me to take off my clothes and lie down on her exam table. It was a gynecologist's office, and my mother had brought me there to examine my so-called purity. I was barely thirteen and had never been touched there before. I felt shocked and embarrassed and felt as if I had no voice. Topics of sex and sexuality were highly taboo and shameful to speak of. Bewildered, I was wondering why I wasn't asked any questions or given a chance to explain that this exam was unnecessary. So I kept quiet to get it over with as soon as possible. Confusing thoughts and emotions blocked my senses. I felt cold, but I tried to tune the moment out.

Then I heard the doctor ask my mother, "Does she have a fiancé?"

My mom responded, "No."

Soon after, I got up and got dressed, and we left as quickly as we'd arrived. Oddly, I have no memory of the actual examination but

16

I clearly remember my sight going dark as soon as my mom said no, and I heard nothing after that. If there was an explanation or anything else exchanged, I didn't hear it. I had no idea why I was being examined.

On the way home, walking side by side with her through the noisy streets, I rehashed that horrifying experience and what it could possibly mean about me. The more I thought about it, the more I concluded that I must have lost my virginity. Otherwise, why would the doctor have asked my mom if I had a fiancé? She must have been looking for a reason for my not being a virgin. That possible conclusion became my truth. I believed it. I felt so unfortunate and ashamed that I silently cried all the way home and for days and nights after that. I rehashed it over and over to make sense of how I might have "lost" my virginity. I had never been touched. Was it because I had fallen down the stairs? I hadn't. Was it because I had run too fast? I hadn't. The fact that my mother never explained the results of the exam reinforced that line of thinking, and I never asked. Talking about sex was taboo, period.

Later, talking to cousins, I found out that some distant relatives with whom my parents socialized a lot had accused me of having sex with their son. Having sexual activity out of wedlock was the worst shame for anyone to bear. Those relatives looked at me with mild disdain anytime they saw me, which was painful and made me feel sad. Because of the lack of clear communication and my multilayered interpretations of the events, this remained a deep trauma and wound in my soul, which carried on throughout most of my adult life.

I interpreted that my own mother distrusted me, and I concluded that she had not stood up for me when someone accused me, which reinforced the times I had felt disconnected from her and her love. The real story was that she had stood up for me and had gotten a certificate of my virginity, or purity, which she'd used as proof to finally put an end to generations of vindictiveness between the families. I just didn't know it. Can you imagine? Being in the dark about all of this made me feel unworthy and broken instead of feeling proud and helpful.

The weeds of sadness and self-doubt had dropped their seeds in my heart by the thousands. The seeds grew and showed up at every turn in my life. They took nourishment from other bad assumptions that filled

17

in the blanks when I didn't know the whole truth. For example, if the elder of the family who had accused me glanced at me, I'd interpret it as her thinking the worst about me, with absolutely no proof.

I had some confidence that my aunts, cousins, grandma, and friends loved me. No one ever questioned me about that event or gave me a hard time. I enjoyed and relied on their love.

When we left the country and I left all my loved ones and the language and system I knew behind, the saplings of happiness, joy, playfulness, and laughter gradually dried out. I felt lonely and disconnected. To become free of that pain, I had a bottomless desire for happiness, and I believe it came from proving that I was good and pure. And society—or, more precisely, Hollywood— conveniently reinforced that desire and perception. Every Disney movie, every song, and every love story I saw growing up was about being special enough to finally be perfectly loved by a prince.

Unfortunately, with social media and other such factors, the same fate is inevitable for any young girls who experience low self-worth and fantasize about being loved. Lacking meaningful connections and clarity about what love is, having other psychological needs unmet, potentially being violated or left without guidance, and missing other supportive conditions, young teen girls in our communities are in serious danger. According to a report from the Centers for Disease Control and Prevention (CDC), from 2011 to 2021, the rate of high school girls attempting suicide was about 13 percent, and 30 percent had seriously considered it. LGBTQ+ teens' rates were much higher: 45 percent had seriously considered it.

Painful experiences and confusion about one's identity are not uncommon for kids and teens. Many people are repeatedly violated and taken through horrendous experiences, which can badly scar their souls and hearts.

I'd like to pause here to say that I am deeply sorry for any pains you, my dear reader, have endured in life, whoever you are and however old you are today. It is unacceptable, and I wish I could take those pains away. I hope that through the Mindful Life Optimization lessons in this book, adults can become aware of the ramifications of their actions and choices on growing minds and can know that every little explanation matters. Assuming that teens get why parents do what they do, don't need to get it, or will get it eventually can lead to teens' acting out and endangering themselves, their families, and society. To avoid these issues, please explain matters to your children, teens, and others clearly and sufficiently; listen to them with care, and learn to be present.

Please review MLOL 56, "Mindfully Healing Perception-Based Traumas," in chapter 21.

INHERENT BIASES

Our interpretations feel real because our brains make them so. According to neuroscientist Amishi Jha, the brain comes with a few built-in biases, including truth, confirmation, and novelty. Although these biases are useful from the brain's perspective, they can lead us astray in life by making us likely to believe things that may not be objectively true. We go through our days making assumptions about anything and everything, with our brains precoded to believe these assumptions. We are preprogrammed to believe that what occurs to us (or even others) is true, even when experience has repeatedly proven us wrong. Even then, we may not see the faultiness of our conclusions. Likewise, the brain's precoded confirmation bias causes us to pay attention to information that confirms previous assumptions and avoid the rest. This function can send us in wrong directions and cause us tremendous hardships.

For example, my assumption during that experience when I was thirteen was that my mom didn't love me enough, didn't trust me, and hadn't stood up for me when someone accused me. During my marriage, I found myself crying hard every time my husband and I made love and I felt intense pleasure. In my mind, I'd see that little girl who'd felt sad and alone at thirteen, wondering how my mother could have thought I had engaged in any sexual activity at that age, especially given the closed culture that made it impossible for boys and girls to be together like that. Every time I experienced that deep grief, my mind would reconfirm that conclusion.

When we are on autopilot, we conjure up and store thousands of false truths, which become the building blocks of future interpretations and conclusions. Any interpretation we have today may be based on at least some past false conclusions. That's right: once again, it's not easy to be human. Read more about inborn biases in chapter 16, MLOL 29.

AUTOPILOT

Our brains' job is to automate things for us so we make fewer mistakes, are safer, and stay alive longer. Being on autopilot makes our lives easier, so we don't have to spend too many resources each time trying to figure things out from scratch. The problem is that while living on autopilot is efficient and simplifies our processes, it does not take into account all the possible faulty perceptions and codes that form our human software or template for life.

The good news is that through the brain's capacity for wiring and rewiring, we can undo our life codes that were created by truth bias, emotional reactivity, automatic interpretation, and other unfavorable conditions and factors. Through understanding and focused effort, healthier and more confident perspectives and strategies can become automatic traits as well.

WATCH OUT FOR MIND VIRUSES

Another factor that influences our development in a way that causes us to become stuck in painful situations is infection by mind viruses, which are all kinds of unhealthy perspectives. In his book Virus of the Mind, Richard Brodie explains how mental memes, like viruses, get passed on and infect a whole society:

> A meme acts as a unit for carrying cultural ideas, symbols, or practices that can be transmitted from one mind to another through writing, speech, gestures, rituals, or other imitable phenomena with a mimicked theme. Supporters of the concept regard memes as cultural analogues to genes, in that they self-replicate, mutate,

and respond to selective pressures. In popular language, a meme may refer to an Internet meme, typically an image, that is remixed, copied, and circulated in a shared cultural experience online.

Think of how easily emoji have found their way into our daily conversations on text or other communication applications. They've caught on like viruses; however harmless they are.

Often, interpretations and assumptions (whether true or false) spread via mental memes and become shared building blocks that our minds and nervous systems use as a template to react to life events. Mind memes may spread through art, movies, and songs. They can spread through religious doctrines, sayings on cups, or poetry that children have to memorize in primary school. They can help to form our emotions, thoughts, boundaries, and adaptation styles.

When a powerful leader has strong negative opinions about something, those opinions become mental viruses that easily proliferate. For example, in Cyrus the Great: The Arts of Leadership and War, Xenophon talks about how the Assyrian king of his time started a false and malicious campaign (meme) to ruin the Persian people's image and reduce their influence in the region. Combating those mental viruses was what allowed Cyrus to become the greatest king who ever lived and the father of humanity.

Memes and mental viruses can spread easily within families and generations, until someone or something stops them, which is not easy to do. Once we are infected by (believe in) unhealthy, untrue mind viruses, not only do we suffer From them, but they also become part of our program—we get stuck in acting them out. On autopilot, people have spread social stigmas, judged others based on race and other categorizations, imposed rigid rules, become combative, and even committed violent crimes and justified their actions by believing others agreed. Because mind memes can spread like viruses, I encourage you to recognize and prevent thoughts and ideas that have negative effects. Once you get infected with the wrong ideas and they become part of your automatic responses, it's difficult to get rid of them or even recognize them as harmful.

On the other hand, we can also use mind memes to spread positive, healthy messages and patterns of conduct in the world.

To disinfect your mind from deadly and painful thoughts (viruses), go to chapter 20, and work on MLOL 47, "Intelligent Mental Action (Wise Effort)."

Next, let's look at the five stages of how stuck human programming is formed.

CHAPTER 3

THE FIVE-STAGE "SMADE" AND STUCK HUMAN SOFTWARE

Stuck Human Software is a model I created as one way to indicate the reasons behind persistent unhappiness and ineffectiveness. It's a result of inherent biases, defective social memes, false information and perception, and habits resulting in a false sense of self (the ego). The Stuck Human Software model has five stages:

1. **Senses** capture data or information.
2. **Meaning** and labels form perceptions.
3. **Adaptation** of strategies or habits occurs.
4. **Disposition** or personality is formed through the above stages.
5. **Engulfed** in this disposition, one becomes stuck.

For ease of remembering it, I've chosen the acronym SMADE: senses, meaning, adaptation, disposition, and engulfed.

The foundational building blocks and codes of this model are conditions that elicit traumatic experiences. They prevent understanding of the truth of things, leaving the person to construct truths based on emotions and biases. The person operates on autopilot, unaware of his or her actions, and finally becomes infected by societal memes, such as mind viruses. Those who have developed within these circumstances are bound to experience chronic dissatisfaction. They often agonize over issues triggered by shame, guilt, and contradiction. They display anger and may feel overcome by anxiety. To offset these feelings, they judge others harshly, and they may exhibit antisocial or racist thoughts and actions. The degree to which a person is stuck can vary, as some people, for example, were exposed to kind and loving grandparents or other key people and learned some sound ways of navigating their lives.

Although people with the SMADE life manual can advance through work and social status, when occupying influential positions, they are bound to cause disharmony, dominate, discriminate, and even start wars. This does not mean that all people with SMADE programming are aggressive, but when leaders have this programming, it can have grave negative effects. They can take things personally, fail to be objective or accountable, blame others for their issues, and look for solutions in all the wrong places. The SMADE programming is a painful, defective, virus-infected inner navigation system that can benefit from debugging, cleansing, and recoding with healthy, kind, and truth-based life intelligence lessons.

The Five-Stage Human Development and Program That Ends in Feeling Stuck in Life

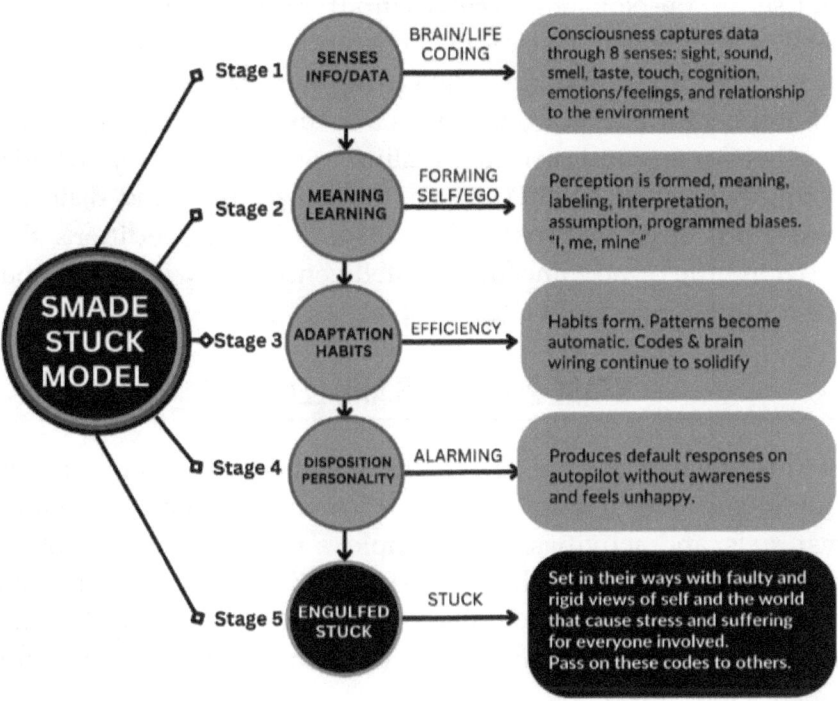

Figure 1

Let's look at how the SMADE inner navigation program is formed.

STAGE 1: SENSES CAPTURE INFORMATION

Our sense consciousness receives input through our eight senses: sight, sound, smell, taste, touch, cognition (mind), emotions and physical feelings, and our relationship with the environment. A lot of the information we take in is inaccurate, biased, and rooted in others' pains and distorted realities. But since our brains wire themselves through other brains, these inaccurate and distorted pieces are often automatically adopted. Given conditions that provide little or no mindful life intelligence, this wiring becomes the foundation to build a life template and program.

STAGE 2: MEANING AND LEARNING

In this stage, a person learns the meanings of things—labels, subtle and implied or explicit references to topics, feelings, materials, and activities. For example, a mother shows an object to her infant, directing her attention, and says, "Look. This is a spoon." Then she points to the food and says, "Yummy," with a smile on her face, to encourage the baby to eat as the spoon touches the baby's lips.

Babies produce various responses, and they eventually get that this activity is about putting something in their mouths and swallowing it. They sense that eating relieves them from the natural discomfort of being hungry. But there is a lot more to take in: noticing sounds, sights, smells, and tastes; paying attention to things; directing their attention; anchoring their attention on what's important; and encountering their own inability to do what they want to or are asked to do. Their brains are still developing those neuropathways—for example, to hold a spoon on their own.

Sensing and self-awareness are two different and necessary inner skills yet to be developed. Unfortunately, many of us don't get to learn self-awareness, unless it's in relation to what the public or others may think of us. That is not self-awareness in its pure sense. It is becoming conscious of being different, in a negative way.

In the meaning stage, at least four situations contribute to emotional and psychological learning that causes an adult to feel stuck in cycles of unhappiness, judgment, anxiety, worry, fear, and disconnection while producing unwise responses and behaviors:

1. Missing information gives birth to an inner fabricated self (ego) to help the person understand things through his or her own best guesses or assumptions to fill in the blanks. Assumptions are often based on the wrong impression of life events, internal experiences, and relationships, but the person is unaware of this.
2. The goal of caretakers and society shifts from caring for the child's well-being and happiness to producing a human who can act appropriately according to his or her family and societal values. The person may learn to be responsible in many ways, but his or her development of autonomous inner happiness and senses of safety and worth is derailed.
3. The child is harshly treated through intense parental or caretaker reactions, neglect, abuse, and negative messages. By young adulthood, the person is fully loaded with all these messages and templates of actions and reactions. The meanings the person assigns to traumatic events become part of his or her life codes, incorporate into the brain's neuropathways, and manifest as unconscious response strategies.
4. The child is overly cared for and not given a chance to build inner skills to regulate his or her emotions, respond appropriately to life's events, value relationships and resources, and stay connected and content.

In all these cases, interpretations, assumptions, and meanings from the person's human software, which operates on autopilot, may also create traumas. Without the opportunity to replace misunderstandings with the truths of experience, assumptions are all a person has to go by. People also perceive and assign characteristics to others through their own unconscious templates and create stories about what's happening relative to their own perceptions and experiences.

We storyize (a term I coined) people and circumstances instead of fully experiencing them as they are in the moment.

The good news is that we can penetrate the truth and achieve transformation by questioning all our meanings and perceptions. When a concept or belief comes up and keeps us stuck, we can look at it and not accept it as fact. This is the stage to make change.

STAGE 3: ADAPTATION AND HABIT

In this stage, whether they were missing key information or were poorly treated, people start adapting to difficult situations, using what the environment teaches them, and believing that their conclusions are true. The habit of creating stories to make sense of things becomes automatic, meaning part of the brain's neuropathways. Being able to make up stories and fill in the missing pieces provides a sense of control over their experiences. Making assumptions becomes the habit of the brain, which needs to predict what to do next and has no time for fact-checking.

STAGE 4: DISPOSITION AND PERSONALITY

Inherent biases (those our brains come with), such as truth and confirmation biases, help to solidify these thoughts, assumptions, and stories. The brain's coding and neuropathways are strengthened. This means individuals automatically think about people, situations, the environment, and themselves with similar meanings and beliefs. As this continues, a set or default disposition or personality solidifies. Lacking developed self-awareness and running on autopilot, they feel their reactions to what they dislike or don't agree with are justified and out of their control. Often, they might say, "This is me. I can't help it."

STAGE 5: ENGULFED AND STUCK

Being engulfed means being stuck with a life manual that is filled with faulty notions and strategies. People who are engulfed in their ways are not open to new or varying viewpoints or perspectives. They have negative or limited views of themselves, others, and their surroundings, even if they do not admit it or act narcissistically. They feel restricted in what they can change, what they can do, and what impact they can have on the world, and they experience cycles of misery.

Being stuck, of course, occurs in various degrees, and it does not mean one is entirely dysfunctional. Most people have developed many strengths and great qualities that could assist in changing the rest.

HOW DO I KNOW I'M STUCK?

It is easy to get caught up in day-to-day life, feel stuck, and not know why. Let's look at a few SMADE program characteristics.

1. **Lacking self-awareness:** Not being in touch with one's feelings and thoughts. Also see MLOL 49 in chapter 20 for more explanation about self-awareness.
2. **Rigidity:**
   a. Resisting new ideas, solutions, and approaches to life and sticking with fixed ideas about how life should be lived or how a situation should be handled. Often, these fixed ideas or traditions don't work for some situations, but one may stick to them anyway out of supposed principle or because of not knowing a better way to handle them.
   b. Judging others who are different or believe in different ways of living. There is a right-and-wrong attitude, and one whose ways are different is the one who is wrong.
   c. Easily getting irritated, stressed out, anxious, and dissatisfied.

1. **Self-absorption:**
   a. Being consistently absorbed in personal agendas and how to get them fulfilled.
   b. Lacking connection with others and awareness of how one's quest for self-satisfaction hinders others' lives or pushes them away.
   c. Feeling lonely, anxious, and dissatisfied, no matter how much one tries to create perfect happiness.
2. **Perfectionism:** Believing in the false notion that everything will be fine only when oneself and others can or should get things or relationships perfectly right. It's a quest for a permanent state of peace and happiness. The only problem is that life's governing laws don't work this way. Things change constantly, making it impossible to account for every unexpected factor. Being a perfectionist causes frequent disappointments, agitation, tension, and self-judgment. (You will learn more about these natural laws and patterns that govern our lives in chapter 12.)
3. **Self-love deficit:** Being focused on caring for others and neglecting oneself, seeking happiness and comfort from relationships and unhealthy habitual preoccupations, and avoiding spending time alone. With a self-love deficit, self-worth and happiness depend on external praise and attachments, and not receiving attention or praise causes anxiety and restlessness.
4. **Chronic self-judgment:** Engaging in self-defeating thoughts, choices, and actions; always comparing oneself to others; and never feeling good enough.
5. **Feeling helpless and lost in the victim loop:** According to Mark Samuel and Sophie Chiche, the authors of The Power of Personal Accountability, there are six signs a person is stuck in the victim loop: denial, ignoring, blaming, rationalizing, resisting, and hiding when problems crop up. Once in the victim loop, one can easily fall into denial, blame others when the situation doesn't resolve on its own, and then hide behind habits and activities, remaining in a feedback loop of suffering.

Perhaps you can pause to reflect on how you feel after reading those characteristics. If you felt uncomfortable when reading any of them, it may be because you partly or fully identify with them. Breathe, and say to yourself, "It's OK. I'm OK. These characteristics do not define me." Say this a few times to neutralize any emotional reaction that might make you ignore or disregard an insight into a piece of your programming. Recognizing areas that can use improvement is the first step to optimizing your HUMAN SOFTWARE and moving to a happier, more satisfying life. Well done.

You can head to the "Supplementary Materials" section at the end of the book to do a self-assessment and see where you or someone you know may fit in the SMADE programming.

CHAPTER 4

AWAKEN THE INNER HERO

In his book The Hero with a Thousand Faces, Joseph Campbell describes a hero as "someone who has given his or her life to something bigger than oneself." Well, I have come to believe that nothing is bigger than freeing oneself from life's deep sufferings and gaining true happiness—along with helping others to do the same. In the documentary Finding Joe, Deepak Chopra describes how Joseph Campbell, the acclaimed literary critic and leading mythology scholar, studied stories, philosophies, and myths from all around the world and found one central theme. Campbell determined there is one mythological story that all humans share: the hero's journey. These mythological symbols give us an insight—an aha moment—about the hero who represents a voice, a call to action. Campbell believes, "The hero in each of us is dragging us through life in quest for the ultimate freedom from 'demons,' whether they are internal or external."

Campbell's hero's journey identifies four simple stages: separation, initiation, reconnection, and return. In my model, I add a fifth stage, which is continuing to optimization. I will cover optimization in the following chapters.

YOUR
Hero's
Journey

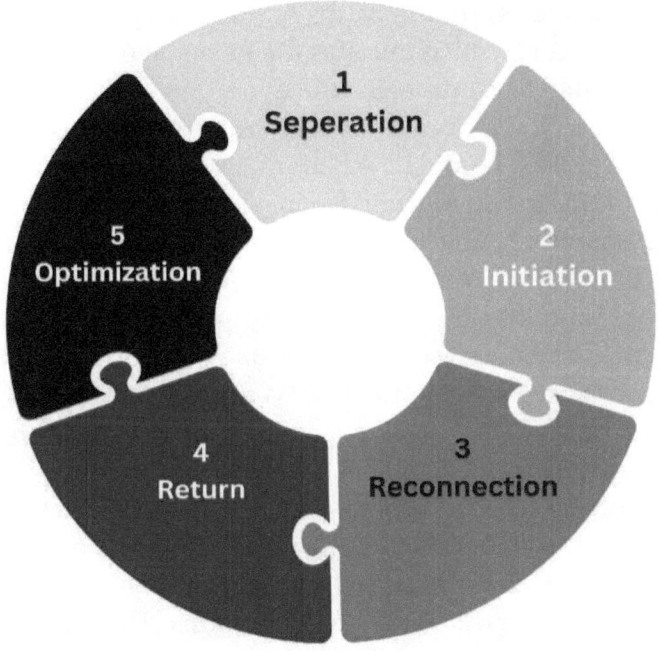

Figure 2

Campbell's model has been used for many purposes and has been interpreted in many ways, sometimes with several other stages added. In the interpretation I use, at birth, we are connected to and one with the universe. We have no separate identities of our own. But as we grow up, we become separated from this oneness with the universe through our experience of being molded by a culture, a system, a way of life full of faulty standards, cultural differences, biases, and inequalities. Then, at some point in life, we come to realize that we are living a lie and are disconnected from the truths of life. We become motivated to find those truths, which initiates the next stage.

According to Campbell, not everyone gets to have such a realization and reconnection to the truth. But that is fine because the one who does become the hero in his or her own story and gets to take on this grand journey for his or her betterment will return and benefit others. The hero, able to discern that he or she has been living separately from the truth of life, sets out to find and reconnect with his or her inner strength and light.

There is a beautiful story about a statue of Buddha made of pure gold that existed a few hundred years ago in Thailand. During wartime, the resident monks covered the golden statue with mud and clay to hide it from the invaders. They hid it so well that it eventually was forgotten. Hundreds of years later, a young monk, sitting in silence and meditation, saw light reflecting through a crack in the mud. He ran to tell the villagers, who carefully and patiently cleaned off the mud and revealed the golden Buddha. This story is symbolic of our own inner golden Buddha, the potential for an awakened being, covered by the layers of mud deposited over time. The mud represents our thoughts, unwholesome intentions, and false notions of life that lead to unwise actions and fully cover our inner knowing. Here is the story of my own connection to light and oneness and how I got separated from it.

Imagine a hot summer day. I was five, running around barefoot on the flat stones of the yard while a relative's memorial service was going on. A man walked out of the ceremony, in agony from the extreme heat. He stopped me and asked if I knew where he could find some drinking water. I pointed to a cooler in the far corner of the building. When he returned, he looked refreshed, as he had also splashed some water onto his head and face.

Satisfied, he said, "What would we do if there was no water?"

Of course, it was a rhetorical question, but I nonchalantly responded, "We wouldn't need any water if there was no water."

He didn't expect that. He shook his head and walked away. It wasn't until much later in life that I realized why the rich, intellectual relatives of my father used to call me Shakespeare as a kid. I never knew who Shakespeare was or what he was known for. As a child, I was thinking of a lack of water not as a deficit but from an existential perspective. If water weren't needed for life to exist, I concluded, nature wouldn't produce it. Simple as that!

I wasn't connected to nature; I *was* nature! As far back as I remember, when I was three, I'd get away from others to go explore on our weekly picnics in the outskirts of Tehran. I'd run through the bushes and branches, immersed in my heartbeats, feeling every sensation, curious about everything. I'd stop along the shimmering stream and say hello to the pebbles and little daisies, who smiled at me. I could hear the water gently murmuring as I'd lean down, gazing at how special each pebble was. I'd reach through the cold water with my skinny little fingers to pick one up and wonder, *What is this pebble doing here?* I had a lot of questions and was eager and excited to know the answers. For example, why were rocks hard and still easy to grab, while the flowing stream was soft and hard to catch? Could they feel my wrinkled palms? Were they as happy to see me as I was to see them?

I communed with every branch and leaf, the little bugs, and the specks of dirt. I can see myself now in my little dress with white daisies. I'd be mesmerized by the sun beaming on a drop of dew on the tip of a blade of grass. Nothing bothered anything in nature. No fallen leaf, no broken branch, and not even my presence took anything away. I'd lie down, feeling utter joy and peace; look up at the sky; and feel that I belonged. There and then, there was no Manijeh but pure oneness

35

with the planet, nature, and the energy of life. Immersed in nature, I somehow knew its process by sensing and intuiting. You may want to reflect on a time when you have felt this way. Let's look at stage one.

SEPARATION

In this phase of the hero's journey, one is separated from that connection, the oneness with the universe, for reasons beyond his or her control. Staying connected with such natural intelligence, as I had as child, requires nourishment, education, others to model it, and development. But like most humans, instead, I was introduced to the made-up version of life and how we supposedly should live it. This signifies the stage of separation in the hero's journey. As I grew older, things changed. The natural insights of my early years were only sporadically nourished, and eventually, they all went dormant. My life template was coded by various people who had some high-grade qualities as well as some false principles they had received or made up on their own.

My mother was only sixteen when I was born. She had been married through matchmaking, which was common. However, she was young and underdeveloped. She worried about how her in-laws might judge or value her. Because she didn't have a chance for continued education, she tended to her image and looks to compensate. She didn't get much of a daily allowance, so by the time I was five, she was working at a hair salon to supplement the household's income. She wanted to make sure I looked perfect. She'd sew me cute little dresses, dress me up, and fix my hair in grown-up styles. I guess she got plenty of praise for it, because looks became everything to her. If we looked better than we felt, then people would think we had it great. That was the message I got from her repeatedly. Later, working through the emotional pains that her behavior caused me, I learned that was a way for her to feel better about herself.

She dreaded drowning and always pulled me away from rivers and the sea. To keep me safe, she instilled a deep fear of open water. I could only dream of being near gentle streams, never the ocean. Fearing oceans and deep waters became a protective code that prevented me from learning to swim well. I even had panic attacks a few times, when I first dropped into a lake and when my ex-husband sent me to a camp to learn waterskiing. Fortunately, while working through various traumas as an adult, I broke through this fear, decoded it, and reprogrammed myself with a healthier and proper mindful life intelligence. I became much more open to understanding the sea and able to feel gratitude and joy in its presence. I go to the beach frequently now and love it, though I'm still building up the courage to go into the deep, where I can't touch the ground.

I learned many strengths from my mother, such as working hard and creating unity and love in the family, but my outlook on life was influenced in other ways. My mother's mom was an amazing storyteller. She told fantastical stories and heroic tales. I remember one about a poor servant girl who hid in a watermelon and rolled under the prince's bed to find a way to his heart. I love that story and asked her to tell it to me every night. The other grandma taught me about traditions, God, and the dos and don'ts of religion, which came with contradictory messages of compassion and fear. She also exhibited an enormous amount of generosity and kindness and many acts of service, which I admired. Overall, though, I picked up that my happiness depended on how good I was—of course, according to others' expectations. This separation from oneness was accommodated by cultural limitations; unexplained, unfamiliar emotions; immigration to a strange, cold society (compared to what I was used to) at a sensitive age; feelings of loneliness; vague guidance in choosing higher education; falling in love for all the wrong reasons; and marrying into a facade. My programming, which I explained previously under the SMADE human software, destined me to walk a path of great suffering.

I now know I had no control over that suffering, as my brain operated from patterns I had learned, interpreted, habituated, and become programmed with. I was stuck in a lot of false notions about life, love, and relationships.

By adulthood, I had little self-awareness and knew of no way out of the emotional turbulence of my life. It was as if I had fallen into a fast-moving river with no end in sight, bumping my head and body through sharp turns, in dark caves, and over cliffs, with no skill to navigate such conditions. Fears I had learned and experienced, as well as confusion regarding what I had known to be true as a child, what I was forced to accept about myself as a female, and the requirements of being a successful adult, overwhelmed me. I had misinterpreted Persian humility as selflessness and a duty to others that required shoving one's soul into solitary confinement.

I struggled to free myself, now having to follow the model of a modern, successful woman and wife, which I had perceived Americans highly valued, at least in Los Angeles, where I've lived for more than forty-five years. On the outside, I was young and beautiful, carried myself well, and was giving and loving. I was proud to manage businesses, care for kids, and live a social and lavish life. But on the inside, it all felt shallow and disconnected. I felt trapped and yearned to be with my true friends: the soft stream, leaves, and pebbles, who were purely themselves and present, with nothing to hide and no reason to pretend. I found nature was serene and indifferent to anyone's opinions and judgments. So I'd escape my improved yet still societally imposed pretend life through hiking and conversing with the moon whenever I could. The moon always appeared, and it lit the sky and my heart right along with it. But it was like getting oxygen not only from a leaky oxygen tank but also through the masks I had to wear to please everyone else. Occasional visits with nature were not enough.

Until one day, stuck in unhappiness, in rage and a powerful determination I had never felt before, I shouted out at the universe for having abandoned me.

"Haven't I suffered enough? Haven't I paid for whatever I am supposed to pay for yet? It's enough! I have paid my dues. It is enough suffering. I will not have it!"

I cried hopelessly, with my head bent into my chest, and quietly continued. "I refuse to continue suffering and not knowing what to do. Please guide me. Please."

And the universe responded.

INITIATION

The universe initiated to unblock the hero in me. It was   spring of 2005. I was finishing my bachelor's degree in psychology. We were to choose our last capstone courses that qualified us to continue for a master's degree. Those were the highest-level research courses in the program. But some strong feelings drew me to another course under multidisciplinary selections. All my friends took the capstone courses and were confused why I took the lower-level course for my final semester. It seemed like a cop-out. But I had to ignore others' expectations and follow my intuition, and my path was forever transformed.

The class was called Asian Thoughts. Up until then, I had heard little of Asian thoughts or philosophies. The closest I had come to learning about Asian philosophies was watching Bruce Lee movies. Back in the 1970s, Bruce Lee was everyone's hero. He was a relatively small and thin young man with strong fists as well as unwavering principles and values. He fought for and defended the weak through his unbeatable karate. He was my hero too.

The Asian Thoughts class covered various religions and philosophies, including Taoism, Hinduism, Zoroastrianism, Confucianism, Islam, and others. I knew about Islam because I had been born into it, and I knew about Zoroastrianism, which was part of my proud Persian heritage. So I made a point of visiting a nearby Hindu temple to get a feel for their philosophies and then a Taoist workshop. I liked them but didn't feel any deep connection to them.

What caught my attention was the story of Siddhartha Gautama — about his yearning to leave home to find the solution for human suffering and then actually finding it. Hearing about his heroism, I felt a jolt of electricity that brought my heart back to life and hope. I knew then that the universe had heard my cries and objections. It was showing me the path to fulfill my longing for solitude and freedom from my structured, empty life.

But how was I going to begin this process? My life was interwoven with family plans, travel, and obligations. Undoing traditions, belief systems, habits, and patterns ingrained in every fiber of my mind seemed daunting. My inner navigation system was filled with neuropathways of judgment, expectations, blame, worry, jealousy, fear, and irritation. My heart was ill with confusion and confinement. I was stuck. I had a long, trying journey ahead of me, of discovering and uprooting the weeds of unhappiness from my mind and heart. But there was no going back.

I thought, If Siddhartha did it, so must I.

How about you? Was there a moment that jolted hope in you for true freedom from a pretend life or others' expectations? Did you follow it? Did you let it go? What happened?

Don't worry if you haven't followed it or if you're experiencing difficulty. Let's look at some of the challenges that all heroes face on their journeys. You're not alone. Together we'll conquer them.

THE HERO'S ARDUOUS JOURNEY

The hero in Campbell's hero's journey encounters dragons, darkness, evil, and all manner of fantastic obstacles along the way, and so does a person who sets out to transform his or her life. The dragons we meet are our own fears and doubts. The challenges we encounter arise from deep within ourselves, not from external dragons or other people. The dark caves we may have to cross are our own confusions and resistance, but with persistence, we will eventually reach the light at the end of the tunnel.

For the hero in us, reaching ordinary daylight doesn't cut it. We can get that feeling from any pleasure we accommodate ourselves with, but eventually, irritation and unhappiness catch up. The hero is searching for or developing that inner light at the end of the inner darkness, looking to reveal the golden Buddha within, the inner light that will not end in the night. Our hero's journey is about the vision and yearning to realize the greatest thing we could ever have: the potential within all of us to reach our inner Buddha, who is steady, joyous, efficient, effective, and full of peace.

PATIENT ENDURANCE

The journey to rewrite the program that caused me suffering sometimes felt like going through multiple painful physical surgeries. Recognizing wrong beliefs and interpretations, whether they were mine or others', was often shocking. I felt as if the universe had taken a video of my inner world, shown it to me, and then asked me to cut out the defective parts.

If my body had been exposed to as many surgeries as I went through mentally and emotionally, I don't think I could have survived. I have a condition called vasovagal syncope, which is fainting as a result of the body's reaction when triggered by certain painful experiences. For me, triggers include fear of blood and needles and physical pain, and a few times, I fainted when I experienced the death of a family member. I'm using this analogy to show you the incredible amount of courage and endurance I had to call upon to rearrange my psyche. Imagine a thick, interwoven web of false perspectives and habits, all extremely sensitive and resistant, not to mention hard to locate and undo. My SMADE faulty wiring included all kinds of half-truths, false truths, convenient truths, mismatched truths, and contaminated truths, such as thinking humility meant being selfless and sacrificing oneself. It was like having veins that were in the wrong places and needed pulling out, half a kidney that was growing in the liver and had to be relocated to its proper position, one eye stuck on the bottom of the foot, or lungs functioning as the stomach—obviously, these are all metaphors for the painful falsities that many humans suffer from, and I had set out for correction. How could I find all the hidden limiting belief systems, false thinking, and unfulfilled needs and the traumas and pains that needed healing?

The SMADE human software and the issues that come with it are not particular to my life. But fully understanding this model gives me an incredible sense of compassion for the suffering of the world—and you, the reader. This is why I tell my students and clients and anyone who'll listen that it's not easy to be human. Most humans operate on some level of badly designed, limited notions and false truths we get stuck in. Then we pass them on to others, and we all suffer for them. It sometimes feels like insanity. I get it.

Not to worry, though. The Human Software Optimization you'll learn about in part 3 is a compassionate methodology that will help you grow organically and as painlessly as possible. But patience and kindness are the keys to meeting restlessness and resistance.

MEETING RESISTANCE AND ESCAPING THE MATRIX

Do you remember the Matrix? In the 1999 movie, people are hooked up to parallel-reality machines, living life through imagined stories they are fed through the machines. But one man figures it out and tries to escape, while facing incredible resistance from those protecting the illusion.

In chapter 2, I spoke of inherent brain biases. These are innate and often hidden biases that make us cling to our ideas and perspectives. If you think your hidden biases are bad, mine were worse. Every time someone had a suggestion to solve a relationship issue or something I was worried about, I had a "Yeah, but ..." for it. Eventually, I was so unhappy that I had no other choice but to see the illusion and find a way out of the matrix of my pretend life. Breaking away from everyone else in my circle was difficult and lonely, as I was about the only one trying to wake up to the realities of life.

But it's because I went through this process of escaping illusions myself that I can see why my clients suffer, and I know how to effectively untangle them from some of their suffering in only one session.

MARCHING FORWARD TO FULFILL THE RIGHT TO HAPPINESS

You may wonder what insight propelled me to where I am today and helped me to recognize these three life-intelligent domains and inner-development needs as the solution to end human and planetary problems. Come with me on a short journey.

It was the fourth day of my first ten-day silent retreat in 2008. On a serene late afternoon, I was lying down in corpse posture, also known as Savasana, which is lying down as the last yoga posture. The instructor guided us to let go completely, with face softening, shoulders relaxing, back letting go, legs becoming heavy, and no more effort. My body relaxed bit by bit into the earth.

Suddenly, an image occurred to me. I saw myself arriving at the front door of my house. My then-partner opened the door. After ten days apart, he showed no excitement to see me — no warm hugs and no kisses, just "Hello." Seeing that image broke my heart. Tears rolled down my face. I felt shame for not being wanted. Luckily, during those four days, we had meditated a lot, and I had been practicing feeling my body, seeing my mind, and bringing myself to the present moment. When tears touched my face, I became aware of how my heart had been broken by just seeing an image. I realized I wasn't home, and my partner wasn't there. It wasn't even certain that he would be cold when he saw me. Yet I had suffered immensely in that moment.

It was then that I became determined to get to the bottom of the business of suffering. There was a saying in the Buddhist circles: "Pain is inevitable, but suffering is optional." Well, that was it. I set my intention and vowed I would not take the option of suffering, period. I saw how I could take charge of my mind by training it so that one day I would be done with all its shenanigans. Mind you, I did separate from that partner, and we became great friends.

The realization that suffering arises in the mind and can be ended in the mind empowered the desire to relieve myself from chronic dissatisfaction. I wanted to live a fulfilling life. The more I learned, the more I felt compassion for others. Thousands of hours of learning; transforming; and realigning my mind, feelings, choices, behaviors, and actions through numerous sources and resources revealed why it's not easy to be human. There is no guarantee we'll learn what's necessary and what's true, and we suffer for this. With a lot of time, attention, and effort, I learned how to live human life with more ease and fulfillment. Out of compassion and the desire to relieve anyone who wanted the same, I taught others very understanding I gained.

To end emotional pain and suffering, I spent every waking minute of every day for more than twenty years undoing a lifetime of wiring — by learning, testing, and implementing every teaching the Buddha offered. I dove into various sciences and learned about the psychology of narcissists and codependents, the selfish gene ruling our minds and bodies, and how to cultivate the intelligence of the heart and purify it. Gaining the wisdom of living blamelessly and setting my intentions to have compassion beyond all judgment and justification became the most important priorities of my life. There was no turning back.

Even while battling with inner doubt, resistance, and clinging, I never wavered. During silent retreat after silent retreat, I journeyed hundreds of rounds into the dark alleys of my soul, meeting painful traumas and relationship disappointments; kneeling and sobbing with regret; and gradually healing the pains I had stored in my system. In the midst of all this, my son died, which shattered my brain and soul. My heart closed to air and life. I became lost in a sea of confusion and sorrow. But I had to continue to hope while swimming through the never-ending night and holding on to the vision of reaching the shores of joy, light, and freedom. That was my human right, and I was not giving that up.

COMPANIONS ON THE JOURNEY

As with Campbell's heroes, no hero goes it alone. Without the compassionate support of my beloved teacher and other Buddhist monks who practiced achieving the same goal with a genuine desire for happiness, as well as other loving companions and students, I could not have pulled through.

It's helpful to stop and think about those who have accompanied you on your journey so far—those who have been genuine, wise, compassionate, and sincere in their own paths to living life authentically. Anyone come to mind? See how you might honor them. There is a beautiful teaching from the Buddha called "The Highest Blessings." One of these highest blessings is to honor those worthy of honor. This is something we can miss in our fast-paced life. Take a moment here to think of ways to honor those who are worthy of it, whether they are directly involved in your life or not. In this way, you can benefit from a brighter mind.

THE GIFT OF SUFFERING: THE HERO'S MISSION

Whether you are a younger person reading this and have yet to harvest the fruits of your labor and life experiences or are older and further in your journey, I'd like to gently invite you to think of the thing that gives you pain in life, brings you sadness, or makes you feel less than or stuck. I want you to then think of ways you can turn this painful experience around and make it a mission to accomplish something that would make you feel extraordinary. Let this suffering bring you its gift, as it definitely has one.

For those of you who are further in your journeys, let's go back a bit into your past experiences to see if you can identify any significant event, a painful incident that could have set you on the path that brought you where you are today — perhaps the career you are in or the determination you've gained to prove something to someone. It may be the root of an innovation you've come up with to solve a problem or cure a disease or of the extraordinary empathy to become a mental health professional. It may be your reason for having the fun qualities and skills that make others laugh or the skills and talents that allow you to fix or design something better than anyone else. Or maybe you are still emerging into what makes you special and unique. Wherever you are, can you pinpoint a single or repeated painful experience that was the seed of the tree whose fruit you are benefiting from today? It could be a situation that caused you to make an assumption about life, yourself, other people, or the world and put you on a specific mission — a gift of a fuller, more meaningful identity that became yours.

This painful incident could have been mixed with some meaningful experience. When you look, you may realize that regardless of what you're doing or not doing to improve your well-being and happiness, the core of this mission that put you on this path may have endured. I knew someone once who said she wanted to become a cop to put her father in prison and free her family of his vicious, harmful behavior. Instead, she became a therapist, and she now helps to heal families and those who were like her father. Many therapists and mental health professionals as well as various types of healers choose their fields through their own processes of healing and rising above their pain. Healing their own wounds and helping others may be a thread that's woven throughout all their deepest desires.

If the suffering you have endured has made you cynical or someone who might deceive and harm others, I am sorry to hear of this and sorry you have had no opportunities to heal and reap the benefits of a healthy, happy inner navigation system.

Many of you, my beloved readers, may not be there yet. The hero within may not be alerted yet. Maybe life is not bad enough, or your inner mission and determination have yet to become clear and empowered. You can continue to watch and explore how you got here. Let me share with you how my sufferings became the gift I am sharing with you today.

THE THIRTEEN-YEAR-OLD GIRL'S MISSION

Do you remember my story of being a child connected to the universe who got disconnected through cultural restrictions and demands and then, when barely a teenager, was falsely accused of having sex out of wedlock? Do you remember that my mother didn't even bother to tell me that my purity or virginity (which played such an important role to calm age-old family feuds) was completely intact? I simply did not exist. Thinking I had been broken without being guilty was the deepest trauma that tainted all my perceptions of myself and life experiences and perpetuated the pains of attachment shame. Addressing that pain and exonerating myself became the mission that awakened and empowered me to become the hero of my own life.

To heal this wound and regain a sense of confidence in myself, my heart became set on a mission: I was going to be as pure as I could be so that no one would ever mistrust me again.

The desire to achieve the highest level of purity and goodness drove me to transformation and optimization. My hero's journey expanded from a yearning to reach purity to the mission of freeing myself from my own unreliable interpretations (the SMADE human software) and others' defective beliefs and outlooks. I had to travel through the ambiguous, dark tunnels of my inner world. I had to sort through layers of anger, sadness, and the desire for fulfillment in order to understand them. I had to be patient with those difficult feelings and finally accept them as part of me. It was painful, but I was not alone. I sought the wisdom of the Buddha's teachings, I learned critical thinking, I cultivated and strengthened the abundant goodness of my heart, and I gained many other life-intelligence qualities and skills.

On this path, I recognized that I was going through a five-stage process that optimized my inner programming. These stages are supported by both the Buddha's teachings and neuroscience. Going through these five stages helped me to become free of chronic discontent and become happy and truly caring. I went from seeking others' approval to seeking inner peace, which came from cultivating and maintaining integrity as well as compassion and goodwill for all beings. This determination and process resulted in great benefits for my life and others', and I could not be more grateful.

RECONNECTION

The third stage of Campbell's hero's journey is reconnection: finding that golden Buddha, the jewel of inner knowing, the oneness with the universe, the optimized inner navigation system and capabilities. As I learned and my traits transformed, I felt more and more at peace and at ease. On my twelfth silent retreat with several days of meditation, while on walking meditation, I encountered complete reconnection, touched pure equanimity, and became one with my maker, The universe. I felt reintegrated, and I understood that I am the universe (I say this not with grandiosity but to mean that I am made up of whatever the universe is made up of, molecule by molecule and intention by intention). I felt beyond grateful for the generosity of the universe. In that state of presence, I saw that gratitude too was a fabrication of the mind, necessary for the limited ego who is never enough or content and who is afraid and worried. What remained obvious to me was that the earth and the sun, and the systems that govern them, are my life. I am partly sun and partly earth, water, and wind. As my body moves, space morphs and shapes within me and all around me to coexist with me. This applies to all beings and you, my dear reader.

I knew everything else had been a fabrication of my mind--and not just mine but our collective human minds.

As I continued walking the hills with focus and immersed in the universe, I heard a dog barking in the distance. I turned to look. It was a small dog standing by its owner, barking in my direction. I wondered how it felt to be a dog, and I spontaneously felt the warmth of its fur coat and its little beating heart within myself. With a soft smile, I sent the dog goodwill (May you be peaceful and happy) and continued. When I reached the top of the hill, I sat on a big rock I regularly sat upon, and I sent kindness to passing drivers. Suddenly, my eyes felt different, as if I were looking at the universe through my son's eyes. He had big, beautiful eyes and long eyelashes. It was so real and peaceful, like nothing I had ever experienced. His eyes became mine. In that moment, I understood that he saw the peace I felt, and I saw what he was looking at with inner peace. He too used to sit on that rock, watching life pass by.

By becoming the barking dog and my son's eyes, I understood that there is no beginning and no ending. My son's birth was not his beginning, and his death was not his ending. He, like all of us, is a soul in transition and transformation. This experience gave me a taste of what it would be like to be free, redesigned, regenerated, and reintegrated — devoid of the obligation to produce meanings and perceptions and one with the fullness of life.

If you'd like to pause here to let what you just read settle in, please do so. Take time; walk away, reflect, and let your mind expand to greater possibilities. You don't have to understand or relate to all of it. You can quiet your mind to allow the universe to reveal whatever is useful at this moment.

CONTINUING TO FULL INTEGRATION

I had touched purity, realized the impersonality of nature, and (for at least those moments) become fully integrated. This was not full enlightenment, at least not for me. I had to continue to nurture, protect, develop, and maintain an integrated brain. I could not merely have this realization and let it become a fantastical memory I could recount, as some might get from hallucinogens. I became even more curious about the intricacies of my impact on life and more open to understanding other things I was blind to.

Soon after I set this intention, I got an invitation to join an inclusive group of folks who care about and discuss the ethics and negative implications of AI (artificial intelligence) for people and the environment. This was a big stretch from the education I had, which was mostly about the human mind, emotions, and conduct. I was eager to be challenged and grow my perspective. During my early participation, I became curious about quantum physics and sought to understand Einstein's theory of relativity and energy. All things are made up of energy. The experience I had of belonging to the universe wasn't just a spiritual insight. Einstein and other scientists proved that since everything is energy, nothing is ever lost, and nothing is ever gained. When something is broken, the missing parts continue to exist, just not in the same shape or form. When water evaporates, those evaporated molecules still exist as gas. Matter is never lost when it changes form.

I realized how this intelligence about existence and life is paramount in protecting every human from the monstrous grief of loss. I was determined to help others understand this and other life intelligences in practical ways so they could live with ease and joy even after losing a loved one and so they could be relieved of many other ways we humans suffer and cause suffering in the world.

RETURN

MAGNIFICENT DOORS OPEN TO THE HERO

When we talk about doors opening in our lives, we usually think of doors to better finances, careers, or status. But these doors could be to accomplish anything our hearts desire. Campbell explains that as a result of this determination and willingness to meet the demons within magnificent doors open to the hero that may not open to anyone else. These are advancements achieved through challenges and failures.

In the final stage of the hero's journey, the hero returns to one's world — one's community — to tell about what one has found. The hero does this to help free others as well — to be of service.

As doors opened to help me accomplish my mission of purity and freedom from being stuck, other doors opened to help me understand the human heart and mind and their makeup. Sometimes these doors looked like those you see reflecting in a hall of mirrors, where there is no end. Like a dream, there is no last door. But you want to open them all. That's how eager and focused I was. These doors came in all kinds of forms — from nature, from science, from others' stories.

One of these doors opened my heart in a profound way. It was the story of Dipa Ma. As a young girl, like me, she suffered through the restrictions of her culture in India, but she became an enlightened being by meditating, calming her mind, and cultivating her heart. She was a heroine I could learn from. Reading Dipa Ma: The Life and Legacy of a Buddhist Master by Amy Schmidt nourished my heart. Schmidt gathered bits and pieces about Dipa Ma's life through interviews with her students. Dipa Ma lived an excruciatingly painful life even for a female in India. She grew up forbidden to meditate or visit any temples. She became ill with immense grief at the losses of her parents, her husband, and her child. But eventually, when everyone who had restricted her was gone from her life, she crawled to the steps of a Buddhist temple and found peace in focusing on a single breath.

Practicing diligently for many years, Dipa Ma reached enlightenment and taught others. What struck me so deeply was not only her overcoming her colossal grief but also her beautiful state of mind.

One of her students, Jack Kornfield, who is a prominent Buddhist teacher, asked Dipa Ma, "What is in your mind?"

She responded, "Loving-kindness."

That meant she could experience only love and kindness for any and all beings, including herself, at all times and under all circumstances. No judgment, just kindness. How amazing is that? That was when I realized that loving-kindness was something I had to fully understand and embody if I wanted to become as pure as I could be and live with joy. I will talk about loving-kindness throughout the book and particularly in chapter 19, MLOL 39.

Think of someone who has been a hero (any gender or race) in your eyes. What are some of his or her qualities, strengths, wishes, desires, and life circumstances? Do you see any of those in yourself or your life? Which of his or her qualities might you aspire to develop in yourself?

OPTIMIZATION

Of course, my version of the hero's journey doesn't end with return and tell. This hero has learned enough about life to know that living fully requires continued development, transformation, and optimization to embody other fundamental life intelligence qualities and skills. I had tasted the good life, the steady emotional well-being and the ability to restore biases to objectivity, resilience and joy. That was due to continuing to the optimization of my perspectives, choices, and actions.

Part 2 will give you my organic and highly effective five-stage Human Software Optimization, which I use to take my clients and students to optimal levels of conduct and experience. Please learn and feel free to transform and optimize yourself or your team, or use it for working with clients in therapy and coaching sessions.

If you have any questions about this model or Mindful Life Optimization professional training, contact us at http://drmotaghy.com.

PART II
MINDFUL LIFE OPTIMIZATION
(MLO)

JOIN

THE MAKING IT EASY TO BE HUMAN CLUB & COMMUNITY

Scan to Register Your Book to Meet the Author.

CHAPTER 5

AN OPTIMIZED INNER NAVIGATION ASSET

In one of the motivational summits I attended, Brendon Buchard said, When you know you have achieved the impossible, being alive, you can have an impossible vision. The vision of this book is for you to have an optimal inner navigation system, an important inner resource that can guide you through life. Inner navigation capabilities become important assets to attract better relationships, employers, and higher quality of life. For those who are stuck in the SMADE programming, change may seem difficult, but it is a worthy vision for this life. Our inner worlds need to be developed and continually transformed to finally be optimized so that we may live meaningfully with love and joy. Let's talk about what a navigation system does.

The Oxford English Dictionary defines navigation as "the process or activity of accurately ascertaining one's position and planning and following a route." With modern urban planning and well-designed gridlines that include streets and highways, it is not so difficult to plan a route to get somewhere. It's even easier to do so with continually optimized navigation applications, such as Google Maps or Waze, or other tools designed to help you get from point A to point B. Google Maps, for instance, takes a given destination and charts the route. It's coded by algorithms that can inform you how long it'll take to get there and tell you about traffic conditions and other obstacles. Not only that, but it also provides options for changing routes. It makes traveling much easier. I, personally, feel much gratitude for the Google Maps app each time I use it and arrive at my destination. However, I also see how dependent I've become on these directions by not using my own memory system to remember routes. So I pull back from using it unless it is absolutely necessary, in an effort not to weaken my inner navigation capabilities, such as discernment and self-confidence.

In his book *Hidden Potential*, renowned organizational psychologist Adam Grant suggests that as our lives become more and more automated, technology takes over our relationships and interactions, and we use our cognitive abilities less and less, we need to master skills that make us human, such as having a solid character. He explains why character is more important than talent and makes the difference between winning and losing in competitions, games, and other aspects of life. Though I do not promote or subscribe to the concepts of winning and losing, I agree that our character development includes getting better at getting better; learning about how we learn, which can be through intuition or even awkwardness; learning by making lots of honest mistakes; being OK with what's uncomfortable; and developing motivation and endurance. Grant also notes that when developing oneself, "It's not about working harder, but about how much you grow."

In comparison to Google Maps or other external navigation systems, the human inner navigation system needs much more comprehensive capabilities. To navigate your way out from wherever you are stuck in life and enjoy an easier, happier life, you may, for example, need to build the heart intelligence (HQ) qualities and character, heal some wounds, create better internal algorithms that include the intelligence of the intuition through bodily sensations, and optimize the cognitive capabilities you already have. Navigating life challenges successfully also requires clearly discerning the intention and purpose of your vision or the end goal.

For example, one of my clients, Shannon (name changed), was in the middle of a divorce she didn't want. Shannon was often uneasy about her newly separated husband, Moshe (name changed), having a good time with his friends. She was obsessed with Moshe and built stories in her mind, as it is so easy to do, that Moshe was already forming an intimate relationship with another woman. This thought was painful for her, and the more she thought about it, the more she felt upset and justified. In a moment of heated perception, unable to sort those feelings out, she sent messages to Moshe, telling him how awful and nasty he was, which escalated an already bitter and hostile relationship. Her inner navigation system didn't have an optimized feature to alert her, saying, "Obstacles or roadblock ahead — going this route will cause you more pain," nor did she have the ability to regulate those emotions so that she could see a better route option. We worked on her recognizing her impatience and jumping to conclusions as ineffective and even harmful reaction and behavior. We continued with practices that helped her to develop self-love, discernment, and inner tools to neutralize her painful subjective perceptions.

Below is the MLO formula, which you can use as a developmental and life-optimization training tool. I will guide you through this as we continue. Depending on your current inner navigation capabilities, you can set some inner development goals and accomplish them incrementally.

There are two parts to developing and optimizing your inner navigation system and assets:

1. A five-stage methodology (the road map)
2. Mindful Life Optimization lessons (MLOLs) that are mindfully thought out and described

I will first lay out the training road map, which is the five-stage Human Software Optimization (HSO) method. Then I will present sixty MLOLs, which you can acquire through those five stages.

If you come across an MLOL for which using the five-stage HSO doesn't feel organic, please give us feedback on your process so we can guide you. You can reach out to me or one of our trained professionals for further assistance by sending an email to http://drmotaghy.com. If you need more learning opportunities, visit perfectlyhere.org.

HUMAN SOFTWARE OPTIMIZATION (HSO)

HSO is a synthesis of lifelong personal and professional success gained through countless lessons and experiential practices from subjects in psychology to business and mindfulness certificate programs; scientific and philosophical perspectives; and insights gained through thousands of hours of silently retreating and experiencing the Buddha's teachings on understanding suffering, its causes, and how to end it. For decades, hour after hour, day after day, I studied, practiced, investigated, asked questions of masters, and put their answers to the test.

This curiosity and determination required me to go deep into the dark caves of my soul to excavate those promised treasures and rebuild the broken foundations of my mind. While digging, I saw faulty mental codes attached to great values and life skills. I learned how to decode them in ways that would not throw away the good with the bad. I learned how to transform each faulty, unhealthy habit of the mind with healthy, strong, honest, organic codes of conduct, and I taught these to others. And now I offer their sweet fruits to you, my beloved reader. With reflection and effort, you can rebuild and optimize your inner navigation capabilities to become your most valuable asset, one that supports you throughout the rest of your life in any context and situation. This inner optimization happens in five organic stages.

THE FIVE STAGES OF HSO

HSO's five stages are as follows: (1) Mindful Life Optimization lessons (MLOLs), (2) mindful authentication, (3) development, (4) transformation, and (5) optimization.

A Whole Human Development Methodology

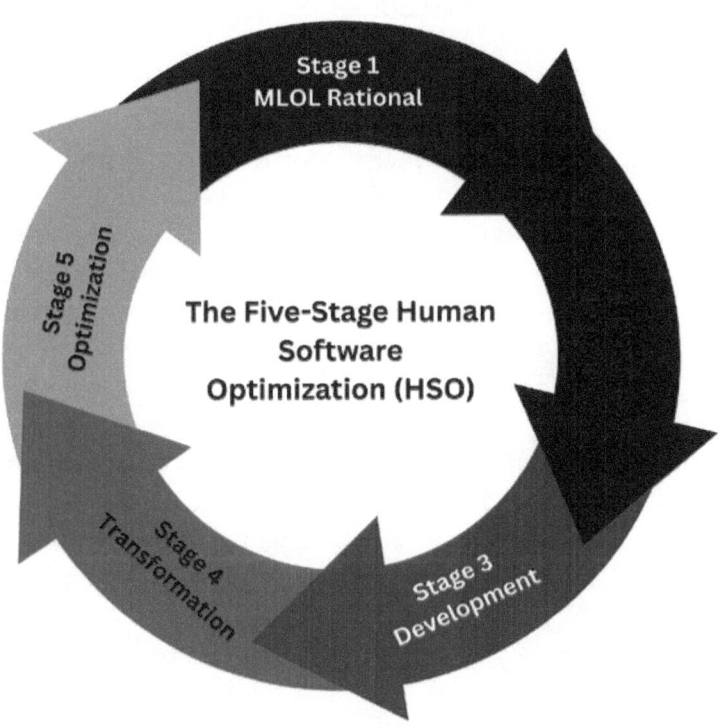

Figure 3

Copyright Dr. Manijeh Motaghy

I am happy to note that there are people who, by being exposed to the right conditions from birth and continuing after, already possess these valuable qualities and inner resources. However, we can all enjoy such programming by putting our minds, focus, and attention toward making our happiness a priority. It's also not about achieving all or nothing. Some aspects of your life may work well, and others may not.

Your inner navigation system can be upgraded wherever needed through the HSO process.

THE FIVE-STAGE SMADE STUCK MODEL VERSUS THE FIVE-STAGE HUMAN SOFTWARE OPTIMIZATION MODEL

Do you remember the five stages of SMADE programming in chapter 3? In that model, people receive false or incomplete information, make incorrect interpretations, and become habituated to telling themselves stories to make sense of situations. They believe their thoughts and perceptions are true, and they end up making mistakes, having relationship issues, causing disharmony, and living without awareness. They live on autopilot, run by their faulty inner navigation program, which constantly steers them wrong and causes them and others undue pain and suffering. On the other hand, people whose inner navigation systems and capabilities are optimized are present and fully aware of their thoughts, feelings, and actions. They are considerate and wise; make fewer mistakes; and would not do anything that would cause themselves, others, or the planet any harm.

The tables across show the two models differ in their processes.

SMADE vs. HSO
Human Development Model Comparison

SMADE Human Software Stuck Model	HSO Human Software Optimization Model
Stage 1: Senses receive information through internal and external sources. Caretakers and others may not have Mindful Life Intelligence to pass on. They may neglect or flood the infant with false notions and painful experiences.	**Stage 1: MLOLs:** Caregivers and others enjoy an optimized human software coded by truths of life, alignment with laws of nature, discernment, presence, compassion, joy, and resilience. They pass on these to the infant, setting the foundation for a fully optimized adult.
Stage 2: Meanings, labels, and explanations are often biased or miss the truth, leaving room for misinterpretations. Distorted realities code the human templates of perception and action.	**Stage 2: Mindful Verification:** The person is taught how to know the nature of truth, lessons, and experiences for oneself. Curiosity, openness, and self-analysis become the building blocks of their development.
Stage 3: Adaptation, habits, and reactionary feelings take root. The skill of storyizing or making up reality becomes practiced and strong.	**Stage 3: Development:** Inner capacities and life intelligence continue to grow as one practices authenticity, conscious living, and other MLO lessons under the three domains.
Stage 4: Disposition or personality is formed. Acting on autopilot, blaming external situations for one's unhappiness. Thinking and behaving through judgment, criticism, outbursts, avoidance, or hiding behind games, activities, drugs, or alcohol. Feeling anxious, restless,	**Stage 4: Transformation:** What has been developed becomes effective habits and traits. Living wisely becomes natural, effortless, and harmless. When transformed in adulthood, one may return to old habits, but they know the pathway to natural, optimized living.
Stage 5: Enervated and engulfed. Without the inner skills of self-analysis, self-regulation, presence, discernment, compassion, and gratitude, one becomes stuck in cycles of suffering with rigid views and causes others and the world pain and suffering.	**Stage 5: Optimization:** Once the person is developed/transformed in all three domains of Mindful Life Intelligence, they are aligned with the laws of nature and have optimal inner-development to lead a life of contentment, non-harming, and joy. They thrive in all aspects of their lives. The world is a better place for it.

Figure 4

Because both these developmental models continue to form from infancy to adulthood, individuals can still begin optimizing their human software or inner navigation capabilities during any stage of their lives. In the chapters that follow, I will describe each of these stages, include scientific and logical explanations, and provide examples to equip you in becoming skilled and fully transformed into a confident and self- loving human.

The next chapter will lay out and describe the first stage of this training roadmap.

CHAPTER 6

STAGE 1: THE LOGIC BEHIND MLOLs

MINDFUL LIFE OPTIMIZATION LESSONS

Chapters 12 through 21 provide fundamental MLOLs that are necessary for human development. These lessons are based on how life works. They can withstand test of time and scrutiny, as opposed to random lessons that may be faulty, incomplete, biased, interpretation, and, in some cases, deceptive and harmful. MLOLs make up the first stage of Human Software Optimization, which draws on critical thinking, encouraging the cultivation of seeing the world wisely. They offer principles, qualities, and skills we all need to understand and become good at. They include some lost wisdom as well as modern scientific knowledge and other best practices that will help reduce stress, worry, anxiety, and other pains we humans create for ourselves.

RESILIENCE AND OBJECTIVITY

We have learned how mind viruses and faulty codes and perspectives cause a person to feel stuck in unhappiness. But you do not have to be completely stuck to have mind viruses and faulty perspectives. You may have developed strengths and capabilities, such as resourcefulness, courage, perseverance, empathy, determination, and creativity that make you resilient and aid you in managing your affairs and succeeding in life. These qualities can lessen that feeling of being stuck.

Objectivity is another great quality you may have. Being objective, you can make things happen, find solutions, and continue moving, despite being stressed, anxious, and burdened by social realities and ineffective perspectives, strategies, and habits. The great news is that you have less work to do, as you are better able to use objectivity and resilience to learn the MLOLs that help your optimization process.

No matter how entangled you are, you're in good hands because the second stage of optimization provides an effective way to fact-check any life lesson or meme or anything that anyone, even your own mind, presents as the truth.

HOW TO TAKE AN MLOL THROUGH STAGE 1

To begin, choose any of the MLOLs from chapters 12 through 21 that seem important or that you feel drawn to, and answer the following questions:

1. What do you think of this MLOL?
2. Do you have prior knowledge of the subject? How does its explanation compare to what you already know or to how you have come to believe it?
3. Can you see how delving deeper into this topic might be helpful to you or someone else?
4. Can you see the logic and intention behind this lesson?

Don't worry if you cannot see the logic behind it. Stage 2 is supposed to help you mindfully authenticate its validity through personal experience, which may then clarify how this MLOL can transform your life.

Let's go to stage 2.

CHAPTER 7

STAGE 2: MINDFUL AUTHENTICATION

This stage is about being present, examining, and realizing through insight. In 1983, Harvard professor and psychologist Howard Gardner put forward a theory that explained the various ways people learn. These include visual and spatial, physical movement and motor control (kinesthetic), rhythm and music, words and language, logic and mathematics, interpersonal, introspection and self-reflection, and seeing and understanding patterns and relationships in nature. We also need to learn with presence and curiosity.

When mindful awareness and the opportunity to verify a lesson are missing from learning processes, the learning can't be sustained, which is the reason for including this second step. For example, you may have heard the theory of the Secret, which claims that the vast power of the universe can give you what you want and that whatever you think about or engage in is what you'll receive. Therefore, it would be to your advantage to think positively, not negatively, and ask for bigger and better things. You might like this idea and want to benefit from it, but you can't constantly stay positive or disengage from negative thinking. Then you forget it without knowing how true such a theory is.

I am not advocating for the theory of the Secret, because I know there is much more to it, such as cause and effect and our actions interfering with the laws of the universe. Positivity is not enough. But if you have simple, consistent ways to verify such theories and lessons for yourself, then your mind and brain will begin to adopt their truths or else will dismiss them because you know their fallacies through insight and wisdom.

Some people are good at doing this—for example, verifying news by fact-checking or looking at all sides before accepting what is presented. This stage helps you to determine if the inner qualities and skills described here can help you to be whole and live with ease. For those you cannot verify for yourself yet, you can be open and curious and keep those principles in mind.

What if you already accept the validity of a lesson? For some MLOLs, you may think, I already get this—I know what change means, what mindfulness is, and what interdependence is. I don't need to verify these. Just tell me how to develop myself to live more effectively. I still encourage you not to skip this part, because it may provide deeper insights, and it will contribute to your overall development.

To authenticate a MLOL, you need to be present and mindful, not lost in a million thoughts. A lack of mindful presence can make it difficult to differentiate truth from habitual ways of thinking. But we all have to start somewhere. As you reflect, observe, and verify MLOLs, you may learn things about your behaviors and patterns, such as where they came from and where they have led you. You may feel uncomfortable and want to stop. Be patient and curious to see what shows up. This is part of your growth.

The mindful authentication stage is broken down into three steps:

1. Become Present
2. Examine.
3. Realize.

BECOME PRESENT

Being present is one of the most valuable qualities and skills our inner navigation system can possess. The more you practice it, the better you become at it. Becoming present can be quickly accomplished through our bodily sensations. Why? Because they are happening at this very moment. You do not feel an itch you had yesterday. Though the brain will always superimpose past related experiences onto this moment's context, the raw experience of sensations and feelings can bring your mind to experience what is happening in the present.

Let's try an exercise to get you to become present. If you are listening to an audio version of this book, close your eyes, and follow my guidance—but not while driving, please. If you are reading, you may leave your eyes open so you can continue reading while experiencing the present moment, or read the instructions, and then close your eyes and do them.

Breathe consciously for a second or two. Then point your attention to feeling something that's touching your body, such as your clothes, your chair, or the ground under your feet. While feeling your body, notice any pain or tightness, high or low energy, or any other feeling: warmth, coolness, or emotions. Breathe, and relax your shoulders. Now concentrate on one point of touch, such as your chest or hands. Notice that when you feel your hands, it's hard to avoid feeling other parts and the whole body, as they are connected. The actual feeling of the body is being present to yourself and your experience in a physical sense. Then, with a kind intention for your body to feel more comfortable, shift your body to straighten up or to correct your posture. Notice if you feel any different by adjusting yourself. Thoughts may have disappeared for a few moments. Consider what else you may need to pay attention to for your mind to experience the present moment. That's all part of being mindful of supporting your purpose and intention.

While you're feeling your hands, your mind may take you away to thinking about this and that, where you become those thoughts. Becoming those thoughts is the opposite of being present.

So keep checking in with yourself through your senses—smell, sound, sight, touch, taste, inner feeling—and your mind to become present and available. This way, you consciously reflect, observe, and gain insights you can trust to make sound conclusions about each of the MLOLs. In chapter 20, you'll find an explanation in MLOL 50 of how to be fully mindful, what it means to be mindful, and how one becomes present.

EXAMINE

Now that you are present, we can go deeper into the MLOL you chose for stage 1 and examine your relationship to it. You may use a journal to respond to these questions. These reflections are just for you to bring you closer to an authentic experience of life.

1. Does this MLOL trigger any feelings or emotions or any attitude? Do you have an opinion about this lesson? After you respond to this question, your mind might be going from one story to another. Pause and come back to being present. Breathe, feel your body, and relax.
2. Look into this MLOL with more conscious awareness. Is it just an idea? Is there any truth to it? Have you experienced it before in your life, in your relationships, at work, or in the environment? You can also check if you might be biased about this through how you have associated with this topic before, or you may not have thought about it.
3. Does it confirm anything for you or reject it?
4. Ask yourself, "If the lesson is true, how would it affect my life and choices? If it isn't true, how would it affect me?"
5. What other question about the MLOL you're looking at might you ask here? Be creative, and allow yourself time to reflect.

REALIZE

With examination of the truth of something come insights and realizations. Insights are usually known for having a positive impact, but realization about the truth of something can have various effects on us. Seeing the truth of something can be freeing, but it can also cause stress and disharmony. Accepting the truth sometimes means we might have to make big changes we're not ready for. If you're not ready for the change at the moment, you don't have to give up the realization. So be kind to yourself. Take as much time as you need for change to happen in its good time. Try to make a note of it in your mind, and keep the light of insight about the truth you have realized alive.

The next chapter will discuss and explain stage 3, development.

CHAPTER 8

STAGE 3: DEVELOPMENT

> Tell me and I will forget; show me and I may remember;
> involve me and I will understand.
>
> —Confucius

This stage is about having clarity, getting the right instructions, focusing on the effects, normalizing these qualities in your life, learning from the right models, and becoming the person you want to be.

In grad school, I was always asking, "How? How do I gain this quality or that skill?" The subject matter revolved around the psychology of humans in the corporate world. We were learning about best practices for leadership, team building, self-management, and so on. While thinking about various theories in leadership, I'd wonder, for example, *How do connective leaders do what they do? Now that I know the style and am inspired by it, how can I do this myself?*

It wasn't until I finally got to do hands-on learning that I felt confident I understood a topic and could perform it. We had projects that had to be done for real organizations with real scenarios. They included strategic planning; creating goals and objectives; drawing visions; and fine-tuning missions, core values, and the like. I knew both intuitively and by experience that if I wanted to truly develop in any area, I had to go beyond getting it conceptually. In *Hidden Potential*, Adam Grant writes, "I've spent much of my career studying the forces that fuel our progress. I've found that the learning process isn't finished

70

when we acquire knowledge. It's complete when we consistently apply that knowledge."

Your development process began with stage 1 and then the effort to authenticate the validity of a life lesson in stage 2. Those two stages engaged your critical thinking and prepared your brain in regenerating the neuropathways that help these life skills become automatic and natural for you.

Once you've mindfully authenticated an MLOL in stage 2 and you feel motivated to develop habits around it, you can partake in exercises, practices, and behaviors that help to cultivate higher standards of care and attentiveness to details of your daily activities. Even though development is an active stage, some of these MLOLs are about laws and principles that govern us, and we don't really have to do anything about them but recognize their presence and stay out of their way. Other MLOLs may require taking varying steps for development. But all are experiential and promote authenticity, truth, and confidence.

It is also not unusual to have some level of development of some of the related MLOLs in each of the three domains. If that's the case, that's great. Just come back to this stage if you need to further improve those skills.

THE FOUR ESSENTIALS IN DEVELOPMENT

1. Clarity
2. Instructions
3. Focus on effects
4. Normalization

CLARITY

By this stage, after you've read and reflected on your chosen MLOL, its lesson must be clear to you. You know the intention behind it and are aware of its benefits to your life. If you come across an MLOL you aren't clear about, go back to stages 1 and 2 before jumping to the next step here.

INSTRUCTIONS

The next thing to do is to try the related instructions. Many of the MLOLs in this book either are guides or include instructions that can help you develop their purpose and intention. You may find other instructions on perfectlyhere.org or in my courses, related books, and resources, for example, how to live a sustainable personal and professional life. You may get them through people you know or models, which I will cover toward the end of this chapter. But instructions and guidance play a key role.

FOCUS ON EFFECTS

As you take instructions and continue to develop your inner capabilities, notice the impact on you and on your surroundings. If they have positive effects, continue using those instructions and developing those qualities. If they have negative effects, stop and ask for help and then modify the practice to improve your situation. I once heard that a person did three thousand days' worth of a specific type of breathing, and she still couldn't get the perfect effect she was told she should experience. Then, one day, a guru told her she had been doing it wrong all along. Can you imagine how she must have felt to hear that? So don't wait that long to ask for clarification and guidance.

Be aware that at first, with some of these practices, you may feel a bit off or clumsy, or you might feel anxious from realizing how you've been living contrary to those truths. Be patient with and kind to yourself. Recognize how far you have come in life— how many things you have learned and how many obstacles you have overcome. Encourage yourself to continue by focusing on the positive effects developing this MLOL can have on your life.

NORMALIZATION

This is when you set up routines to practice a skill and make it a habit. "Practice makes perfect," they say. While we're not looking for perfection, we are looking to bring consistency to our beneficial actions so they become automatic — so we can experience them as traits and not as effortful. This is the way to transformation.

LEARNING FROM BEST MODELS

We all need models in life — those who embody and exhibit qualities we seek, who can show us the way and show us that we can too. Models who have traveled the road can tell us where the bumps are and how to get around them. We need them to show us where and how to refuel and teach us to be patient with mistakes. The best thing about connecting with these models is that their evolved wiring can help to wire our brains (create connections and new neuropathways for understanding) and make our process of development easier.

For example, for a few years, I closely interacted with a relative who is extremely organized, tidy, and punctual. Most importantly, he puts his happiness first. As a result of proximity and regular interaction, I learned the importance of being attentive, organized, and tidy and of keeping track of time and not ignoring any little odd symptoms in my body. These skills have contributed to lessening my self-judgment, wasting less time looking for things, becoming more efficient, and having better self-care. As you explore any of the MLOLs, think of people in your life who may be great models for you. You've already learned so much from so many people. Maybe you have an exceptional aunt or uncle; a wise grandmother; or a friend, teacher, or neighbor who displays qualities and skills you seek to embody. Spend time with those people. Ask them questions. Watch how they manifest, perform, or live their qualities. The models may also show up in media, such as documentaries and biographies of great people who appeal to you, ones who raise your bar on some MLOL. Let your mind capture the how of it.

INTENTION

To benefit from any of the MLOL qualities and skills, you must also work on wise intention, or it will backfire. (Read about wise intention in chapter 18, MLOL 37.) No matter how enticing the act, if it takes anything away from anyone or causes harm to anyone, you are connected to that harm. You will feel its negative energy. Your mind will remain restless and not a tease. It always boggles my mind when the bad guy in a movie gets killed in the end. I think, *Didn't he know that he too could get hit with a bullet and die? I feel sad for him.*

As you are learning from others, be careful not to pick up habits that are partly effective and partly negative and that you'll later want to give up. For example, if you learn from a successful salesperson or businessperson to become great in sales, that's a useful skill, but part of it may depend on knowing how to deceive others. Using deceptive methods will eventually run you into problems. To check for this in the models you're aiming to follow, ask yourself the following:

1. Do they act with integrity and with genuine care and attention to the impact of their actions?
2. If not, how have their underlying intentions to deceive, take, or twist the truth panned out? Was it all success, or did a lot of stress and suffering come with it?
3. How should I revise the steps they took?
4. What can I add to improve the benefits of that skill for myself and others?

Cyrus the Great always instructed his generals to be models their soldiers could follow. For example, they were to treat their subjects as equal to themselves and to eat and sleep in the same tents on the battlefield, keeping the morale up and not making any man feel less important or envious, which might turn him into an enemy.

BECOME THE PERSON YOU WANT TO BE

James Clear, in his book *Atomic Habits*, advises that when trying to change a habit or pick up a good one, you should not think of the end goal, because that may not turn out to be the actual goal you want to achieve. Also, if your goal is lofty and hard to achieve, you may give up too soon. Instead, think of the new habit as an identity you're taking on "the kind of person you want to be." By focusing on the kind of people we want to be, we get to examine how we might be stuck in an identity that holds us back and, hopefully, free ourselves from it. By focusing on the kind of people we want to be, we realize that the stakes are higher, and therefore, we are motivated to set identity goals with care and wisely.

Next, we'll look at stage four, transformation.

CHAPTER 9

STAGE 4: TRANSFORMATION

WHAT IS TRANSFORMATION?

Transformation is when things change for the better. You change. Your life changes. You no longer respond to things in old ways that may not have been as skillful. You realize something is different. Your habits have changed. You're calmer, wiser, more understanding, less reactive, and more patient. Your life and work become easier. Others notice it too. They feel it and are pleasantly surprised.

Some people, such as family members, may still be stuck on the old version of you until you point it out. Those who can benefit from your transformation stick around; those who are stuck in the old ways tend to disappear. Or you move on.

It means you have actualized one or more of the MLOLs you've been working on. Now you know for yourself what living an MLOL looks like and feels like, and you also are skilled at performing them and, more importantly, being them. These skillful behaviors have become your new responses, and if you ever go back to old ways, you can quickly catch yourself and get back to doing things your new and improved way.

That's transformation. It feels peaceful and confident, and life, in many ways, becomes easier and more enjoyable.

HOW IS TRANSFORMATION ACHIEVED?

Achieving transformation requires going through the first three stages of Human Software Optimization and normalizing the practices you were given into your daily life. By doing so, you understand the rationale behind an MLOL, have verified its validity and benefit, and have followed directions to develop related skills. Continued practice and development of each MLOL finally becomes your natural response. If you realize you still can't do something skillfully, such as interacting with a sibling without being triggered, please seek advice and learn more about those emotions and how you may handle them — and keep at it.

RESOLVE DISAPPOINTMENTS

More importantly, try not to get disappointed or give up too early before making these inner qualities and skills new traits and automatic. I've seen this perception too often while teaching mindfulness courses; beginning students expressed that they still couldn't keep themselves from self- judgment, couldn't keep their attention on the breath during meditation, couldn't remember to meditate, and so on. They usually made these comments after two or three sessions in an introductory class. It always surprised me how much they expected of themselves so soon. By the end of the sixth session, though, almost no one who did the exercises said they couldn't do the practices. As long as you keep practicing, you will always progress, even if it may not be as fast or as much as you'd like.

MANAGE CONDITIONS THAT HINDER YOUR PROGRESS

To improve your odds for learning, you can look at the environment and conditions that might hinder your progress. In chapter 12, MLOL 4, I talk about causes and conditions and how they affect change. You can always improve conditions in your surrounding environment to support your transformation.

An internal condition that hinders progress is impatience. Impatience can distort our perception of growth. I know this from gardening.

When I plant a seed, depending on the type, it takes several days to a couple of weeks to germinate and sprout. Normally, germination takes place under the soil, so I cannot see how the seed is activated, growing and bursting out of its skin and trying to emerge into the light. When I look for the sprout before the germination process has transformed into the sprouting stage, I think something is wrong. I wonder if I've done it wrong, or maybe the seed is not good. That uncomfortable feeling of uncertainty kicks in, and I end up losing hope that it will ever happen. Of course, now these doubtful thoughts last for just a few moments for me, and they pass quickly as I feel them and let them go. The same analogy applies to seeds of wisdom and the process of behavior change. So be patient. Endure the discomfort of waiting for the right amount of time and practice to see considerable change. Water and nourish the seeds of the MLOLs you're working on. That means you seek to understand, develop to embody them, and acknowledge their benefits. Be willing to fail and make mistakes.

Failure, mistakes, and clumsiness are signs that your brain is working on creating new neuropathways and is not yet ready to put your intended new habits on autopilot. But if you persist, that time will come. If you let go too fast, those essential neuropathways won't develop, and the sapling of new knowledge, intelligence, and inner navigation capabilities won't grow. You are here, so at least your attention and self-love must be stronger by now.

SEEK OPPORTUNITIES THAT SUPPORT TRANSFORMATION

Similar to having great models we can learn from, participating in groups and communities focused on creating the same qualities in their lives is of utmost value for transformation. Taking into account neurodiversity and learning variations, following guidelines and routines shared through a community and structured environments can be especially conducive to learning and growth.

For example, my own transformation in these MLOLs is heavily due to my spending days at Buddhist monasteries under Ajahn Chah, who revived the way of forest practice in alignment with how the Buddha lived his life. Abhayagiri, the Northern California branch, is like a university, with lectures, daily practice structure, a library with diverse books from all kinds of topics, and lots of opportunities for anyone who seeks to dig in and explore his or her own mind. One gets to learn about the causes of suffering, the obstacles in the way of happiness, and how to achieve peacefulness. Then one can use silence in meditation and quiet time like a science laboratory to explore.

The experience there is so deep and fulfilling that any other fun vacation feels to me like a waste of time. Being in the presence of kind, mindful, and compassionate practicing monks and lay visitors and following the daily work and meditation structure create plenty of fruitful opportunities for mindfulness practice. When I'm there, I feel not only peaceful but also respected and loved unconditionally. I have learned what it means to feel loved and to love another with no strings attached. Even when people get annoyed at someone, the environment encourages compassion. On his first trip, my son, sitting on the top of the hill next to the golden Buddha overlooking the forest below, said, "Mom, I cannot believe how happy I am here without my phone and iPod and without chatting with my friends on social media. I never thought such a thing was possible." He said this with tears of joy.

When you live in a city, following the conventions of mainstream life and trying to implement those teachings into your daily routine, it is a different experience. Therefore, making an effort to visit and spend time with those whose lives are dedicated to cultivating these excellent inner qualities and skills offers opportunities to experience these teachings in actions and interactions. Through the brain's capacity for being wired by others, one can gain a profound understanding and adopt those principles. As your transformation in how you view the world and act in it becomes regular, you will also realize its benefits for others in your life. You'll become more aware, nonjudgmental, patient, and understanding, and others will be grateful for it. As you become more aware and act with consideration, the quality of your relationships will also transform. They will improve over time. So keep looking forward to that transformation that awaits you.

Next comes the fifth and final stage: optimization.

CHAPTER 10

STAGE 5: OPTIMIZATION

Congratulations on making it this far! It's taken much interest and dedication to get here. Optimization is about achieving transformation in all three domains of mindful life intelligence.

Let's recap the past four stages of Human Software Optimization (HSO) before we get to the final stage.

- **Stage 1: Logic behind MLOLs** provides an objective and reasonable look at the lessons from the three domains of mindful life intelligence. Do they make enough sense for you to test them out?
- **Stage 2: Mindful Authentication** offers the means for you to verify these lessons by becoming present, examining them with your own personal experience, and testing if they're true.
- **Stage 3: Development** offers the means to develop each MLOL's fundamental principles, inner qualities, and skills and to normalize their presence in your life.
- **Stage 4: Transformation** is gained when the new mindsets and effective responses and habits become automatic traits. They become effortless. Should you fall back to the old habit, you know the path to get back on track.

The fifth stage, Optimization, provides a wider path to inspire you to continue developing and transforming in all MLOLs in each domain until you have covered them all. Here you discover what else needs your attention. Can you pinpoint something that will empower you to release yourself and the world from suffering? This is a holistic strategy for transformation, in which you zoom out and look at the bigger picture of life to gain growth and development through effective means of spirituality, psychology, neuroscience, environmental sciences, AI, commerce, and so forth. We human scan benefit from being fully integrated by becoming better equipped and collaborating to resolve both individual and world issues. So please don't stop before reaching the end of the process — keep striving to optimize your human software and that incredible inner navigation system filled with capabilities that can move all of us toward a thriving and fulfilling experience of life.

RECOGNIZING AND NEUTRALIZING SELF-DOUBT

As you grow, develop, and transform, before reaching full optimization, you may lose motivation for various reasons. For example, you may feel frustrated with other people who are not on this path of growth and development and feel discouraged to continue. One of my students expressed that she felt that working on herself was useless, when most of her family and others she interacted with were in denial, lived carelessly, and had no compassion for others. She thought, What's the use anyway? This sense of hopelessness can cause confusion and doubt, which can fog up your view and direction in life and hinder your flow and continuation. It is said that in the last stages of the Buddha's enlightenment, Mara, or Satan, appeared to him to try to stop him from advancing to his final destination of freedom from delusion and of knowing the whole truth of life. Mara brought several obstacles to trick him and to knock him off his concentration and connection to the truth. His first four obstacles — craving, hate, restlessness, and lethargy — didn't work. Mara's last weapon was to generate self-doubt in Prince Siddhartha, the Buddha-to-be, but because Siddhartha's development and attainment were complete, doubt couldn't hinder his clarity.

Self-doubt is tricky and can be subtle. We may doubt our own capacity or worthiness or doubt the process itself. Doubt can get a foothold when we forget our vision and the benefits we've gained on the journey to optimization so far. However, experiencing doubt is a great opportunity to learn more about oneself, what it means to be human, and what is left to work on. It shows us what it feels like to be disappointed. It gives us a chance to develop more empathy and compassion for others who doubt themselves and lose their way in life.

We can keep it light. Laugh at these findings. Continuing to gain such insights in to human experience can brighten a dimmed heart and keep previous insights lit, allowing us to remember that our perceptions as well as the time we have left in this life are relentlessly passing. This reminds me of a retreat attendee who came to set mindful intentions for 2024. She shared that the process I took them through reminded her that more than a decade ago, she had learned from a one-year trip that creating meaningful connections and relationships was much more important in her life than material things. Ten years later, this day retreat revealed to her that she had lost that insight and had resumed neglecting her happiness. This can easily happen to any of us—stopping or breaking the chain of presence and awareness and falling into old habits and autopilot, causing the insights we've had to dim or be lost to us. Gradually, we rebuild a strong and healthy sense of self, no matter how many of our perceptions and delusions we have to come back to destroy and rebuild.

Rumi, one of the greatest poets and philosophers of all time, demonstrates how destruction is a natural part of building new foundations:

> When a tailor cuts the cloth for a garment piece by
> piece, does anyone strike him, saying, "Why have you
> torn this choice satin?"
> Whenever the builders repair an old building,
> don't they first ruin the first one?
> Likewise, the carpenter, the blacksmith, and the butcher,
> with them too, there is destruction before restoration.

Unless you crush the wheat in the mill,
how will there be bread on your table?

Let us persevere to reach transformation in all three domains and reap the benefits of an optimized inner navigation system.

WHICH LESSON TO PICK FIRST?

When you're picking from the list of MLOLs from chapter 12 and after, some may not seem as urgent. Just make a note of those and continue with any that you feel drawn to. Developing and gaining wisdom and insight from one MLOL can positively affect all other areas, as our lives consist of a web of interconnected and interdependent physiological, psychological, biological, neurological, spiritual, and environmental conditions, causes, and effects. Improving perspective or skill in one area can have ripple effects and improve your perspective or skill in another. For example, developing mindfulness of body, mind, feelings, and events through self-awareness and attentiveness can have immeasurable positive effects on skills you may not have even developed. Let me explain through an example.

One day I was sitting with my family on a bench at a park, where my siblings and their partners were playing tennis, my sister came over to me, huffing and agitated, because she couldn't get it right. She put the racket in my hands and sternly said, "It's your turn, Sis."

I insisted that I couldn't play and refused, but I eventually caved in to please her, thinking, *I'm so bad, and when she sees it, it will make her feel better.* So I agreed and went on to the court.

Surprisingly, I played really well! My sister kept making fun of me: "Yeah, she can't play, ha ha." I believed I couldn't play because of an embarrassing experience I'd had as a teenager new to the United States, which had caused me never to pick up a racket again. I was really shy and knew only a few words and phrases in English when they placed me in physical education to play tennis. The first time I ever held and served the ball, it and the tennis racket flew into the air and hit my partner, who was a good-looking lad standing in the front on the left side. The ball hit his neck, and the racket hit the back of his legs. Out of shock and embarrassment, I stood there silently, unable even to express how sorry I was. The wave of shame was so powerful that I ran out, and that was the last time I ever played tennis.

When replacing my sister and doing so well that day, I realized I wasn't triggered with the shame of that trauma, which could have easily disabled me. But more importantly, because I didn't want to hit and harm anyone again, I held on to the racket tightly and focused on the ball as it moved in the air toward me and back to the other side. I was calm, fully aware, and attentive. I realized because I had been training and developing my attention and self-awareness, I was able to direct my attention to be aware of my thoughts, emotions, and physical sensations and to keep my attention anchored in my body. I stood firmly and tied my attention to the bottom of my feet (as I had done many times in walking meditation), and I didn't get distracted by what others were saying or the chaos of the park. Having developed those inner capabilities helped me to perform a task I hadn't developed. It was a great joy to hit the ball back and forth for a few rounds.

You will benefit from developing any and all of these MLOLs. Simply run any of them, or other lessons in this book, through the five stages of Human Software Optimization. Most importantly, enjoy the process.

MY SECRET RECIPE FOR TRANSFORMING OTHERS

I'll give therapists and coaches a little secret to the recipe I use when working to transform and optimize my students' and clients' cognition and internal navigation capabilities. Of course, they come to me for help with something they're stuck in or suffer from, not to optimize their navigation capabilities. But that's what happens at the end.

It's a three-step process. First, I listen to find the glitch in their perspectives and weakness in their inner skills. These glitches could be false notions or mental viruses that cause them pain and suffering, or

They might lack knowledge of how things work. Second, I debug the fallacy and treat the mental virus that causes pain in their lives by gently introducing some truth or MLOL codes. Third, I reveal and nourish the inner strengths and goodness they already have developed within them. There is no linear order here, but I use these three steps in every session, and it works like a charm. You can go about your process in this way as well. Reach out to me via http://drmotaghy.com if you have any questions about this process. I have also included a case study at the end of chapter 21 to illustrate how I went about influencing and transforming someone who is a possible narcissist (NPD).

Now let us move to the universal and timeless Mindful Life Optimization lessons I've been rooting for. You have the path and the knowledge regarding how to achieve them via the five-stage human optimization method. Let's look at what these MLOLs are.

PART III
MLO LESSONS
(DOMAINS ONE AND TWO)

JOIN
THE MAKING IT EASY TO BE HUMAN CLUB & COMMUNITY

Scan to Register Your Book to Meet the Author. Get Support on Your Transformation Journey.

CHAPTER 11

MINDFUL LIFE INTELLIGENCE

LIFE

Life is a complex subject we can look at from many angles and with many definitions. From a personal angle, we can see life through our human experience as physical beings, including aging and health; our wishes, hopes, and desires; the pain and suffering we may have endured; or the meaning or quality of life we seek. We can look at life in relation to our material belongings, the relationships we build, or our social status. For some people, life and love, or being with the right mate, are valued the same. For others, life boils down to one's roles, responsibilities, or identities, such as being a parent or having a particular race, gender, color, background, class, education, talent, or neurologically diverse identity. Life can also be viewed from a religious perspective, with importance given to gods, creators, or karma accumulated through eons of lives lived. It can be seen from the perspective of the universe or nature, proven through mathematics and physics and through chemistry, biology, and genetics. The list is endless. Life is a multifaceted phenomenon that has been investigated through scientific inquiry and philosophy. Each perspective offers valuable insights into the nature of life and human experience.

Just for fun, I asked ChatGPT, "What does AI think of life? How does AI describe life?" It came back with "Asa n AI, I don't have personal experiences or emotions, but I can provide a description of life based on a synthesis of human perspectives and scientific understanding." Then it provided a list of categories it had grabbed from the internet. It finished by saying, "As an AI, I can present these perspectives without personal bias."

I thought, Isn't that something? No personal bias! Huh.

That was when my friend Lou came in to say dinner was ready. He pointed out that AI is biased by extension because all its information originates with people.

So the lens through which we can consider life is open for discussion, debate, and scrutiny. This book uses a combination of psychological, ecological, philosophical, scientific, and practical perspectives of life. Let's look at intelligence.

INTELLIGENCE

Intelligence and the ability to understand have important implications for human development and advancement. There are many types of intelligence, including emotional intelligence (partly debunked), cultural intelligence, and others. A popular standard measurement of intelligence is IQ (intelligence quotient), which was created by French researchers Alfred Binet and Théodore Simon. In 1904, the two men were asked by the French Ministry of Education to develop a test that would reveal why some children were unable to do work that others were able to do. As it was more widely used, IQ became a popular test to measure overall intelligence.

That these cognitive tests are culturally biased and exclusionary, even discriminatory, has been the subject of extensive discussion. They are so because questions on the test may refer to knowledge or situations that are more familiar to white and middle or upper-class test takers than those of diverse backgrounds, leading to the false impression that these groups are more intelligent.

MINDFUL LIFE INTELLIGENCE

I'd like to focus on a combination of intelligences that are universal and timeless, that anyone can acquire, and that all humans must learn in addition to any other intelligence or skill they may possess. I call this collection mindful life intelligence, which includes source intelligence, mindful heart intelligence, intelligent mental actions, and others related to human experience and conduct and to the greater life. I've organized them under three overarching domains: systems, planet, and humans. I provide them as lessons for you to develop to optimize your life by using the five-stage Human Software Optimization method from the previous chapters. Together, these three domains and five stages make up Mindful Life Optimization (MLO). These MLO lessons (MLOLs) are introduced and discussed in chapters 12 through 21 and include insights about natural and human-made systems; our planet and what it needs to remain sustainable; the human brain and mind; the necessary balance among wisdom, compassion, and clarity; and how to heal emotional wounds.

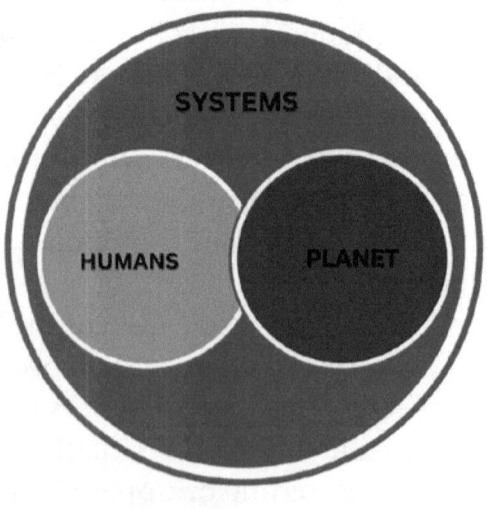

**Three Domains
of Mindful Life Intelligence**

Figure 5
Copyright Dr. Manijeh Motaghy

THE GOAL OF THE THREE DOMAINS OF MINDFUL LIFE INTELLIGENCE

1. **Natural Laws and Constructed Systems:** This domain covers MLOLs that help us to develop insight and alignment with the fundamentals of specific natural systems that govern our lives. Once individuals adopt these, they are able to create systems, AI innovations, and material goods that have zero or minimal negative impact on our individual lives, society, future generations, and the environment. They create more effective policies and governance rooted in wisdom, adaptability, flexibility, and heart intelligence, which will benefit all involved. No one suffers.

2. **Our Planet and Sustainable Living:** This domain covers MLOLs that aim to reconnect humanity to the planet and provide insight about the planet's role in our lives, its boundaries and limitations, and our role and responsibilities in stewarding it. By developing a more intimate relationship with nature and various life-forms, we can experience its immense source of generosity and be nourished by this realization. With a deep sense of connection, fulfillment, and joy, we become inspired to refrain from destroying it, instead helping nature's regenerative design, which keeps all life on our planet healthy and thriving.

3. **Human Experience, Conduct, and Happiness:** This domain includes MLOLs about how the brain works; how and why emotions arise and what to do with difficult emotions; how mental struggles and biases form; how our internal obstacles keep us stuck in reoccurring unhappiness; and how to balance wisdom, heart intelligence, and peacefulness and deal with grief and heal our wounds. As you continue optimizing your inner navigation capabilities, you will develop a solid character, enjoy harmonious relationships with yourself and others, and become more successful within the society you live in.

All of this will be accomplished through the application of the five-stage HSO.

THE GLOBAL IMPACT OF INDIVIDUAL OPTIMIZATION

Societies are made up of individuals who share many beliefs and actions, which also makes individual and systemic issues interconnected and interdependent. Consequently, great numbers of people behaving unskillfully can have a great negative impact. It may be any idea or behavior that becomes a social reality. For example, millions of people consume food in plastic containers that end up polluting the environment and killing animals, with a chain effect of diminishing natural resources and causing illnesses. For various reasons, some people don't want to hear about these types of problems. They may think they can't do anything about it, or they may consider certain subjects, such as climate change and related topics, a hindrance to creating wealth or a political agenda. They get caught up in arguments about how politicians and scientists gain by pushing global warming and related issues. The fact is, there will always be cases in which politicians and other groups take advantage of public agendas. Guess what. Politicians, like most people, may be underdeveloped. They can be great in some respects yet not understand or ignore that natural laws and patterns govern everything and that going against them will have detrimental negative effects. I'll talk about faulty constructed systems in chapter

If all of us, including advocates, policymakers, and those who implement and govern, learned how to think and live more consciously, we could realize the positive effects systemically to eliminate both personal and global issues. To still have a positive impact regarding issues you may not agree with, such as climate change, you can become more curious about some of its aspects — for example, mountains of trash piling up and contaminating our oceans and hurting other creatures on our planet. In those respects, you might choose to reform personal choices to avoid adding to the problem.

SUSTAINABLE DEVELOPMENT AND
INNER DEVELOPMENT GOALS (SDGS AND IDGS)

In 2015, the members of the United Nations drafted a proposal that outlined "a blueprint of peace and prosperity for people and the planet, now and into the future." They proposed the "17 Sustainable Development Goals to Transform Our World," to be accomplished by the year 2030. These all-inclusive goals consisted of the following:

1. Solutions regarding clean water and sanitation
2. Affordable and clean energy
3. Decent work and economic growth
4. Industry, innovation, and infrastructure
5. Reduced inequalities
6. Sustainable cities and communities
7. Responsible consumption and production
8. Climate action
9. Life below water
10. Life on land
11. Poverty
12. Hunger
13. Health and well-being
14. Education
15. Gender equality
16. Peace, justice, and strong institutions
17. Strengthening partnerships for achieving these goals

The time to accomplish these seventeen goals was chosen based on scientific data determining how much time we had to turn around the planet to avoid natural disasters that could end this era of abundance and begin another era of hardship and intensified suffering. It was a seemingly lofty goal.

In 2020, a group of researchers, experts, educators, and leaders realized that the sustainable development goals (SDGs) will not be met in time to remedy climate issues if we all continue thinking and living the ways we do. They determined that this wide spectrum of goals will be met only if humans develop some key inner qualities and skills, which validated my warning people of this reality long before the research came out. They launched a global study, called Inner Developmental Goals, to determine which important inner qualities and skills could prepare us to better care for ourselves and help our planet have a sustainable future.

To anyone around the world who answered their survey (including me), they posed one question: "What qualities, abilities, or skills do we need to develop in order to build a sustainable future for people and the planet?" With the answers they collected, they created the Inner Development Goals (IDG) framework in support of the seventeen SDGs. According to the IDG website, "This framework simplifies a complex field of human development to help us better identify, understand, communicate and integrate and develop the inner skills needed for sustainable development." The results provide five basic categories necessary for inner development so that we can effectively address external issues:

1. **Being (relationship to self):** Inner compass, integrity and authenticity, openness and learning mindset, self-awareness, presence
2. **Thinking (cognitive skills):** Critical thinking, complexity awareness, perspective skills, sense-making, long-term orientation and visioning
3. **Relating (caring for others and the world):** Appreciation, connectedness, humility, empathy, compassion
4. **Collaborating (social skills):** Communication skills, cocreation skills, inclusive mindset and intercultural competence, trust, mobilization skills
5. **Acting (enabling change):** Courage, creativity, optimism, perseverance

The IDG website also explains that this is a "naked framework" to bridge capacities between cultures and traditions. The ways to develop them are left to others to create. I am happy to report that the five-stage Human Software Optimization and the MLOLs that follow can be used as a training manual for developing the IDGs as well as other fundamental principles, inner navigational qualities, and skills that will support the achievement of the seventeen SDGs.

AN EFFECTIVE PATHWAY TO DEVELOP IDGS AND OTHER INNER-GROWTH MODELS

There are sixty MLOLs under the three domains of mindful life intelligence (systemic view; relationship to the planet; and human experience, conduct, and happiness). Many of these lessons address the development of qualities in the IDGs. For example, IDG skills under the category of *thinking* include complexity awareness, described as "understanding of and skills in working with complex and systemic conditions and casualties." The first domain of Mindful Life Optimization begins with explanations of this complexity awareness by looking at some natural laws and patterns that affect us and at the importance of understanding them and how to align with them. Both this domain and the thinking IDGs address perspective skills, sense- making, and long-term orientation and visioning.

The third MLOL in the first domain of life intelligence delves into dependency and interdependence and the relationship we have with our planet, which help to develop the IDG skills included in both thinking and collaborating. Other MLOLs under the second and third domains of life intelligence cover pertinent topics that support the development of most of the IDGs related to being, relating, collaborating, and acting, as well as covering additional fundamental qualities and skills not included in the IDGs.

Applying the Five-Stage HSO to Develop
The Three Domains of Mindful Life Intelligence

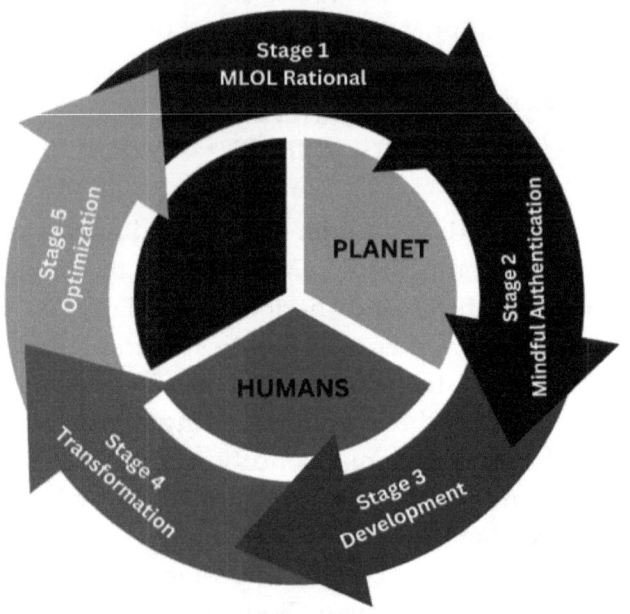

Figure 6

Copyright Dr. Manijeh Motaghy

INTEGRATING MLOLS INTO DAILY AFFAIRS

Related MLOLs in each domain encourage compassionate consideration by consistently revealing why it is not easy to be human and showing how seeing life from a holistic approach and aspiring to live accordingly can end individual as well as global suffering. It is a three-dimensional mindfulness approach that aims to engage you in what it looks and feels like to be mindful. Hence, if you seek to gain the benefits of mindfully optimizing your inner navigation system and capabilities and possess a powerful personal asset, the MLOLs under each domain must gradually become a regular part of your daily affairs.

Next, we get into MLOLs in each domain, starting with natural and constructed systems and principles.

As a reminder, you can further understand and develop any MLOL by taking it through the five stages of HSO.

CHAPTER 12

THE FIRST DOMAIN: NATURAL LAWS AND CONSTRUCTED SYSTEMS

OK, the fun begins here. Let's look at some glitches and begin debugging the fallacies of our lives from the system's perspective—the first domain of mindful life intelligence. This first domain covers two types of systems: natural systems and principles and systems that we humans construct. They are interrelated.

Life needs governing rules and ways of reinforcing them. The natural laws and systems in this chapter are like policies, procedures, and resources that create and maintain life for all living beings, including us. There are many natural laws and systems, which are explained through mathematics, calculus, physics, chemistry, biology, astrology, and other sciences. Every time we utilize these natural laws and systems, such as physics and mathematics, what we create has a reliable foundation and can be everlasting, as in ancient historical structures and formulas. These have certainties I will not be discussing here, as they are not directly related to developing inner skills and qualities. I will discuss the following natural laws and systems as frames of reference or tools for exploring solutions for human problems: change, regenerative design, dependency and interdependence, cause and effect, and the law of intentionality.

By aligning w/these natural laws or patterns in your daily life, you gain their power, are able to harness their effectiveness, and can enjoy optimal happiness and success. This domain includes MLOLs 1 through 15, discussed in chapters 12 and 13.

NATURAL LAWS AND SYSTEMS

DOMAIN I:

NATURAL LAWS AND SYSTEMS

FUNDAMENTAL LESSONS

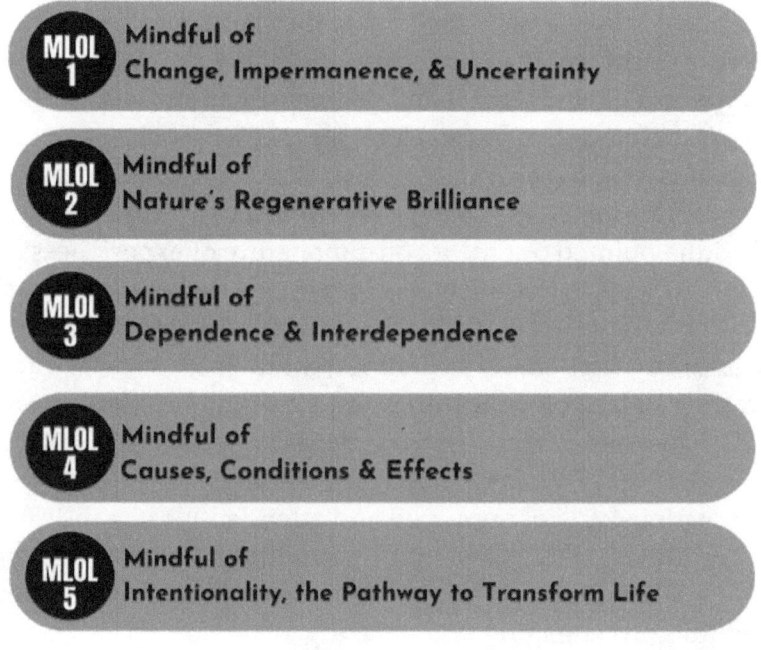

Figure 7

Copyright by Dr. Manijeh Motaghy

MLOL 1: MINDFUL OF CHANGE, IMPERMANENCE, AND UNCERTAINTY: THE FORCES OF LIFE

I have chosen change as your first MLOL because embracing change, impermanence, and uncertainty as fundamental forces that shape the essence of life can have a tremendous positive effect in reducing stress and creating successful systems and life experiences. Although change seems simple enough to understand, it's not always easy to go with its flow. We forget that change is an unavoidable natural phenomenon; as a result, we fight it, dismiss it, or force it, and we experience discord and problems we cannot solve. These are typical reactions to the demands of human life.

For our lives to work in the way they have been set up, we need to be consistent, reliable, and responsible in following routines. Then things change, and what we become consistent and responsible toward needs to change too. But we don't see it as simple change or see how it works as a natural system. We experience conflict and agitation.

In Buddhist texts, change is referred to as impermanence. The Buddha pointed out the inconstant nature of experiences and how this can lead to dissatisfaction when we don't understand it and accept it. My first introduction to the concept of impermanence was at my first ten-day silent retreat in 2008. I was a total rookie in the practice of mindfulness and meditation. (How I ended up at an austere, monastic silent retreat has a beautiful and perhaps karmic story, which I will tell another time. But somehow, miraculously, I got approved and attended.) While the retreat was incredibly challenging, involving sitting for long periods and being silent for days, at the same time, I had never experienced anything so engaging and amazing.

When Ajahn Amaro, the leading monastic teacher at the retreat, spoke of impermanence, I didn't know what he was talking about. I'd never heard that word. We were silent, and I had no dictionary or quick AI companion. But from the description, I tried hard to find it, to see it, and to understand it. I couldn't. Finally, after a few days, during one of the walking meditations, I looked up and saw a yellowed leaf separate from its branch and make its way down toward the ground. The leaf's stem tail moved from side to side, teetering to the right and left, in slow motion before it landed. My eyes were pinned to the falling leaf. I saw it make incremental change from one location in space to another.

All of a sudden, my mind said, *That must be impermanence!* But I wasn't sure which part was impermanence. The location of this leaf in the air was changing by the moment. I followed it closely until it landed on a bush. I sat down on a bench and looked around. It was a beautiful fall day, sunny but cool. I was surrounded by autumn's deep shades of red, yellow, brown, and orange.

I asked myself, *Is impermanence change in time? Or change in location? Or both?*

Something deep had caught my attention. It felt peaceful and pleasant. This was a seed planted, which would grow into a sapling insight and later into a full grasp of how impermanence plays out within every aspect of human life and experience.

I continued to hear teachings around impermanence, probably hundreds of times, as uncertainty, inconstancy, instability, and the adage that nothing is for sure or forever. I taught the same to others. I explained that things don't always go our way and that many factors, known and unknown, can change our plans or whatever is happening at every moment. Though this understanding was useful to keep my mind steady and peaceful, I would still circumstantially forget it or not accept it. I watched many of my students have trouble accepting the impermanence of things, especially when experiencing the loss of loved ones or other unfavorable changes and fear of the unknown. In many cases, it seemed as though if they accepted the impermanence of all things, then life would lose its meaning and purpose: *If I'm dying anyway, then what's the use?* Denial of death and loss as natural phenomena gave them some sense of stability — though it was not helpful in any real sense. I continued believing and teaching about impermanence, not realizing there was a deeper place, a direct understanding, that could open the doors of insight and change everything for me.

One night in class, beginning, as always, with meditation, I asked the students what topic they wanted me to guide them on. I asked them to reflect on what was suitable for their minds at the moment and tell me. They called out different requests, mainly about calming stress. So I started with the guidance of breathing, body awareness, and mental-activity awareness. I guided them to notice how things arise and pass in their field of awareness—the breath arising and passing, physical tightness and tension arising and changing, thoughts appearing and building, moments of awareness emerging and then being lost in thoughts, sensations of hot and cold changing inside the body, attention moving from one thing to another, and so forth.

In the quiet space of my attention, I guided them with what I was aware of in my own meditation. Suddenly, a vast door of knowledge opened for me and allowed me to see more deeply into the nature of change and impermanence. I saw change functioning as a natural phenomenon—one that occurs within us as well as outside us. I realized change is a powerful natural event we can use to make things happen—to shift things, create better mental states, and eliminate what is burdensome. It's not just about the ending of things, as impermanence implies. I saw change and impermanence as one and the same, so from here on, I will refer to them interchangeably.

Before the meditation ended, I saw change as the power to existence. During a ten-minute break, I devised a lesson around it to present following the meditation. As I thought about how what people don't understand causes them stress, the insight arose in me that change is an unbeatable phenomenon, a true force of nature. There is no force big enough that can bring the phenomenon of change to a halt. If we try to stop or avoid it, we will fail and then suffer for it with stress and anxiety. But when we understand the unique attributes of change, we can harness its power, shift its direction, and create results that are reliable and sustainable.

From a systemic point of view, change is one of the most necessary phenomena in life. It is a simple, unavoidable, and commanding natural mechanism that runs everything. We need changeability, for example, when we cook, walk, grow, innovate, and build economies. Change, or impermanence, is a natural law that affects all systems, the universe, our planet, and everything within it.

But why am I harping on this point? Because we humans have

self-centered opinions about change. Sometimes we like it; other times, we don't. We want circumstances to go our way, and when they don't, we get annoyed and agitated. For example, one day I approached the elevator of the building my new mindfulness center had just moved into. I was hauling boxes on a dolly. It was a heavy load. The door of the elevator opened, and I began to move in. When I was halfway in, the door started closing. It bumped into the boxes, almost knocking them off the dolly. I felt frustrated and thought the door must have been malfunctioning. I finally managed to get the stuff in, and the door closed. Leaving the elevator, I fussed in my head about how awful that experience had been and thought I should have my office manager call the building manager to complain. After all, we had just moved in and signed a five-year lease, and it felt as if we could be stuck with a malfunctioning elevator and other issues. Luckily, that day, my office manager wasn't in, and I forgot all about it.

Two days later, I came back to the office. This time, I had nothing to haul. I pressed the button, the elevator door opened, and I went in. Standing there for a few seconds, I became agitated again, this time because the elevator door didn't close fast enough. Thanks to my continual work on being present and mindful, I suddenly realized it was the same elevator, acting in the same way, taking the same amount of time to close. I wanted it to behave differently, according to my desires each time. As I walked out of the elevator, I laughed at my mind. I couldn't believe my expectation had caused me to become so upset. The not-so-funny thing about the situation was the story I had come up with to blame the building manager for an issue that didn't exist. How could the elevator's timing have been too fast one day and too slow another day? I was glad I had seen the truth soon enough not to let myself start a list of things I was unhappy about with the building, especially a list based on associations with prior agitations.

Can you relate to this in your daily life? How many things do you get agitated about because you think they should be this way or that way?

To write about change in this book, I looked for any scientific claims about change as a natural phenomenon, and I couldn't find any, but I can vouch for it here as a firsthand insight. Throughout a lifetime of education, observation, and practice, I've come to the conclusion that change is not only inevitable and constant but also a necessary mechanism for life. Think of it: Without the change phenomenon, the world might be frozen, remaining solid in space, or simply be nothing. Change has been there from the birth of our universe, our stars, our planet, and the process of growing life in all its multitude of forms. Could we even exist at all if there were no such thing as change?

Furthermore, everything human-made can exist only due to the possibility of changing from one form into another, whether in combinations or complex forms. For example, blood can flow because of the ability to change, enabling biology, chemistry, and neurology to function. As this and every other aspect of existence proceed, change is at work, moment by moment. I saw change not only as an outcome but also as a movement, an energy that can be both the condition and the cause of various outcomes. The energy that moves through the body also moves the breath, the mind, the lungs, the heart, the eyes, and so on—billions of cells moving, shifting, and shaping. All this complexity and more are due to the existence of the simple phenomenon of change. It's best that we know it and learn to go with its flow.

Note: Use the HSO stages to develop your own insights into this MLOL.

MLOL 2: MINDFUL OF NATURE'S REGENERATIVE BRILLIANCE

Knowledge about nature's regenerative design can inspire us to create impeccable systems. Even without scientific research, observing and communing with nature can offer us insights into how life happens and perseveres. You can witness nature's undying will for regeneration and continuation through every blade of grass that pushes its head through the mud after a rainy day. You can see it in every seed perfectly laid in the center of a piece of fruit and in the hundreds of seeds in one eggplant, a cucumber, a bell pepper, or a tomato; the enormous number of fruits that an almond tree produces; and the thousands of salmon that swim upstream to get back to their origin and lay their eggs. Many salmon become food for bears and birds, but enough of them make it to continue producing their kind. It's nature's way of ensuring that its species will survive and continue to thrive. This design is not just for the benefit of that one species but for the sustenance of all life-forms, including ours.

As I've learned more about ecosystems and the regenerative system they contribute to, I've realized how much our lives rely on other species' doing their part so we can survive and thrive. Moreover, there is an ingenious systemic design that ensures a waste-free environment and fosters balanced, thriving ecosystems through the collaborative efforts of all that's alive. It is completely efficient and, miraculously, does not leave useless or toxic waste behind. Green leaves take energy from sunlight and turn it into food and medicine that feed and preserve life, and there are armies of creatures in various ecosystems who effectively recycle or reuse whatever is left behind.

TRASH HAS VALUE

Trees and plants produce fruits and shed leaves, bugs pollinate the fruits and clean up the dead leaves, birds and lizards eat the bugs, and animals and humans consume the fruits. The bacteria inhabit human bodies, and the human bodies become food for the worms that create compost for trees and cycle back into food as fruits. Everything in this chain effect is food for something else. There are no waste products left behind in nature, as the death of one living thing is nourishment for another. Life is designed to keep life going, without prejudice. This is the heart of nature's regeneration. Miraculously, no other creature leaves any useless trash behind. But we do.

Interestingly, the concept of trash as we understand it today, referring to waste or discarded materials, has English-language origins dating back to the sixteenth century. The word likely has Scandinavian roots, with similarities to the Old Norse *tros*, meaning "rubbish" or "fallen leaves," and Norwegian *trask*, meaning "lumber" or "trash," according to *Wiktionary*. These terms indicate that early uses of *trash* were associated with bits of broken sticks and twigs found under trees, which were often collected for fuel or other uses. This etymology reflects a practical aspect of waste management in historical societies, emphasizing the repurposing of what was deemed discarded by nature. What humans in the modern era perceive as trash and throw away had a purpose for the members of some older cultures, such as the Aztecs. Everything had a value; nothing was useless. We can reflect on this brilliant model and become mindful of something's worth and value. Understanding regenerative design in depth and shifting our mindset from thinking of objects as useless to thinking of them as useful can help us to figure out how to create lasting systems. Mimicking regenerative systems can help us to create processes that benefit all ecosystems and handle waste products systematically and effectively. Next, let's look at the natural law of dependency and interdependence.

MLOL 3: MINDFUL OF THE LAW OF DEPENDENCY AND INTERDEPENDENCE

Often, modern or materialistic societies fail to teach us how interdependent everything and everyone are. Not recognizing the gravity of interdependence that governs everything in our lives is one of the key reasons for poor mental health, emotional issues, and a sense of failure.

Scientists have examined nature and gained incredible insights into how the universe works. They've produced fascinating and insightful studies about how everything is linked in the universe. Our planet is but a speck of dust compared to the whole. But those reports and inferences don't help to improve our day-to-day circumstances, such as our livelihoods, how we relate to in-laws or raise children, or any other human affair. We end up seeing and considering limited versions of interdependence, and our problems in life persist.

Let's take it a step back to the truth of dependency: everything and everyone are created with conditions and causes that depend on other conditions and causes. For this reason, I am calling interdependence *the law of dependency*, which, like change, cannot be overruled.

Of course, we get what it means for us to be dependent on another

To provide for us, for our bosses to like us and keep us employed, and so on. Sometimes we like it because it works, and other times, we don't. We then wish for freedom and independence from all of it.

The *Cambridge Dictionary* defines *independence* as "the state of wanting or being able to do things for yourself and make your own decisions, without help or influence from other people." This is how language, concepts, and frames of reference create our realities, which may be partly true but may also negate the bigger truth. The problem comes when we move from dependency to independence and forget all about interdependence.

When dependency, which is a naturally imposed rule or process, becomes tough or off-balance or is taken advantage of, some of us seek independence. Examples are countless: youths leaving their parents' homes to create their own destinies, employees leaving their jobs to own their own business, and new nations being born. Independence is appealing. Enduring incredible struggle and hardship, people all over the world have managed to get out of oppressive situations. They've bravely fought to be free so they can pursue their own belief systems, live as they wish, or accumulate wealth and gain power. In each case, they have to depend on the people within the new scenario to do the right thing—to respect and protect their freedom, their belongings, their safety, and their equality. No matter the circumstance, we cannot avoid the natural law of dependency. Not accounting for it makes our experience one of dissatisfaction and results in a sense of failure.

We fail to see that even when we gain independence from those things and people and achieve our goals, we are still dependent on some things and some people. This is not to promote staying in bad relationships or avoid creating positive change for yourself and the world. It's pushing to the surface of consciousness the false belief that our happiness can be achieved through self-ruling, self-governing, and autonomously self-sustaining. Complete independence is not a choice we can make, because it doesn't exist in nature. Even a hermit who moves into the mountains to live in solitude needs the mountain and the caves to do so. He or she needs food for sustenance and clothes for safety from the harsh elements. The hermit too can never have complete independence.

Life is ruled by the natural law of dependency. Everything and everyone benefit from an invisible web of interdependence that we rarely ever realize, let alone acknowledge. Life works through a chain of links, relationships, and interactions that satisfy varying needs and create varying results. Nothing on this planet as we know it exists independently. Different life-forms, materials, and systems rely on and need one another and affect one another in many ways. It's really the law of dependency we need to honor and work with.

Then we can comprehend the inner workings of the chain of interdependence and be able to equally appreciate all who have a part in it and recognize the necessity of properly caring for everything and everyone.

Another important natural law is the law of causes, conditions, and effects. This often is not taken seriously, which can end in pain and suffering.

MLOL 4: MINDFUL OF THE LAW OF CAUSES, CONDITIONS, AND EFFECTS: OBJECTIVITY

As we grow up and develop awareness, we learn about cause and effect in various ways. Children learn that when they touch a hot pan, they get burned and feel pain. So they quickly learn about heat and are careful when close to it. The natural law of causes, conditions, and effects is another law that governs everything we door experience. This applies to our personal and relational lives as well as the systems we create, which I will cover in chapter 13.

There also are conditions that affect causes or act as causes. But the end result (the effect) happens whether or not we realize and acknowledge it. It's a process that exists everywhere all the time: for every effect and outcome, there is a starter cause that may be influenced by some condition. For example, we have come to believe in a certain perspective (the effect) because we learned it in a particular way (the cause). We trusted the source of the information (the condition) that helped to form our viewpoint. Sometimes there are multiple causes and conditions for an effect. Great. So far, it's just a formula.

The problem arises when we lose our objectivity, react, and create problems out of this process. An example would be dropping something important—say, a pair of expensive glasses—that breaks when it falls. The causes include a loosening grip and the impact of the glasses hitting the hard surface. Conditions include the breakability of the glass and the hardness of the surface. Gravity can also be seen as a condition and the hard surface as a cause. All of this leads to the effect of the glasses breaking into pieces.

We don't like that our expensive glasses are broken, of course, but the breaking itself is not personal. Anything that is breakable will eventually break. But we easily forget or ignore such principles and stress needlessly. Even though conditions, causes, and even effects may not always be easily discernible, we can count on this law to play a constant role in our daily experiences. Having deep insight into this law and seeking to understand the causes and conditions of a situation instead of the associated stories or filters we put upon a situation can reduce our stress, tension, and unskillful actions. You've probably had an experience in which you learned about someone acting inappropriately or hurtfully, but when you discovered some of the conditions that caused his or her actions, you couldn't help but forgive the person. Painful emotions can give way to objectivity because you realize there is more than one reason, cause, or condition that plays into what happens. Therefore, it's always best to withhold absolute and harsh judgments about anything that is going on with yourself, others, a system, or the world. Instead, learn to inquire and find out more about conditions and causes before drawing conclusions.

Knowing this natural law well, watching it carefully, and analyzing it prudently can also have substantial benefits in our finding the reasons and conditions that create systemic flaws and other issues in our lives. Once we're able to identify causes or conditions that lead to problematic outcomes, we can focus on ways to eliminate or modify them. An example of this exploration became a formula in perfecting manufacturing: Lean Six Sigma, a business strategy developed in 1986 at Motorola to eliminate errors during the production process, became a popular methodology for companies to focus on operational excellence, reduce waste, and address flaws in design and other aspects of the process. Motorola was able to identify conditions that cause errors and reduce the rate of errors to only six out of a million tries. Letting go of resistance, opinions, and judgment and taking time to observe and find conditions that cause errors or disharmony can help us to eliminate them and peacefully improve life on all fronts.

In the next lesson, we'll explore intention, which makes our actions have karmic effects and become consequential.

MLOL 5: MINDFUL OF THE LAW OF INTENTIONALITY, THE PATHWAY TO TRANSFORM OUR LIVES

Intentionality

Intentions play a huge role in how our lives turn out, how happy or unhappy we are, and how easy or difficult our lives feel. Many people don't have a full grasp of the law of intentionality and karma and its ramifications and benefits. Most people think of karma as our negative consequences because we did something bad and we deserve the harsh outcomes. Some pretend karma doesn't exist or doesn't apply to them, and when caught doing something wrong, they may claim their intentions were other than what panned out, so they can get off the hook. Of course, my encouragement is to not be judgmental of anyone who does this; it's easy to become deluded about or be oblivious to one's harmful thoughts, speech, and actions.

To remedy this condition, the oldest established religion in the world, Zoroastrianism, offered three simple tenets: good thoughts, good words, and good deeds. Growing up as a Persian, I always heard these three principles. We understood that good meant thinking, intending, speaking, and acting kindly, compassionately, fairly, justly, generously, beneficially, healthily, and peacefully. It was believed that if people learned to think, speak, and act in those ways, then their intentions were aligned with the nature of life and would naturally yield positive results.

Zoroastrianism also holds that there is no good or evil in nature and that all life-forms live according to life's plan. For example, a lion that hunts down a deer and eats it is not evil. It's just killing to eat and live. That survival quality is ingrained in the lion. Other animals benefit when the lion hunts and leaves the leftovers behind, so there is an act of generosity and sharing encoded in this killing. Animals of any kind don't kill or take more than they need. But that natural intention to be generous and not intentionally cause harm hasn't always been understood by humans, who took more than they needed, enslaved the weak and dominated others, and lied and cheated, all for personal gain. Therefore, later religions found it necessary to distinguish good and evil from the whole and create punishments for those who engaged in so-called evil acts. Still, some take advantage of these rules to gain status, power, and profit. With greater inequalities, stress and unfulfillment continue to rise. The irony is that this sense of unfulfillment is not only for the oppressed but also for the oppressor. It's just the way it is. We cannot be separate from the outcome of our intentional actions.

Karma Can Transform Our Lives

The law of karma basically says that we inherit the results of our intentional actions. When our intentional actions are good, beneficial, and considerate, we inherit the results of those positive intentions, and through positive intentions, we can change the results of the negative ones. The heart of the law of karma is action with intention.

Some people think karma is just about "What goes around comes around." They believe whatever bad thing you do to others, the same will happen to you. While there is some possibility for this, fortunately, that is not the whole picture. We are not necessarily stuck with getting the same bad things we did to others. We can sometimes, to a great extent, remedy those consequences by acting from better intentions. The purer these intentions to undo a harm are, the greater potential they have to transform our lives.

Other aspects of karma include rebirth and inheriting the karma of past lives, which I won't get into here. Let's focus on what we can verify and how our actions and intentions can help us to yield healthier outcomes, transform hardships and suffering, and reduce the negative results of our unskillful past actions. For example, even those who have killed another person and ended up in prison for life can transform their intention to one of kindness and generosity and generate thoughts, speech, and actions that can help them to reduce the pain of being locked in. With the intention to not harm, to have goodwill for all, and to let go of all hatred and animosity, they can meditate, clear their minds, and become peaceful. With better mental health and improved responsiveness, they become able to see and accept their lives as they are and not struggle as much with painful thoughts and emotions. The ripple effect of accepting their situation with ease and kindness is that they can engage in skillful acts that keep other inmates calm. They can remain present and productive through a radical knowing that nothing is permanent. The more present and well intentioned we can remain, the more potential and opportunity we have for cleaning up the harm of past negative actions.

You may ask, "What about deserving to suffer? Shouldn't one who has killed another suffer the maximum suffering possible?" Well, if there is a real, tangible benefit to suffering, such as learning, growing, and transforming, then maybe.

This view of karma, which the Buddha revised from its more punitive form, does not entertain the concept of deserving or not deserving the consequences of our past actions. Instead, it gives the individual the power to become more accountable and responsible for his or her life and well-being in every moment, now and into the future. In fact, thinking that someone deserves hardship and pain would be unwise intention, which creates painful consequential karma for the one who thinks it. This is not a theory. You can test it for yourself. Hate someone, and see how you feel. Let go of hating the person, and see the results of it for yourself. It is wise to be careful not to hate others for their negative actions, for you could get tangled up in their karma and also inherit the consequences of their actions.

The freeing aspect of the Buddha's stance is that no one, including ourselves, Is stuck with our bad karmas (actions with intention). We can

Always awaken, change our paths, and begin cleaning up our intentions, because they drive our thoughts, words, and actions. Just think about it: We always have action at our disposal in the present moment, and with clear, wise, compassionate intentions, we can create positive actions and change the experience of those consequences.

Next, let's look at lessons that pertain to clusters of constructed systems and how they can go wrong and create hardship and suffering in our personal lives, in society, and for nature.

CHAPTER 13

CONSTRUCTED SYSTEMS

This chapter includes MLOLs 6 through 15: natural laws or patterns ruling constructed systems, belief systems and rigidity, systems favoring those in power, invisible systems, one-dimensional capitalism, issues with maintaining competitive edge, consumerism and circular anxiety economy, abandonment of stress-producing activities, solutions to wicked problems, and the building of systems as a force for good. And doing all of it with mindfulness.

NATURAL LAWS IN ORGANIZATIONAL DESIGN
AHEAD OF ITS TIME

Studying various management systems in my doctoral program, I wondered if the business world could mimic nature's design in its strategies, innovation, and management style. Having communed with nature and observed its incredible systemic process — with plants going from seeds to saplings, budding and blossoming, fruiting, dying or going dormant, and then repeating that consistent and effective design — I was in awe of its mystery, and I wrote a poem called "Life Wants to Live." I didn't have any scientific understanding of this, but I thought, *What better to copy than nature's system, which works flawlessly?* But I had no idea how that could translate into human behavior and strategic actions.

In 2006, to finish my doctorate in psychology of management, I requested to do my dissertation research project on the inner workings of natural systems. I wanted to learn as much as I could about how nature works and design a management model that corporations could implement and benefit from. But my program director flat out rejected it. She said no one cared about something like that. She claimed that profit, productivity, and employee satisfaction were key focus areas, and modeling after nature was too soft and ambiguous a model for business management. She couldn't yet see a business case to justify researching ideas about ecology or environmental sciences. These disciplines didn't cross fields in the academic world then as much as they do today.

With climate change concerns, advancements in AI, and the reemergence of transdisciplinary approaches, these barriers have been lifted. So I am delighted to join many others who have been examining and mimicking natural systems more directly. Chapter 15, MLOL 26, offers an effective management system I have modeled after nature's regenerative system: RIMS (regenerative integration management system).

DOMAIN I:
CONSTRUCTED SYSTEMS

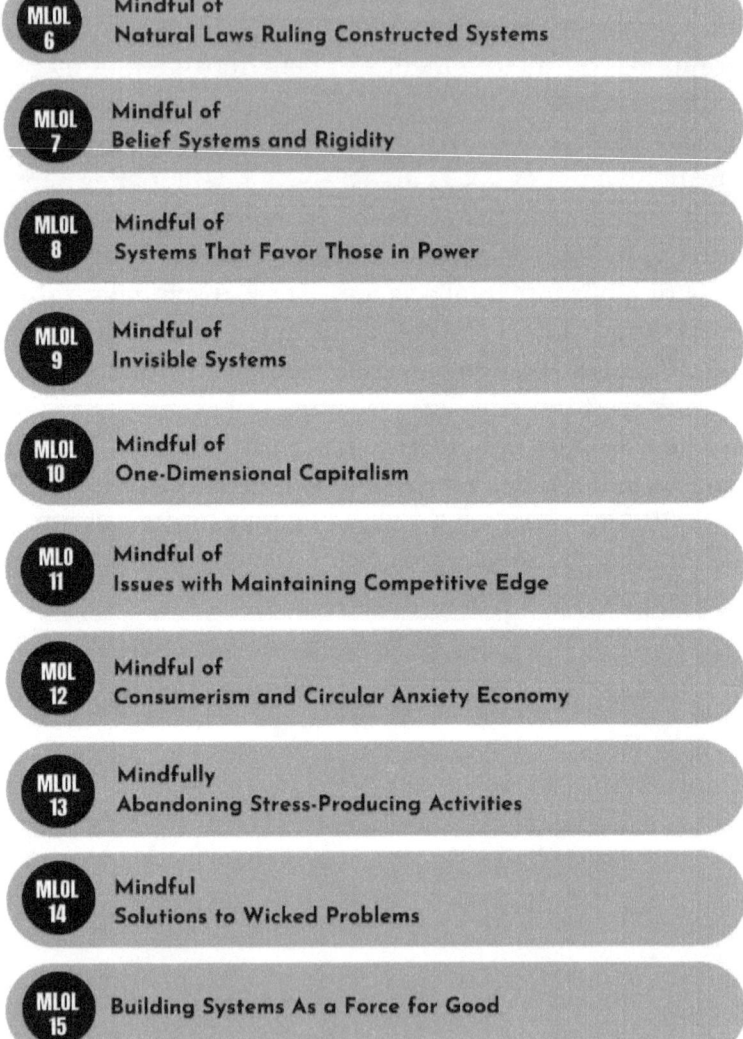

MLOL 6 — Mindful of Natural Laws Ruling Constructed Systems

MLOL 7 — Mindful of Belief Systems and Rigidity

MLOL 8 — Mindful of Systems That Favor Those in Power

MLOL 9 — Mindful of Invisible Systems

MLOL 10 — Mindful of One-Dimensional Capitalism

MLO 11 — Mindful of Issues with Maintaining Competitive Edge

MOL 12 — Mindful of Consumerism and Circular Anxiety Economy

MLOL 13 — Mindfully Abandoning Stress-Producing Activities

MLOL 14 — Mindful Solutions to Wicked Problems

MLOL 15 — Building Systems As a Force for Good

Figure 8 - Copyright by Dr. Manijeh Motaghy

MLOL 6: MINDFUL OF NATURAL LAWS RULING CONSTRUCTED SYSTEMS

Understanding that our constructed systems are also bound by natural laws can keep fear, greed, and delusion in check. Take the law of dependency and interdependence in our constructed systems, for example. A technological network depends on various hardware and software components, design, ample power, and hundreds of other factors to function. The failure of one component, such as a server, can hinder the performance or accessibility of the network. In business, different departments (e.g., sales, production, and logistics) depend on one another to perform their parts properly. In addition, countless known and unknown conditions affect the chain of interdependence: the way customers behave, the quality of vendors' products, services provided by financial sectors, landlords, lawyers, agreements, and various laws and policies that affect the business. The effectiveness of one aspect depends on the effectiveness of another.

In social systems, individuals, communities, and institutions also depend on the proper functioning of everything else. The actions of an individual can affect the larger community, and societal structures, in turn, influence individual behaviors, opportunities, happiness, and unhappiness. You may think this lesson is obvious too, but when you're in the thick of problems, it's difficult to think of a negative result as natural and impersonal and remain objective and not see how the laws of dependency rule.

Keeping this law in mind when resolving systemic issues through analysis of how components within a system influence one another, we may see that caring for the people and other beings involved is central to the success of the overall system. We can craft social and environmental policies and sustainable designs by respecting the dependency and interdependence of humans and technology on nature and vice versa. Understanding how natural laws govern our systems is fundamental to devising solutions that are both ecologically safe and socially equitable.

We can pause, notice, account for, and learn how to flow with fundamental laws that govern life. In doing so, we create fewer problems and communicate our understandings more effectively. Every individual on the planet can learn, grow, and develop him- or herself to be responsible and accountable to produce best actions, innovations, and impacts.

MLOL 7: MINDFUL OF BELIEF SYSTEMS AND RIGIDITY

Throughout human history, numerous belief systems in the form of religions or social movements have arisen. Many have provided beneficial direction for their followers: instructions that people can carry out in their lives, relationships, work, and governance and principles, such as being fair, truthful, just, caring, and merciful. However, followers often adopt these tenets rigidly and without compassion or discernment; they become judgmental, unmerciful, and unfair. They end up believing the core intention as absolute truth and feel hate or resentment toward those who don't act according to such beliefs. The belief becomes their identity. I have witnessed people become vegan because of compassion for animals yet end up hating humans who use animal products. They can't see that loving one while hating another is contradictory to the heart's intention and goodness—that if we possess compassion and kindness exclusively, we continue to experience and cause stress, anxiety, worry, and disharmony. Examples of rigidity and contradiction are many.

Years ago, a friend of mine agreed to have her two-year-old daughter initiated into her husband's religion. When the time came to get the child ready, my friend was told she couldn't attend her daughter's initiation ceremony, because she wasn't from that religion. She was devastated. She was willing to have her daughter initiated into a belief system she wasn't from and was willing to learn and attend their gatherings to please her husband and his family. But they said she wasn't pure enough to attend the ceremony. It seemed counterproductive that the leaders of this religion believed in humanity, kindness, and compassion yet had no openness to embrace the child's mother. This rigidity made no sense and didn't seem beneficial. It was about to tear their family apart. Thankfully, the husband didn't allow this initiation to be forced on his child, and neither got initiated.

Persons and communities with strict tenets and beliefs who seek to push their own ideas are generally inflexible to changing conditions and exclusive as well. You're in if you are willing to agree with them and live as they deem right. Otherwise, you're disregarded, shamed, or out. These conditions can cause tension and unhappiness. How often have you felt tight and tense because someone didn't agree with your beliefs? Or you may have witnessed others be treated unkindly because their violators were sticking to what they believed was true. Unfortunately, when we get stuck in rigidity and persist in our positions, we cause more harm. The more harm we cause, the more we experience tension and tightness, irritation, and unhappiness. Nature's laws of intentionality and causes, conditions, and effects will always be at work. When we recognize these tensions, whether in our own minds and bodies or in other people, we can investigate conditions present in each moment and consider a modified application of these tenets to create well-being, safety, and happiness for all involved.

Next, we'll look at issues caused by favoring those in power.

MLOL 8: MINDFUL OF SYSTEMS THAT FAVOR THOSE IN POWER

History shows that systemically favoring those in power, unless they are of the utmost development in wisdom, compassion, and contentment and can use their power to benefit others, usually ends in exploitation and suffering, even for those who have the power and those who gain some privileges. Some come to power through virtuous ideals, heroic acts, and genuine desire to relieve others from some sort of suffering. Many powerful people use their privileges through a combination of these negative and positive factors and can both benefit and hinder society.

Most people in the world, though, are not in positions of social, political, financial, or military power. They are followers, adapters, and doers, including scientists, scholars, and innovators. For the majority of people of any background, it's easier to be followers. It's how our brains are designed to be efficient — by copying and doing life on autopilot. Followers do their jobs and let the ones who lead set standards and provide procedures, trusting or hoping that the leaders do their due diligence to act with knowledge, care, and wisdom.

When systems provide power, there's a whole other level of impact. Systemic power comes in various forms and depends on various factors. People may have power through their wealth, through their brands or inherited names, through their enthusiasm and gaining followers, or through governing and leadership. Whether consciously or unconsciously, many of these systemic powers embed favoritism toward the one(s) in power. The more obvious and treacherous power-favoring systems are created by individual tyrants or tyrant regimes fueled by their constituents' fear, shame, and submission and by coercion to abide by unjust rules. A less obvious example could be a professor whose name might be advantageous for a university to keep despite his or her being unjust to students. Such systems may continue functioning through force or by offering benefits to those who can keep them in power. In time, though, the inherent imbalance, inequality, hardship, and disharmony in these systems will cause them to collapse, regardless of whom they are unfair to. Retaliation is a natural reaction shared by all species.

Throughout time, it became obvious that power left in the hands of one or a few could cause even the most virtuous to stray. Hence, systematic plans for power distribution, such as a well-designed democratic system, came into existence. When it's not taken advantage of or disrupted, democracy can combat the abuse of power and account for all stakeholders' needs by giving them a voice. However, history has also shown that democratic systems can fail to prevent favoring people in power. This is not a surprise, as such systems are made up of humans who don't possess fully developed programming with life intelligence that keeps them connected to balancing their input and output with wisdom, compassion, and clarity. Therefore, once again, we can withhold judgment and seek to understand.

Power and Anxiety

There are several logical reasons why people favor those in power. For one, they may believe the person in power knows more and will guide them to get the job done in the best way. But when power is misused, it can cause fear and anxiety for anyone involved. For example, people may praise or favor someone in power for personal gain, as with politicians backing one another to get their agendas moving forward, regardless of whether another's agenda might be corrupt or produce chain effects of suffering. There are sleepless nights, fear of being exposed, and living a restless life.

This is true even when people in power create their own immunity or enjoy the favor of immunity given them by the system to avoid being caught or persecuted for their wrongdoing. However, regardless of how lavish and comfortable their lives might be and regardless of whether they are heartless, psychotic, or just plain greedy, unfortunately, they experience fear, anger, worry, and anxiety rather than honor, joy, fulfillment, and peace. I say *unfortunately* because if they could experience honor, joy, fulfillment, and peace and experience a deeper level of happiness, then they might not intend and act unwisely. From the perspective of this book, their operating system, the SMADE model, makes them oblivious to the laws of nature we are all subject to: the laws of cause and effect; the laws of intention and its karmic effects; and most, importantly, the laws of change and impermanence. Death, or the ending of this life in this body, applies to every living and nonliving thing. In the end, one may never be relieved of his or her hunger for power, and what remains are anxiety over losing one's power and an undying need for satisfaction.

EMPOWERING LEADERS OF BENEVOLENCE

Thankfully, we do have great models, such as Gandhi and Nelson Mandela, who were able to defuse favoritism with tact. Another powerful example is Xenophon's *Cyrus the Great: The Arts of Leadership and War*, which I spoke about in the preface of this book. Xenophon described Cyrus the Great as a strategist and tactician who planned like a CEO and managed his people like a middle manager. Cyrus embodied virtuous qualities, mindful life intelligence, and other skills to lead others through examples. He held them to the highest standards of performance and integrity, was able to quickly right a wrong, and gained trust by always keeping the benefit of all in mind. When Cyrus strayed from the path of virtue and reason, he was overcome by a sense of remorse that pushed him to reverse his course. He had an optimized inner-navigation system.

Xenophon, who himself was an exemplary model of strategic genius and virtue, was in awe of Cyrus's compassion and generosity toward the people of territories he captured and the ways in which he improved the lives of the citizens he conquered. He explained that when people of other territories heard of Cyrus's advancing to conquer them, they showed no resistance. They instead welcomed him and his troops with open arms and a deep trust for their safety and rule by a benevolent leader. Xenophon explained that each time, Cyrus would carefully and equally divide all material gains among his troops and the people he invaded, never indulging or allowing his men to indulge in lavish living, hence warding off greed and the games of the ego.

There are many lessons today's leaders can learn from Cyrus the Great's tactics and strategic examples, especially when merging with or acquiring a corporation. After all, he conquered half the ancient world, which lasted for more than two hundred years, until Alexander — who, by the account of historians, was nothing like Cyrus — divided the Persian Empire. Alexander's reign and accomplishment did not last long, as his tactics were not as virtuous and merciful. By using Cyrus's war strategies, Alexander became great at conquering but missed the part about the good of humanity. Brutally, he caused a great deal of grief in people's lives and destroyed cities and massive libraries of knowledge.

When a system (e.g., a government, a corporation, a belief system, or a community) favors someone in power who is not developed with the three domains of mindful life intelligence, this can create social imbalance, inequality, hardship, and disharmony. For the members of a business, a culture, a religion, a political system, or any other system to remain healthy and thriving, the system must act with integrity and enable, respect, and empower all its members and resources properly.

MLOL 9: MINDFUL OF INVISIBLE SYSTEMS

Continuing with systems that favor those in power, there is another system that may not be as obvious, but it resides in the psyches of humans and has a negative impact on the health and well-being of society: benefit from what's called *invisible privilege*. Some people experience privileges (are treated better) for being taller, more educated, or prettier; in some cultures, for being older; and for belonging to particular groups perceived as better or groups who dominate through their power, money, confidence, intelligence, or malicious intentions. Others can be treated poorly, unfairly, and with disdain and be taken advantage of due to how they look, how little money they have, how vulnerable they are, or which racial groups they're labeled with. In extreme cases, many have lost their lives, their freedom, their loved ones, or their livelihoods, and their pain and suffering have been immense.

Invisible privilege, though, can be difficult to recognize as a condition that causes pain and suffering for those who don't have it. In 1989, Peggy McIntosh, the founder of the National SEED Project, published a profound essay about how people of the white race, as well as men, enjoy much more unearned automatic privilege in their average daily lives than people of other races. She remarked, "I was taught to see racism only in individual acts of meanness, not in invisible systems conferring dominance on my group." As a white woman in the workplace, she had been told by her colleagues of color that she was privileged over them and that no matter how hard they worked, they could not advance as easily as she could. Thus, McIntosh became determined to understand what it felt like for the women of other races to have to work much harder to prove themselves worthy and still never get to advance as a white person could. She was moved to understand this from a first- person perspective. She set out to practice the second stage of Human Software Optimization, which is to mindfully authentic an experience for oneself. To do so, she observed and recorded her daily experiences. She was astonished how many examples she found, twenty-six of which she recorded, of having advantages because of belonging to the greater population, which valued her race and skin color over others. Here are three of her observations:

- I can go home from most meetings of organizations I belong to feeling somewhat tied in, rather than isolated, out-of-place, outnumbered, unheard, held at a distance, or feared.
- When I am told about our national heritage or about "civilization," I am shown that people of my color made it what it is.
- I can criticize our government and talk about how much I fear its policies and behavior without being seen as a cultural outsider.

Many of her examples may no longer be relevant today, but there are other ways in which we may enjoy unearned privilege and, by doing so, hinder others' lives.

Most of us can understand how one way of being treated makes us feel confident and another way causes us low self-worth and anxiety. Two of the most helpful inner qualities and skills are compassion and self-awareness, which I cover in chapters 19 and 20. Like McIntosh, one can observe how others in the collective are affected by one's presence and style of participation. This is not to reduce oneself in the service of caring for another but, rather, to become aware of getting unearned favors and pull back when possible to even things out. This awareness may not be easy, as one may not relate to the experiences of those without these subtle privileges. One also may not have developed the skill of self-appraisal, which is the ability to see the effect of one's words and actions on others. This is especially true for people with diverse nervous systems, such as ADHD (attention deficit hyperactivity disorder), a population I often train to live more mindfully and successfully.

On the plus side, many imbalances can be remedied through cultivating awareness of what goes on in our environment, connecting with the pain of others, and working to neutralize the negative effects of the unearned privileges we may not even know we enjoy.

For these gaps and their associated pains and suffering to be uprooted, the heart of compassion must be active and present. For example, let's say you are at a meeting, discussing an important issue. Someone tries to voice her perspective but has a hard time because her first language is not the language of the group. You or someone else might be more articulate and enthusiastic and unintentionally dominate the conversation. This is the time to become self-aware and not let your enthusiasm and language skills become privilege over another human who may have the same eagerness and knowledge to express. You may, always kindly and nonjudgmentally, take a slow breath and gently back off. Give the person time to gather her thoughts and, if possible, help her to tease out her thoughts without making her feel less than. Another example is having conversations with people who are different from you (e.g., people who have a different skin color, nationality, gender, or race) and making it safe for them to be who they are by making kind comments and asking genuine questions to understand their experiences. While it is not anyone's fault for having these invisible privileges, it is important to become aware of them and make suitable adjustments.

Next, let's look at how one-dimensional, profit-focused business systems became harmful.

MLOL 10: MINDFUL OF ONE-DIMENSIONAL CAPITALISM

As I've discussed thus far, constructed systems become problematic because the humans who design and run them lack development in some of the qualities and skills in the three mindful life intelligence domains. When we acknowledge first that it's not easy to be human, because no one is born with a perfect template of inner development to follow, we may then be motivated to understand the root causes of our human suffering; aspire to improve our knowledge and skills so we may live with the least amount of anxiety, judgment, conflict, and dissatisfaction; and even move into sustainable happiness.

Throughout the history of advancement, humans have adopted theories, goals, strategies, and even doctrines that made sense and felt beneficial, and they fully pursued them, only to find out decades later that those concepts were at least partly damaging and should not have become the ultimate mission and goal of humanity.

An excellent example of this is a theory the economist Milton Friedman introduced in his influential 1962 book Capitalism and Freedom. Friedman advocated for the standard that the goal of a business and its leaders should be to create profit for the shareholders. In Friedman's mind, this principle ensured a free society that could pursue its own advancement. The Friedman doctrine, or shareholder theory, became widely accepted and practiced by corporations across America (and eventually worldwide). Indeed, it gave power to a free society and perhaps reduced the rate of hostility and inequality among people. Instead of raiding, killing, and taking others' fortunes, people could innovate, create business, and profit. Industrialization and profit could be the most important factors that more than doubled the world population and, in turn, led to the need for more resources and production. While capitalism contributed to many opportunities that increased wealth and improved health, comfort, and lifestyle, it finally became highly criticized in 2007–2008, when a financial crisis hit America and crushed the economy Friedman had advocated for, ruining many lives.

The missing piece was that Friedman believed doing social good was not the responsibility of a business and, moreover, espoused the faulty notion that using business to do good would "undermine the basis of a free society." He strongly maintained that the ultimate mission of a business should be to make profit for its owners and shareholders, who could spend that profit in any way they wished.

This pursuit of financial gain and living in a free society came from an idea that showed great potential making America perceived as the "land of opportunity." Businesspeople started regarding the opportunity for great wealth as an absolute truth that could liberate them. Doors were opened to immigrants who became self-made millionaires. Innovators became billionaires. However, decades later, we find ourselves gaining a tremendous amount of comfort through material goods but also witnessing tremendous amounts of stress-related illnesses, cancers, anxiety, inequality and damage to our planet. A direct result of lacking clear understanding of how natural systems, such as cause and effect, intention-based actions, dependency and interdependence, and change and impermanence, ultimately govern our lives.

The encouragement here is that as we experience the results of our ideas and strategies, we can look at them objectively — without harsh judgment but with curiosity — with intentions that are more suited for keeping our constructed systems effective without harmful impacts. We can make ample and genuine effort to understand these natural systems and employ them in our plans. As we align with natural laws, we develop a strong character that can be wise and discerning.

If we don't train ourselves to produce ideas and strategies that are mindful of life's intelligence, we will face business as usual: unending rounds of suffering. Let us reflect on what it's like to be wronged, to be hurt, and to suffer, as it's NOT EASY to be human. We can set our minds to develop ourselves in these MLOLs so we may make wiser choices and actions.

MLOL 11: MINDFUL OF ISSUES WITH MAINTAINING COMPETITIVE EDGE

Livelihood is a primal need that fulfills other primal needs for humans. It provides the safety and security humans need against the wild. Unfortunately, in systems that aim only to maintain growth and monopolize markets, no one is secure in his or her job. There are many business strategies that empower employees to attain their companies' competitive edge by pushing results at any cost. Everyone in the chain, from the CEOs to other executives, employees, and their families, suffers stress, anxiety, and burnout due to the fear of losing his or her livelihood. Knowing and feeling replaceable can have grave psychological effects, with the same fear, worry, and anxiety as if one's life were in danger.

Following capitalism, creating wealth and remaining competitive became a hamster wheel that no one could get off. For example, Purdue Pharma filed bankruptcy to defend against litigation for its role in the opioid epidemic — doctors endorsed and overprescribed OxyContin while looking past widespread signs of addiction and loss of lives and despite the enormous amount of suffering it caused. The suffering experienced did not exclude the CEOs, the VPs, the directors, the promoters, the vendors, and a whole web of interconnected and interdependent systems. As they marched in the magnified direction— to get more of the market share, to earn more, and to be endlessly competitive to stay in the game—all involved were stressed out and losing sleep at night. As the result of staying in the rat race, people lose connection with the human heart, peace, and joy, often neglecting their families and harming society, and then life comes to an end. That's it. It is all for nothing!

When we recognize the damage caused by using any strategy to win and making employees who work hard to gain a livelihood feel replaceable and insecure, we can stop, rethink the greater loss to ourselves, and course-correct to minimize harm and damage.

MLOL 12: MINDFUL OF CONSUMERISM AND CIRCULAR ANXIETY ECONOMY

Have you ever taken an inventory of all you have and all you are and asked yourself why possessing the next thing you're about to get is so important? Have you imagined already having that next better thing and thought of some of the problems that may come with owning it? Most people in consumer societies rarely do. There is no pausing. Once a craving for something shows up, we try to satisfy it, believing our happiness is guaranteed by owning new and better things. This reliance on external things and conditions to bring steady pleasure or a sense of confidence and belonging can cause stress and anxiety, weaken our immune systems, and cause disharmony in our lives.

The circular anxiety economy is a theory I came up with to point to an entire economy built on maintaining people's anxiety. It is circular because it pushes people to continually get more, have more, and be more—a systemic economic anxiety that makes some people rich and robs others of emotional stability, fulfilling relationships, and even life. If you are not falling for this economic strategy, good for you. But let's see how a circular anxiety economy works.

CIRCULAR ANXIETY
· ECONOMY

Self-Perpetuating System

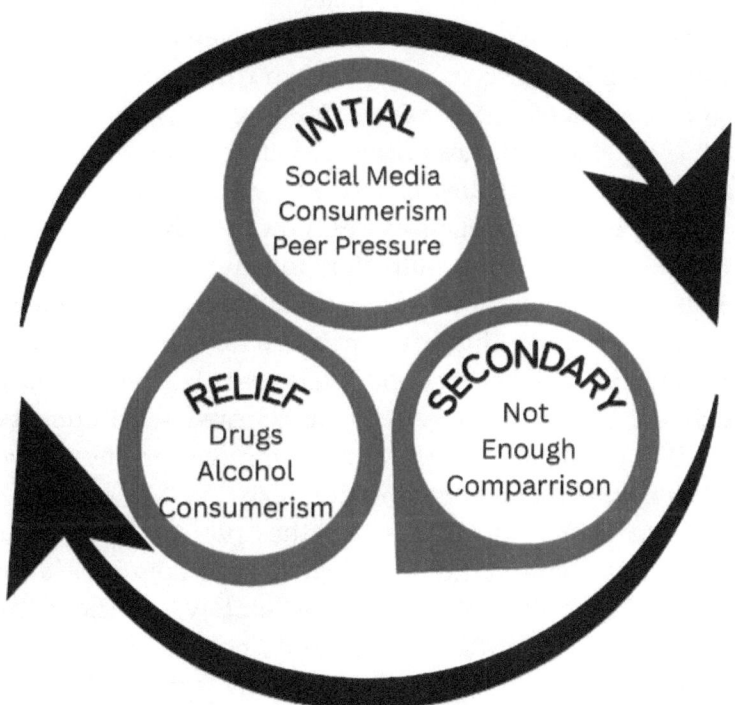

Figure 9, Copyright by Dr. Manijeh Motaghy

As I see it, there are three parts to the circular anxiety economy: initial, secondary, and relief. The initial anxiety is induced by the creation of perceptions and expectations that one needs to have more or better possessions (e.g., the next generation of iPhone) or higher achievements, make more money, be more beautiful and less wrinkled, become more likable, and so on, which preys on humanity's natural

130

desire for safety, comfort, and happiness. The secondary anxiety comes as a result of never catching up with this perpetual pursuit of having more or being more. This secondary anxiety caused by financial imbalance and feelings of inadequacy fuels the circular anxiety economy, which conveniently pushes all kinds of remedies to relieve these anxieties.

The circular anxiety economy is invisible to most and hard to detect. One falls for the allure of a materialistic and shallow life. But it is a powerful economic strategy that takes advantage of the cyclic and self-perpetuating nature of consumerism driven by profit motives. Through consistent, persuasive messages that we don't have enough— whether in terms of possessions, experiences, or personal attributes— business creates anxiety over what we supposedly need, in order to sell products and services. When we live on autopilot and are moved by novelty bias (attraction to new), ads and promotional materials drive us into a relentless pursuit of getting the next new product or experience. This drive can lead us to be even more unaware of our choices and overextend ourselves, both financially and emotionally. When the novelty or anticipated satisfaction fails to materialize or is only temporary, it results in even greater anxiety and dissatisfaction, perpetuating the cycle.

This hamster wheel creates the perfect conditions for pharmaceutical companies to step in with solutions aimed at alleviating these symptoms. Unfortunately, medications can address only the symptoms of anxiety, not its root causes, thus preserving the circular anxiety economy system. Sadly, most humans who are involved in these circular anxiety cycles— and are beneficiaries of the economic rewards— are unaware that they share the same painful restlessness and unease.

There is a saying in the Persian language: "The grander your roof, the more snow to plow." This refers to flat roofs that need to be kept free from snow, as the weight of snow could cause them to collapse. It means that the more stuff or bigger things you possess, the harder you have to work to maintain them. So the next time you are about to make a purchase, pause and ask, "Do I really need this? Or do I want to care for another thing?" Keeping the money might prove more beneficial and bring you a sense of security and peace. In fact, one of the seven rules of becoming wealthy or having financial security is to have a budget for everything you need and let go of things you don't need — a new shirt, a glittery pair of sandals, a plastic toy that'll end up in the trash. You may read more about this in the book *The Richest Man in Babylon* by George S. Clason.

For Vendors

This MLOL, being mindful of consumerism and the circular anxiety economy, I understand may not suit you if your livelihood depends on selling products and staying competitive by presenting new ideas. To you I say, you are smart. Those smarts can be used to alleviate root causes of anxiety and stress. Think of ways to create your livelihood that don't perpetuate anxiety or harm the planet. The more stuff is produced and owned, the more waste gets dropped on earth and the more our waters and natural resources become depleted and poisoned. Our children and families and our own bodies suffer for it. So why not use your intelligence to be on the side of a healthy, peaceful, and joyful life and engage others to do so as well? I know you can.

Next, see how the Buddha advised his son to avoid causing stress and anxiety or harm.

MLOL 13: MINDFULLY ABANDONING STRESS-PRODUCING ACTIVITIES

The Buddha gave his son, Rāhula, great advice that can be adopted by leaders, vendors, and consumers as well as by governing bodies, activists, and families — a perfect life lesson we can cultivate within ourselves and give our children. The Buddha knew the human mind; the tricks it can play on us; and the ways we can get caught by desire, hatred, and a lack of understanding. Below is a summation of his teaching.

If you want to live a happy life in harmony and happiness and without stress and anxiety, follow these instructions:

1. When a thought or an idea occurs to you, you can stop and think, *Where is this thought or idea leading?* If you find that it

leads to satisfaction, harmony, and beneficial results for you and everyone involved, continue developing that thought or idea. If the thought leads to ineffective or stressful results for you or others involved, then abandon it.

2. When your thought or idea becomes a choice, you can stop and think, *Where is this choice leading?* If you realize this choice leads to satisfaction, harmony, and beneficial results for you and everyone involved, continue with that choice. If the choice leads to dissatisfaction, disharmony, and ineffective or stressful results for anyone involved, then abandon it. You can think of other choices and continue with the same process until you find the best choice possible.

3. When your choice has become an action and you find yourself in the middle of this action, you can stop and think, *Where is this action leading?* If you realize that it leads to satisfaction, harmony, and beneficial results for everyone involved, continue with the action. If you realize that continuing this action will lead to ineffective or stressful results for anyone involved, abandon it. You can look for or consider other effective and harmonious actions.

4. When you find yourself experiencing the outcome of your actions, if you recognize that your actions led to satisfaction, harmony, and beneficial results for you and others, then repeat such actions. If you find yourself or others involved experiencing dissatisfaction, disharmony, and negative or stressful results, stay in the painful experience to feel the impact. Remember those painful feelings so you understand them and do not repeat the same actions again.

Taking Preventative Measures

Last year, I created a preventative accountability model (PAM), a nine-step guide for creating, selling, or utilizing AI ethically and responsibly. It includes detailed instruction and an expanded version of the lesson the Buddha gave his son. When one of my colleagues who is an expert in AI and related matters read this preventative accountability model and the nine steps, she commented that it is hard to stop in the middle of coding algorithms, for example, and think about the thoughts, choices, and actions and their consequences. You're on a roll, focused on creating and designing. Besides, you are not having thoughts, choices, and actions on your own; there are other people and factors involved.

I get it, but I also know that the human mind needs development and realignment. We are intelligent beings who create and follow guidelines, philosophies, and traditions; abide by social realities; and, most of all, are guided by our intentions. We can set our intentions to keep in mind instructions that bring awareness to our thoughts and ideas, to our choices and actions, and to the outcomes we create. We can consider whether they are stress-producing for anyone. If so, we can rethink and find a way to avoid creating disharmony. This applies to any context in which we have to think, choose, and act.

Part 4 of this book offers MLOLs to understand and develop such abilities.

MLOL 14: MINDFUL SOLUTIONS TO WICKED PROBLEMS

We experience life as we perceive, as we assume, as we desire, as we associate and understand situations, and as we are skilled at handling them. We see a problem from our angle and genuinely seek to resolve it. Then we encounter obstacles and realize some of these issues are complex and systemic. These conditions may exist within small systems, such as family systems, or large and global systems, such as environmental and economic systems, and every system in between. We may let those issues be because we don't know what to do with them. We may come up with solutions that end up causing other problems.

As these negative results compound, they create even more complicated issues that are hard to trace, decipher, and resolve. Scientists call these wicked problems. Some of these wicked problems arise from systems that prioritize growth, profit, and a competitive edge over long- term sustainability. False perspectives and underdeveloped wisdom and heart intelligence lead to the design and manufacture of products that create social realities and cultural norms, inspire dependency, need frequent upgrades and replacements, cause mental and physical health problems, and end up in landfills.

Wicked problems can have multiple causes and be interconnected with other problems, with no one solution to resolve them. A prime example of this is climate change, which is caused by a chain of errors in constructed systems. For example, part of climate disturbance is due to overconsumption and mountains of trash in the oceans, which disrupt oceanic undercurrents that keep the water temperature cool and suitable for life. Other factors that have contributed are well known. They include clear-cutting trees (deforestation), polluting the air, disposing of toxins in the environment, and harming creatures that play instrumental roles in maintaining the brilliant regenerative design of our planet's natural system.

When economic and industrial systems prioritize financial growth and take advantage of natural resources without regard for limitations or the damage they cause to ecosystems, they cause and contribute to unsolvable problems. The interconnection of various industries, such as energy production, transportation, agriculture, fishery, textile, and others, along with the lack of a unified global accountability mechanism (i.e., disagreement among scientists and other stakeholders), has made climate change an incredibly complex issue.

Wicked problems are difficult to resolve because often solutions threaten the very existence of a whole system that people depend on. For example, how do you resolve the issue of an economy created on people's anxiety without resolving the conditions that demand businesses to maintain a competitive edge? How do you resolve the negative side effects of having to be competitive without causing corporations or industries to collapse or become obsolete? How do you resolve the chaos and anxiety that come from putting harmful industries out of business and leaving people jobless, homeless, and lost?

These are some examples that help us to see how the natural laws of dependency and interdependence govern us, our actions, and our systems. Hence, before taking any action, we can be mindful not to create or contribute to wicked problems. Also, in the same way that

One idea, such as capitalism and the accompanying strategies, can cause wicked problems, a wiser idea and skill development can save us from them. These solutions include developing oneself, CEOs, executives, employees, and anyone possible in the qualities and skills of IDGs as well as in the MLOLs that equip them for resilience, integrity, and life intelligence.

With a change in perspective and the understanding that some problems can become big and out of control, we can be equipped to look meticulously and rigorously to consider the impact of our choices on various stakeholders, including those who do not have a voice — as the Buddha guided his son to abandon or modify potentially harmful choices. It takes understanding and mindful life intelligence.

Next, let's look at solutions to some of these systemic issues.

MLOL 15: BUILDING SYSTEMS AS A FORCE FOR GOOD

Aside from nonprofit organizations set up to do good in the world, there are now corporate systems that have moved away from Friedman's one-dimensional philosophy of creating wealth with no other social responsibility. After all, corporations are made up of humans, and humans have the potential to wake up. Thankfully, corporations designed to be forces for good are increasing in number. While these businesses are profitable, they equally prioritize care for their people and the well-being of our planet. These corporations are mindful of their strategies, implementation, waste products, and use of natural resources. They use innovation to do good.

A successful example of movement for positive change in the corporate world is the advent of B corporations. In 2006, B Lab created a for-profit structure to make business a force for good and began a campaign to certify every company that meets a high standard of social and environmental performance as a B corporation, as a legal business structure. Often, leaders and business owners wish to make their businesses forces for good but do not have the know-how. B Lab offers opportunities to organizations to develop their goals, strategies, and execution plans by responding to a set of criteria that account for

136

The well-being of people and the planet while creating healthy profit. As of February 2024, some 8,254 corporations have been certified as B corporations. Some of these are large corporations that employ hundreds of thousands of people around the globe.

For example, the clothing company Patagonia was certified as a B corporation in 2011. Patagonia is known for the simplicity and durability of its clothing. Those who run the company understand that all the activities that go into their business, from the lighting of their stores to the dyeing of the material, are a burden on the environment. Thus, they strive to find ways to make their products repairable and last for generations. For example, you can trade in a piece of clothing you bought from them for a new one. They've designated hub cities where local shop owners can make a livelihood out of repairing, reusing, and recycling that clothing. In addition, Patagonia participates in activism that has a positive impact on the planet.

So it is possible to run a business, even a very large one, as a force for the good of all while making a decent profit. Let yourself feel hope, confidence, and resilience for a brighter future. Look into establishing your organization as a force for good and achieving B-corporation status. It is a great feeling to be part of a company that works toward the well-being of people as well as the planet while staying profitable.

To develop wiser ways of managing your occupation, go to chapter 19, MLOL 46: "HQ for Occupation Fulfillment (Wise Livelihood)."

In the next two chapters, we will look intently at MLOLs that relate to our planet, pointing out its generosity and abundance, its boundaries and limitations, and our relationship and responsibility to it. Let us encourage a forward-looking, compassionate approach to inner development that leads to responsible environmental stewardship.

CHAPTER 14

THE SECOND DOMAIN: OUR PLANET AND SUSTAINABLE LIVING

This domain includes MLOLs 16 through 26 in this chapter and chapter 15. They include "Mindful of the Falsehood of Ownership"; "Mindfully Flowing to Relieve Death Anxiety"; "Mindful of Evolution: Humans Are Not Better Evolved"; "Mindfully Transforming Learned Nature Anxieties"; "Mindfully Transforming Narcissism and Climate Anxiety"; "Mindful of Life Source Intelligence: A Regenerative Generosity"; "Mindful of Oneness: The Antidote to Separation and Loneliness Anxiety"; "Mindful of the Boundaries and Limitations of Earth's Resilience"; "Mindfully Stewarding Earth Through Conscious Action"; "Being Mindful Ancestors"; and "Mindful Manufacturing: Regenerative Integration Management System (RIMS)."

AWAKENED NATURE, HUMAN NATURE

The reason for designating the second domain as our planet and sustainable living occurred to me during a course I taught at Perfectly Here in 2018, using Ajahn Sucitto's book *Buddha Nature, Human Nature*. The book is filled with statistics and data on how humans have caused destruction on the planet by disrupting the food chain, leading to many imbalances in nature, and continue to do so—how we have been consuming without regard for the safety and maintenance of how nature has designed ecosystems to feed every living thing.

To expand my students' development in mindfulness and reduce other types of stress and anxieties, I assigned them a surprising research project. The project goal was to have students explore their relationship with nature and challenge their view of any creature they hated or feared and felt anxiety toward, ultimately creating more ease within them through understanding, connection, gratitude, and compassion. They were to take the one animal or insect they hated or feared most and find the answer to three questions:

1. What is the role of this creature in the world?
2. What would happen if its type were all gone?
3. What negative consequences would their extinction have on our human lives?

This last question was especially designed to engender relatability, because we usually think of extinctions from the animal's point of view and may not be touched much. But if the extinction affects us, then we might pay more attention. For example, most people think if koalas were completely extinct, it would be awful for them, so we have to do something for them out of compassion. While this is an important point, this assignment was to reveal the laws of dependence and interdependence and show a direct correlation between an animal's role and its extinction's negative impact on all life, including our human lives.

Through this assignment, as a class, we learned about insects and their contributions to the cultivation and thriving of the planet and how every creature on Earth plays an important part in the food chain. We were astonished to learn how various animals clean up after themselves; clear the environment of natural waste, such as dead trees; and even assist in the decomposition of our dead bodies. Some of these creatures, such as rats, provide benefits we were unaware of. One student's research argued that if rats didn't exist, viruses that use rats as hosts could instead possibly use human bodies as their hosts because we have biology similar to rats' — and that could be catastrophic. Students realized that if we knew these things, we wouldn't hate or fear rats when we saw them. We can humanely make sure our living space is free of them while still giving them respect for the important role they play.

If you'd like to be amazed at the dependency and links among all living things, watch the 2011 documentary *The Wolves of Yellowstone*, which shows how, when a pack of wolves was reintroduced to the park, within a few years, the desolate landscapes of the park were transformed into thriving habitats filled with new plants, trees, birds, insects, and other animals. The wolves created the means for a perfect ecosystem by living, hunting, and providing food for the rest to thrive. Now, that is something to be overjoyed about.

OPTIMIZING OUR RELATIONSHIP WITH NATURE MLOLS

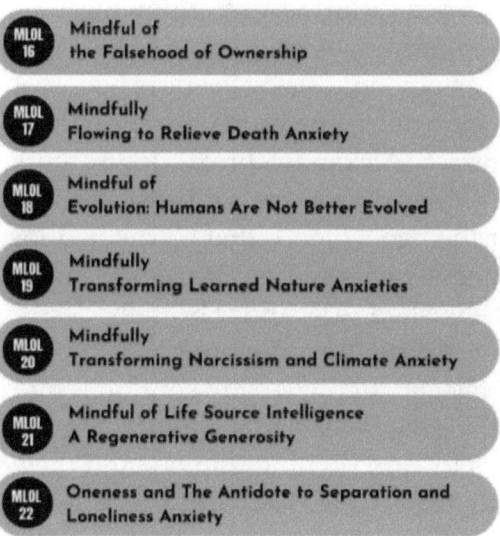

DOMAIN II
PLANET AND SUSTAINABLE LIVING
OPTIMIZING OUR RELATIONSHIP WITH NATURE

MLOL 16 Mindful of the Falsehood of Ownership

MLOL 17 Mindfully Flowing to Relieve Death Anxiety

MLOL 18 Mindful of Evolution: Humans Are Not Better Evolved

MLOL 19 Mindfully Transforming Learned Nature Anxieties

MLOL 20 Mindfully Transforming Narcissism and Climate Anxiety

MLOL 21 Mindful of Life Source Intelligence A Regenerative Generosity

MLOL 22 Oneness and The Antidote to Separation and Loneliness Anxiety

Figure 10
Copyright by Dr. Manijeh Motaghy

MLOL 16: MINDFUL OF THE FALSEHOOD OF OWNERSHIP

Ownership has become a foundational concept in human worth and happiness. A person's quality or degree of belonging determines his or her societal worth, and his or her ego and sense of identity feed on such societal recognition. Unfortunately, because ego is a fabricated self, it cannot recognize that everything is in flux, ever-changing, and that we can get separated from our belongings at any time. Circumstances that cause a person to lose financial and other societal status can involve great suffering. Feelings of failure, shame, and hopelessness can set in, all due to misalignment with the nature of things. People have been known to commit suicide over losing their companies or meeting financial ruin. Humans fall into the delusion of ownership as an absolute reality. But those who are wise and programmed with mindful life intelligence know better.

On his deathbed, Cyrus the Great said, "When I am dead, don't bury my body in an expensive coffin. Just give it back to Earth. What can be better than lying in the lap of the mother and nurse of all beautiful things?" Knowing he owned nothing and could take nothing with him, King Cyrus trod with caution throughout his conquests by keeping his ego in check and his eyes on his mission of freeing humanity from itself.

In contrast, Alexander broke down the Persian Empire and became known as the Great for his strategic mastery — not for his virtues or the benevolence that Cyrus had instilled in the people he governed. Conquered by the idea of ownership and the right to do as he wished, Alexander brutally destroyed valuable assets and enslaved those he conquered.

This belief about ownership continues into modern times. Our small-minded egos are constantly trying to look out for us by pushing us toward owning things — and they continually lead us to fear and anxiety. We can easily become deluded, thinking we own things if we allocate names to them. This misunderstanding traps us in suffering. Believing we actually own things, as an absolute fact, creates heartaches and hardships we cannot resolve.

141

The truth is that nature owns everything, even us. But we grow up with a me-over-nature mindset. We take its resources, create documents that indicate ownership of land, build up walls, and even go to war and kill one another over our belief in owning little patches of Earth. There are other animals who are territorial. They are so in order to protect their food source and ensure their survival. I see this in hummingbirds that come to feed on the sugar-water feeders hung off my front porch. One hummingbird fights off others but allows its partner or family members feed. While humans also instinctually push to satisfy their innate needs, some of us push to possess much more than we need.

Possessiveness and ownership are only shared social realities, not natural reality. As with anything that goes against laws of nature, this too causes many problems, some of which are discussed in the natural laws and constructed systems domain. This is important because in nature, everything that integrates eventually disintegrates and becomes otherwise. Understanding this can help us to see how an ego-driven relationship with nature can throw life off-balance in the ways we innovate, produce, and proliferate synthetic materials with the false notion that we are the owners of these things and that we have the right to do so.

It's About the Elements

To explore why and how everything ends up being disintegrated, changed, or lost and we lose ownership, let's use the five elements as a frame of reference. There are many perspectives that explain these elements, including philosophical alchemy, psychology, medicine, motivation, energy balance, and others. Here I take the simple versions of these as elements and their functions in nature.

1. *Fire*
   Fire represents energy and temperature; both heat and cold. The fire element exists within us and outside us and can transform states of being.

2. *Water*

   Water is the basic fluid running through our bodies in the form of mucus, urine, blood, and so on, as well as in rivers that fill oceans, vapor that forms clouds, and the same water that runs through our household plumbing.

3. *Wind or Air*

   The wind or air element is the ability for anything to move internally in our bodies, as our hearts and lungs do, and externally, as in moving our hands, bending to pick things up, or needing movement for walking and talking. It enables things to shift and change directions and makes mechanics function. The wind or air element also helps to cool things down, as with the undercurrents in oceans keeping the water temperatures cool enough for underwater life. The phenomenon of change itself needs the collaboration of the wind or air element.

4. *Earth*

   Anything that is solid is the earth element: a flower; a piece of clothing; a rock; a tree; a plastic bottle; a jet; and our hair, muscles, and bones.

5. *Space*

   Space is the emptiness — which may or may not be so empty — around other elements, within atoms, or between objects. It must be present for things to function well and to have room to grow and change without friction.

Note that all the elements above are both within us and outside us. They make up the material world.

All of these elements are of nature, no matter their form or shape. It also doesn't matter if they are combined in a naturally occurring form, such as an orange, or in a manufactured form, such as a car. Once they are integrated, they will also disintegrate. Integrated, assembled, or combined elements are subject to the natural phenomenon of change and susceptible to change and transition. Because of the inevitability of disintegration, we can lose anything at any time. When we hang on to the idea that we're the owners of things we've lost, we face fighting nature. When we fail, we agonize immensely and cause harm to others.

Understanding that everything comes from nature and goes back to nature can prevent anxiety and stress related to loss. If we know that we don't really own anything and that our concepts of ownership are not natural, we won't be as hurt when those so-called possessions separate from us. We can replace the disconnected, ego-driven intention with appreciation for nature and be one with nature. In this way, even when we are in the presence of cars, cell phones, and other constructed objects, we can feel at one with them, because in essence, we are made up of the same elements. When we discard the false notion that we are able to keep anything indefinitely, we can avoid conflict, war, and other harmful competitions that lead only to suffering.

MLOL 17: MINDFULLY FLOWING TO RELIEVE DEATH ANXIETY

Now let's talk about how to suffer less at the loss of things and relationships we supposedly own. From the fact of elements disintegrating comes the reality that with every moment that passes, you and I, and everything and everyone on this planet, get closer to that point of disintegration, or death. Death is something most people don't want to talk about. But we need to talk about birth and death — in particular about death — because for some of us, grief of loss can be overwhelming, even debilitating. While some cultures have a level of equanimity with death and loss, others can be very emotional and experience deep, long-lasting pain and sorrow.

In many societies, discussing death is taboo and unwelcome. When someone speaks of his or her death, we often hear responses like "God forbid," "You're too young," "You have a long way to go," or "You shouldn't talk like that." Because our parents and our communities don't speak of death enough, we grow up trying to avoid it and push it off into an unknown distance. Then we're taken by surprise when it happens. When my grandmother, who was ninety-four years old, passed away, I was in my twenties, and I became extremely distraught. She was my backbone, my sense of trust in goodness and in myself. I was lost at times and lonely, and at other times, I was angry at her for not telling me she would one day pass away — for not teaching me about this fact of life. Perhaps she thought I would learn it on my own. But these things are not discussed much, for fear they may cause hopelessness.

The Cause of Death

From one view, the cause of death is birth itself. If one is not born, one won't have to suffer death. This view can feel cold and abstract and not helpful when we lose someone we love or lose our own health or a relationship. While the pain of loss is real, our reactions to death in general are both natural and learned. While we have to live this life and experience loss and death, we can reflect on truths that can help to ease our pain and free us from it in any degree possible.

Flowing With Change

If we can see that birth and death are manifestations of change, we can see that they are a natural flow, consisting of various processes moving from one state of existence to another. The process of elements in nature becoming a sperm driven by energy and movement to join an egg, more processes forming a fetus, growing a body made up of the five elements, and entering the world as we know it represents flow and transformation — change. Aging too is just change, helping living things and even non-living things to transition through various states. Then comes the dismantling of all these elements; they're sent back to their original forms or transformed into other forms that continue to exist somewhere in the environment. Take the LA fires, for example, which disintegrated thousands of houses and millions of objects. These materials no longer exist in their integrated forms but continue to exist as ashes, gases, and other forms.

One of the ways Buddhists monks contemplate death to become free of its suffering is by contemplating a body at the time of death. When observing a person on his or her deathbed, a patient person can see the wind element leave the body and the organs stop moving. Then the fire element leaves, and the body becomes cold. Water leaves as the body decomposes and dries out, and the earth element is the last to disintegrate. When archaeologists discover bones from long ago, they may give them some identity that explains the events and history, but the actual thing is just the solid earth element.

From this angle, you can see how this change, which we call *death* and suffer immensely for, Is a natural process and impersonal. When we get this immutable law of nature, we naturally let go of the prolonged grief of loss; the pain of attachment to others, things, and situations; and feelings of abandonment, and we become peaceful. A dear friend of mine who lost her home and everything she owned in the LA fires said that while walking through the ashes, she couldn't cry or be upset. Nothing was recognizable, not even the boundaries between her property and the neighbors'. She was surprised to have so much equanimity with the situation. Though she has moments of grief and bewilderment over so much loss, the truth—and the finality—of everything being gone is so undeniable that her mind goes into natural acceptance. Truth can set us free.

Now, you may think, *I get that, but the unbearable sorrow I feel for losing someone I love is too deep and real. How do I get relief from that?* Of course it is. Loss and grief are not fabricated or imagined. I know this firsthand from losing many I've loved but most painfully from the loss of my child. You can read about how you may overcome grief in chapter 21, MLOL 59.

MLOL 18: MINDFUL OF EVOLUTION: HUMANS ARE NOT BETTER EVOLVED

Throughout our history of understanding ourselves, we've made many assumptions that were false or became outdated. We've heard philosophers, poets, religious entities, educators, and our parents tell us that we are superior to animals and should value ourselves over them because we've evolved to have language and cognitive intelligence, are civilized and have feelings, and can dominate other animals. Therefore, we are better and more valued.

146

Today neuroscience has found that natural selection, or evolution, did not favor us or make us a superior species. We are, at best, another interesting species with our own adaptation mechanisms, which allowed humans to migrate from one region of the planet to another to find better food sources and living conditions.

In *Seven and a Half Lessons About the Brain*, neuropsychologist Lisa Feldman Barrett explains that rats, lizards, birds, insects, worms, and all other forms of life have their own perfect brains evolved to do what they are intended to do. While we have evolved with the ability to strategize, innovate, create, communicate, collaborate, copy, and conceptualize— characteristics that are mostly attributed to the human species—Barrett emphasizes that "other animals are not inferior to humans. They are uniquely and effectively adapted to their environments. Your brain is not more evolved than the rat or lizard brain, just differently evolved." There are no lower or higher levels of importance in nature. Every creature and plant has a unique place and role. This is true regardless of species' strength, size, or quantity. Otherwise, bacteria, which monitor and balance our bodies and play an immense role in our existence, could be given the highest ranking. Even so, the interconnection and interrelation of all participants of life are what make life work. Similarly, within the human species, various environments determine some of our adaptations—for example darker skin tones protecting against the severity of sunlight; survival skills, such as fishing; or social realities, such as driving a car in busy cities. The ideas that separate us into *more valued* and *less valued* are constructed by the human mind and are in conflict with the nature of things.

Understanding that we're neither better nor more important than other creatures that live on this planet can undo the delusion that we are more intelligent or valuable than bacteria, for example, and can protect us from doing things that are not in our best interest.

MLOL 19: MINDFULLY TRANSFORMING LEARNED NATURE ANXIETIES

From the moment children become aware of their environment, they also become aware of the responses and reactions of the adults around them. They realize that when they cry, they will be tended to. When they scream, someone notices. When they smile, others' faces soften and smile too. With every little action and socialization, their human realities form. They closest people around them. These learned emotions and emotional expressions end up as response codes in their brains. Some of these response codes become anxiety codes.

Anxiety codes often form in relation to nature, especially for those who live in cities and are not as connected with the natural world. These anxieties grow with the child and become another form of needless suffering and unhappiness.

For example, a mother may scream when she sees a cockroach and run to get a shoe or something to kill it. Her reaction teaches the child that this creature is rejected from the house; one should dislike it and end its life as quickly as possible. The child not only experiences and records the energy of anxiety in the mind and feels the emotion in the body but also misses out on an opportunity to get to know this creature and its direct role in the child's life and survival.

The human child learns to hate the cockroach because it looks different or is ugly by some human standards. A child doesn't realize that ugliness is just a concept and a subjective judgment. It is biased and, in this case, discriminating against the *cockroach*. Even the name cockroach is just a word or label we gave this noble creature so we could refer to it, and we refer to it from our perspective. But we don't realize that the names, labels, and perceptions we create are not, by themselves, facts of life. If you happen to love nature and understand it, you most likely know the importance of all that exists. But most who live in modern cities don't, and they suffer for it.

The Noble Cockroach

Let's get to know the cockroach for a minute.

The *Moment of Science* radio program describes cockroaches as professional recyclers and explains that they love to live in our homes because there are plenty of food crumbs on floors or counters and plenty of dark, cool corners and other hiding places to live in. According to Web MD, the American cockroach is known to eat almost anything, including our trash, which we should be thankful for. They decompose waste material and turn it into nutrient-rich soil for the growth of nutrient-rich plants, which we should be grateful for, because we can't do that for ourselves. Can we?

Cockroaches are also food for lots of other animals that themselves are important to the chain of life, such as lizards, birds, and mice. Even some other bugs, such as spiders, praying mantises, and centipedes, feast on cockroaches. Additionally, while moving through green areas and flowers, cockroaches transport pollen, which helps with plant reproduction. In some areas of the world, cockroaches area high-protein food source for humans; they are not seen as vermin. In Costa Rica, it is common for people to refer to household bugs, such as spiders, as *amigos de la casa*, or friends of the house. This expression comes from the cultural perspective that these creatures help keep harmful insects at bay and play a beneficial role in the household ecosystem.

These types of MLOLs were known and passed down through generations by native cultures, such as the aboriginals of Australia. These ancestors lived lives intimately connected to nature, as they needed to find food; make clothing, medicine, and shelter; and keep themselves safe from predators and other environmental dangers. They spent a lot of time observing natural processes, understood themselves as part of the world, and saw that they were responsible for caring for nature. So did the indigenous people of America and other ancient cultures all around the planet, such as the Aztecs, Chinese, Japanese, and Persians. Some still have some connection to all these ecosystems.

For us, in the modern world, these bits of knowledge and benefits are lost, replaced by fear, dislike, and anxiety. But why would we want to be scared more than we have to be? Or be anxious that another living being is alive, when it is just nature, and everything about nature is part of our lives and existence anyway? Instead of experiencing disharmony and fear, we can work on transforming our mindsets about a creature from disgust to neutrality and even compassion. From there, perhaps you can become more understanding and curious about it. Maybe you can even feel grateful and live with joy when you see one.

I recently walked up to an executive who was a speaker on a panel during Climate Week in New York. She had spoken about how she takes morning walks to clear her head and notices ants, birds, and plants. I commended her and said, "That is so beautiful. Do you want to know what I do on my walks?" She eagerly nodded, and I said, "When I walk and see ants, trees, bugs, and birds, I say to them, 'I see you, and I am rooting for you. I have your back.'" She was overjoyed to hear that and said she would add that to her walks.

Communicating with nature is magical indeed. Nature understands us. All you have to do is connect and speak from your heart's intelligence and goodwill. In fact, I have experienced this a lot with little bugs and things. When I communicate with them, they respond. A few weeks ago, my family got to witness this firsthand. A tarantula was walking toward several of us who were standing outside the cabin we had rented in the Sequoias. While everyone was scared and trying to figure out what to do, I gently spoke to it: "Go back. It is not safe for you here. Go home; there is nothing here for you. Go home; it's not safe here." Still fifteen feet away, it suddenly stopped shriveling itself up and, after a moment, turned around and walked away. My family was stunned, but to me, that was normal.

Developing a proper relationship with the world around us can mitigate some of these learned anxieties. Children and adults encountering a cockroach, a spider, or a wolf can express curiosity and appreciation for the creature's role in keeping our environment flourishing, while protecting themselves from potential harm. The point is, you can be protective, avoid, or run when you feel danger and can learn how to manage the harmful effects of creatures without having to harbor hate and ill will toward them. This will increase your inner peace, well-being, and confidence.

MLOL 20: MINDFULLY TRANSFORMING RESOURCE NARCISSISM AND CLIMATE ANXIETY

In many parts of the planet, natural resources are still abundant and seem unlimited. However, the pursuit of capitalism and the increase in human population have caused exploitation, destruction, and depletion of natural resources. It's like how a narcissistic partner in a relationship takes and takes while the other gives and gives. Eventually, this imbalance causes the giver to burn out, become ill and, with no chance to recover from loss of energy and resources, finally stops giving. That's how we've been treating our planet's natural resources.

We've extracted and extracted from nature without regard for its regenerative process and renewal needs. Desertification, whereby a perfectly fertile land becomes dry and infertile, is typically a result of drought, deforestation, or inappropriate agricultural methods and over farming, which have had significant effects on the environment, the global economy, and human life. The US Department of Agriculture reported $520 billion in total cash receipts from agriculture for 2023, a big portion of which went toward feeding cattle that were food for humans.

With rich land and economic incentives, the United States has developed the largest beef industry and the largest population of consumers of beef in the world. Having to feed such vast numbers of cattle every year with monoculture farming has burdened land and contributes to desertification. Monoculture farming is an agricultural practice in which a single crop or plant species is grown over a large area, often repeatedly season after season. While it allows for high efficiency and large-scale production, it depletes soil nutrients, increases vulnerability to pests and diseases, and requires heavy use of chemical fertilizers and pesticides, ultimately reducing biodiversity and long-term soil health.

Moreover, scientists found that these massive numbers of cows release more methane emission (toxic air) than all types of transportation worldwide combined. That includes all the airplanes, cargo ships, cars, buses, trucks, and trains. Can you believe that cattle farming, a major source of meat, dairy, and other products for humans, plays such a major role in climate change and climate catastrophes? This is one of those wicked problems.

Worse, experts say that the poorer countries who don't benefit from US cattle farming are the ones affected the most. Many of these catastrophes happen in poor areas of the planet, where people are not overconsuming and overproducing. In January 2023, the World Economic Forum reported the following:

> The World Bank reports that only one-tenth of the world's greenhouse gases are emitted by the 74 lowest- income countries, but they will be most affected by the effects of climate change. Compared to the 1980s, they have already experienced approximately eight times as many natural disasters in the past 10 years. By 2050, unchecked climate change might force more than 200 million people to migrate within their own countries, pushing up to 130 million people into poverty and unraveling decades of hard-won development achievements.

As scientists figure these things out, projects spring up to resolve the issues. However, some of these projects that aim to reduce our toxic footprint on the planet fail or create more issues, because those solutions aim to accommodate the same level of narcissistic consumption, rather than changing the culture of wasteful living.

For example, to resolve the problem of wild salmon depletion, salmon farmers started rearing thousands of wild salmon in enclosed cages in the sea. The goal was to sell these salmon in order not to fish from the natural resources of the rivers and seas, allowing those overfished areas to rebound. Later, investigators found that salmon locked in enclosed spaces produce enormous amounts of toxins in the water, which makes them ill and harms other sea life and humans who consume them. You can learn more about this in *You Are What You Eat*, a documentary on Netflix.

Climate Anxiety

These negative results continue due to a lack of understanding of the realities of life, which I have described under the three domains of mindful life intelligence. We are kept locked in like the salmon. While farmed salmon have no choice but to release toxins in small areas, we keep acting unskillfully and produce toxins in the world. With our learned anxieties about nature compounded by all the news about climate change and similar threats, a new type of anxiety called climate anxiety has flared up. For example, executives and employees at large corporations are suffering from climate anxiety due to concerns about not being able to resolve environmental issues, not being able to comply with new regulations, or having to make drastic changes in the way they operate. These corporate climate anxieties may be reduced by new laws and changes that reduce such restrictions, such as the use of plastic straws.

However, for the average person, every time we learn of climate catastrophes or the health hazards of microplastics and other contaminating agents in our water and food sources, we lose joy, peace, and our sense of security in what we can consume. Feeling helpless and worrying about the future perpetuate and increase our mental health problems and dependence on medication and requiring more from the planet. A vicious cycle!

Let's stop for a moment to breathe here. Relax your shoulders, relax your face, and reflect on your life. How much do you really need? Reflect on the importance of nature as our source of life. Think of ways you can be compassionate and mindful of our shared inheritance— what nature gives and leaves in our hands and what bonds you and me to every other living being.

Solutions for Positive Individual Impact

Once we learn that depleting natural resources in one area is not wise, as it can lead to a chain of demise for living beings and the health of an entire ecosystem, we can explore and balance this relationship by learning skills and ways of living that our ancestors all knew, plus some newer ones that suit our modern lives.

Here are some examples:

- Avoid single-use plastic products
- When farming, use best practices, such as switching crops or periodically letting the land sit fallow to allow it time to recover
- Separate food waste from trash to reduce the production of methane gas in land fills
- Plant your own fruits and vegetables
- Forage foods and medicinal herbs in our own areas
- Reduce family meat consumption to reduce the need for cattle breeding or salmon rearing to reduce methane gas in the atmosphere and toxins in the water and improve the balance for all life
- Aim to use less water by not letting water run needlessly while washing dishes
- Buy products that don't need packages, such as dried nuts and fruits placed in open containers

For more suggestions on how to reduce the negative impact of your consumption, download Handbook of *How-to Bring Life Back to Earth*: https://perfectlyhere.org/handbook-of-how-to-bring-life-back-to-earth/.

MLDL 21: MINDFUL OF LIFE SOURCE INTELLIGENCE: A REGENERATIVE GENEROSITY

As I discussed under the first domain, nature's regenerative design produces what is necessary to continue life efficiently, and it has incorporated ranks of creatures and ecosystems that handle waste and by-products, keeping the system functioning well, free of pollutants, and in an abundant, thriving state. I use the term life source intelligence to help describe our planet and the universe as a massive source of generosity. This type of mindful life intelligence is about recognizing the vast, unconditional, continual, giving nature of natural creation that powers life and makes existence possible. Some may refer to this source of creation as a God who created everything. When we eat, we can also give thanks to each item of food for offering itself to us, becoming our bodies, and maintaining our lives. If we pause and look, we can see the immensity of offerings in each spoonful of food. In my mind, I bow to each item every time. When you see lettuce in your bowl, you can think of the land, the seed, the sapling, the sun, and water; the farmer bending over to plow, dig, sow, and look after the harvest; and the store owner carefully shelving the lettuce. The fish on your plate, once swimming freely in water, now offers its body to you for your benefit, and then it goes back into the cycle of life. I cannot but bow my head to these truths in gratitude.

We can experience this with each item in our homes and the homes themselves. There is only one source everything comes from. That source is nature's generosity. Observing nature as the ultimate source of generosity for its ability to continually regenerate through its many natural systems is an essential MLOL that can help to reduce your stress and anxiety and the false notion that you do not have enough. This highly effective, systemic generosity that helps life to operate well is a perfect model we can mimic in our constructed systems. It's a great topic to reflect on and take through the five stages of Human Software Optimization.

MLOL 22: MINDFUL OF ONENESS: THE ANTIDOTE TO SEPARATION AND LONELINESS ANXIETY

Loneliness and the perception of loneliness are painful feelings that include feeling insecure, rejected, or as if you don't matter in life. This can create unpleasant energies that run through the body, making a person feel restless, imbalanced, and anxious.

Loneliness does not occur only when you're alone. You may be with others—family, partners, friends, coworkers, and other communities— yet feel deeply lonely. We regulate one another's body budgets. Our brains make us dependent on one another. Supposedly, people are to take our loneliness away, but they don't always do a good job of it.

IT'S NOT EASY TO BE HUMAN

When we feel judged for not being good enough or not doing the right thing or saying the right words, we may pull away, go inward, and feel separate. To remedy their loneliness, some people just complain about it. Others become good at emotional manipulation to get what they want.

Some focus on learning and growing, while others isolate and lose themselves in video games or other addictive activities. We learn the hard way sometimes that depending on other humans to make us feel whole, wanted, and as if we belong is not a reliable strategy. Others too have to address their issues that arise from underdeveloped qualities and skills, which is why it's not easy to be human for any of us.

We try to work on our relationships, improve communication, become more present, and provide a space where people feel comfortable around us. Those steps are positive and beneficial, but as the natural phenomena of impermanence and change would have it, we can lose those relationships and go back to feeling alone and dysregulated. However, there is one sure way to banish loneliness anxiety for good, and that is to experience oneness with everything around us, which all comes from nature.

Most of us, especially in the modern world, are brought up to experience nature as something apart from ourselves. We're told, "Look out there; that is the sky, and those are the clouds. That's rain, river, ocean, beach, forest, flower, rock, and mountain," or "It is a sunny and beautiful day," or "It is peaceful." It is implied that none of those things are us. We are humans, and the rest is nature. Then we hear about oneness and its blissful feelings, but we don't know how to get it.

For some, the concept of oneness can seem philosophical, religious, or perhaps distant and unrelated to daily activities. Gurus, philosophers, and even scientists have tried to explain what oneness is. Some call it *nonduality* and encourage people to accept that they are part of the universe and that the universe will take care of them. Others believe that you have to develop a sense of oneness and that you will feel it when you are enlightened or freed from suffering. Some can feel it and then lose it. For most people in Western societies, oneness is a far-fetched concept, hard to feel and hard to grasp, and they may not even see it as useful to develop. Fortunately, the second stage of HSO, mindful authentication, in chapter 7 shows you how to verify abstract lessons through your own experience to help make them useful, practical, and achievable.

So how can we achieve oneness and relieve loneliness?

Let's talk about what oneness may feel like. Perhaps you have felt oneness when fully immersed in making love with another or when you were deeply ingrained in nature, as when skiing in mountains or hiking beside a stream. Some feel it in meditation or while worshipping a sole creator. They feel connected to boundlessness and to the universe or feel one with the entity they are worshipping, which they believe is vaster, more meaningful, and more powerful than they are. Though it may be short-lived, this experience can produce a profound sense of trust and security — a feeling of joy in knowing you are precious, loved, taken care of and safe. In those moments, loneliness vanishes.

Because impermanence is constant, that level of oneness too can disappear and give its place once again to separation and anxiety. But you can develop it within yourself so that you can benefit from that same feeling without any special circumstances. But it takes love and dedication to develop such insights.

It is not unusual that insights and experiences of this type are not valued in the average lives of society, especially if one has to make a lot of arrangements, spend time and money, and go away to gain them. Most people are lost in their busy lives of daily routines, responsibilities, and commitments that supposedly cannot be broken. To feel connected and escape that deeply rooted loneliness anxiety, people remedy it with cosmetic surgery and other attempts to be accepted. In some groups, these procedures are norms or even requirements.

Then, to cover up that they're still feeling those anxieties and caught up in their self-image, people (usually women, due to gendered social pressures) claim they use the gamut of cosmetic surgeries to feel better for themselves: "It's not for others. It's for me." This is one of those examples that is easily created, empowered, and exploited by the circular anxiety economy I talked about in chapter 13, MLOL 12. With this insatiable desire for having and being more comes the need for greater financial success, which can become its own vicious cycle of stress, separation anxiety, and unspoken loneliness. Luckily, we can learn immensely from nature and our acceptance of its imperfections.

One day on a hike on Mount Baldy in Southern California, where a fast-moving stream gushes through enormous rocks, I had a profound insight. Getting splashed by the overzealous river, I was immersed in the moment. While I communed with nature amid giant rocks, fallen tree trunks, and leaves, I noticed many dead, broken branches, and I had an epiphany: No one ever judges a broken branch, a brown bush, or fallen leaves for what they look like or why they are there. We never say things like "I hate these broken tree trunks." Well, unless they're a nuisance to what you deem your home. But when walking in nature, we accept these seeming imperfections. They are not even imperfections. They just are.

I wondered, *Why, then, do we have so much judgment about ourselves — about the way we look, talk, walk, or act? Why do we feel shame or feel less than with what we think are imperfections? It makes no sense.*

I smiled with joy, as I felt loved by the river; my true mother, Earth; and my true father, the sun.

To undo this separation and loneliness anxiety, you don't have to be out in the wilderness. You can feel the ultimate sense of being good enough and having enough anywhere, anytime, and during any activity. You can do this by reflecting on the five elements I described in MLOL 16 earlier in this chapter and how everything is from nature. You can open to the reality that everything around you is nature, and you can reconnect, instantly or gradually, with the ultimate source of life.

When you feel disconnected from yourself or other people, it may be due to inattention, being lost in thoughts or worries and disconnecting from everything around you. Right now, feel your body; take three deep breaths; and connect with the presence of Earth, the sun, the moon, and all you have. Thank the galaxies for offering you what you need — for sustaining your life.

CHAPTER 15

OUR PLANET AND REGENERATIVE LIVING

This chapter continues with MLOLs regarding the planet and optimizing our relationship with it. Now that you have explored perspectives that are more aligned with the nature of life, let's explore our planet's boundaries and ways we can live more consciously with the awareness that we are the ancestors of the future generations and that what we do will directly affect them.

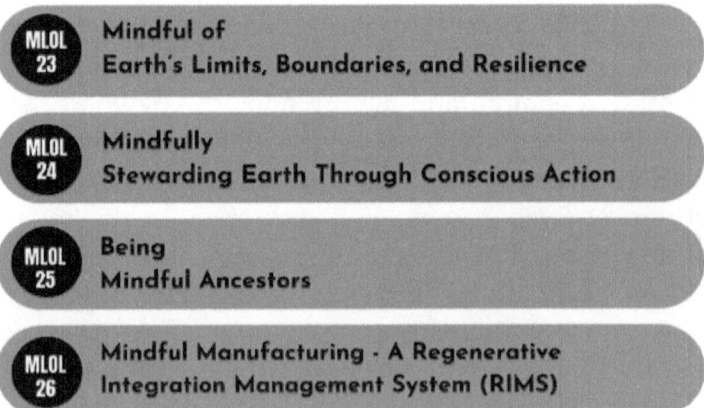

DOMAIN II:

OUR PLANET AND REGENERATIVE LIVING

MLOL 23 Mindful of
Earth's Limits, Boundaries, and Resilience

MLOL 24 Mindfully
Stewarding Earth Through Conscious Action

MLOL 25 Being
Mindful Ancestors

MLOL 26 Mindful Manufacturing - A Regenerative
Integration Management System (RIMS)

Figure 11

Copyright by Dr. Manijeh Motaghy

MLOL 23: MINDFUL OF THE BOUNDARIES AND LIMITATIONS OF EARTH'S RESILIENCE

Scientists led by professor and researcher Johan Rockström of the University of Stockholm in Sweden determined nine natural systems and boundaries and limitations that are being surpassed, causing problems for our planet:

1. Climate change
2. Change in biosphere integrity (biodiversity loss and species extinction)
3. Stratospheric ozone depletion
4. Ocean acidification
5. Biogeochemical flows (phosphorus and nitrogen cycles)
6. Land-system change (desertification and deforestation)
7. Freshwater use
8. Atmospheric aerosol loading (microscopic particles in the atmosphere that affect climate and living organisms)
9. Introduction of novel entities (e.g., organic pollutants, radioactive materials, nanomaterials, and microplastics)

Rockström's goal was to measure the capacity of Earth's resources to understand the dynamic between nature and humans and the ramifications of our lifestyles so we can improve social and planetary resiliency. According to the Stockholm Resilience Centre, "Science shows that these nine processes and systems regulate the stability and resilience of the Earth System—the interactions of land, ocean, atmosphere, and life that together provide conditions upon which our societies depend." The 2023 report quantified all boundaries.

It also concluded that six of the nine boundaries have been transgressed. Crossing boundaries increases the risk of generating large- scale abrupt or irreversible environmental changes. Drastic changes will not necessarily happen overnight, but together the boundaries mark a critical threshold for increasing risks to people and the ecosystems we are part of.

These consequences have also been discovered by ordinary citizens of the world who have witnessed the changes firsthand. Travelers have reported that polar ice caps, which reflect the sun's heat back into space and keep our planet at a livable temperature, are melting at rapid rates. Greenland is losing massive amounts of ice, enough each second to supply a day's water needs to a city often million people. These are massive amounts of water adding to our ocean and rising levels.

Since his findings, Rockström has given numerous talks warning people globally that all planet systems are interconnected, and once we cross a tipping point in one or more of these planetary systems, our planet will undergo a domino effect of destruction with no point of return.

As time passes, there are more reports and awareness of and personal experience with these disasters. Millions of people, including children and youth, are painfully affected by the situation. Our Children's Trust, an American nonprofit law firm, reported the following:

In 2015, 21 young Americans filed their constitutional climate lawsuit, Juliana v. United States, against the U.S. government. Their complaint asserts that, through the government's affirmative actions that cause climate change, it has violated the youngest generation's constitutional rights to life, liberty, and property, as well as failed to protect essential public trust resources.

As of this writing, many locations in the world are devastated. The small island of Tuvalu in the Pacific Ocean, for example, is sinking due to sea levels rising around it. In January 2024, Earth.org reported the following:

Tuvalu's vulnerability to climate change, particularly rising sea levels, is rooted in its geographical makeup. Comprising nine low-lying coral atolls and islands, Tuvalu faces the dual threats of global warming and the subsequent melting of polar ice caps and glaciers.

These factors will lead to the demise of an entire nation with more than eleven thousand citizens who share a rich heritage. Other islands are in similar straits. In 2023, the *Guardian* reported that nine small island states, including the Bahamas, are suffering the devastating impacts of climate change. They have taken the most pollution- producing countries before the United Nations maritime court to seek a ruling to designate ocean-heating carbon emissions as pollution and, therefore, a violation of international law.

Many other regions and countries are experiencing undue disease and hardship because of natural disasters. We can no longer ignore the cries of humanity. And this is only the tip of the (melting) iceberg.

We must remember that the abundance of the planet and the generosity of nature depend on Earth's operating systems functioning at healthy levels. Having scientific proof and experience, we can support nature's regenerative design by avoiding overconsumption and overindulgence in materialistic living. I hope the MLOLs in this book will help the people of the world to become aware of, attentive to, and aligned with the laws of nature.

MLOL 24: MINDFULLY STEWARDING EARTH THROUGH CONSCIOUS ACTION

Now that we know what our earth means to us and what it's facing, let's go back to the law of karma and its powerful natural effect in order to understand conscious actions. As the inner workings of karma indicate, we humans make an impact through the power of our intentions, choices, and actions. (Choice, as I previously mentioned, is not always up to us but is made for us by social realities programmed in us and other conditions that influence or dictate them.) However, as we become optimized, we become more able to choose intentions and actions that are efficient, effective, and in harmony with nature.

Luckily, scientific advancement is now capable of measuring various sources of pollution, with an interest in finding where we can make the most impact to end the many causes of disruption and suffering. Scientists say one of the most powerful conscious actions is to transform our food consumption, which can potentially fix many of these issues all at once. Now, that sounds amazing. Doesn't it?

As described before, one major opportunity to address the environment via our food consumption is the problem of excessive cattle farming and the amount of toxic methane emissions cattle release into the atmosphere. The CLEAR (Clarity and Leadership for Environmental Awareness and Research) Center at the University of California, Davis, has determined that methane gas emissions produced by cattle have climate-warming potential more than twenty-eight times that of carbon dioxide (CO_2), consistent with the finding of the United States's EPA (Environmental Protection Agency). Furthermore, when it comes to livestock and climate change, several other characteristics make biogenic (from cattle) methane more hazardous than CO_2. Here are the important two:

1. Methane stays in our atmosphere for about twelve years, whereas CO_2 is reabsorbed into plants and the soil.
2. Methane eventually returns to the atmosphere as CO_2, which makes it recycled carbon.

It's easy to just live our lives day after day, tending to what's needed to maintain our personal and family affairs, and let others take care of bigger issues, such as food distribution and resource shortages. This is reasonable. We depend on governments and the economy for all of this. However, most humans, including those who run governments and corporations, are also on autopilot and can get stuck in fabricated social realities. We experience individual, global, and planetary issues in large part because we live and act unconsciously and habitually. So we must engage and align ourselves to ensure we can enjoy a planet that continues to provide for all of us; we need to think consciously and regeneratively, choosing actions that produce better results.

To develop conscious actions, refer to chapter 19, MLOL 45. Wise and conscious actions ensure and protect our planet's regenerative nature and do not disrupt the harmony and balance of systems that are beneficial to all living beings, including ourselves. Such actions require not only wisdom and compassion but also a clear understanding of the situation, as well as discovering best choices.

For example, because we know that methane gas produced into the environment will take much longer to dissipate than atmospheric carbon, reduction of cattle farming seems vital if we are to repair our atmosphere and reverse climate change.

Please check out the US Climate Resilience Toolkit website (in the "Resources" section) to learn more about research, resources, and tools for preparation and prevention of disasters in your area.

MLOL 25: BEING MINDFUL ANCESTORS

You may be already doing so, but with your knowing as much as you do now, I hope you are willing to join those who are taking actions to eliminate or minimize inevitable environmental hardship. As more of us begin living consciously and sustainably, we can hopefully stop the domino effect of exploitative lifestyles and live in harmony with nature once again. Perpetuating planetary balance through wise stewardship is one of the most important MLOLs to partake in and embody.

We want to begin with sustainability, which the United Nations defines as "meeting the needs of the present without compromising the ability of future generations to meet their own needs." This is a simple and clear definition we can work with to do right by our future generations. In many regions of the world, ancestors understood that they were part of nature; they knew they were dependent on natural systems and resources, and they acted with responsibility and cared wisely for the resources they consumed. Like many magnificent animals in the wild, humans moved from location to location so as not to deplete the resources of one territory. This moving on gave the land a chance to replenish itself. These migration patterns prevented certain environmental issues, such as desertification. Those who settled in one place also learned to use nature intelligently. For example, by rotating crop types when farming, they kept the soil replenished with necessary nutrients. Their lives might have been physically demanding but were not necessarily more demanding than our lives today.

USING ADVANCED TECHNOLOGY AND MINIMALISTIC LIVING AS CONSCIOUS ACTIONS

Most of us today are not able to migrate periodically, as our homes are relatively permanent structures, and we hang on to the mindset of ownership, which may be hard to let go of. But given our advancements in science and technology, we can learn to employ ancient insights and practices that are more attuned to nature. For example, today we can send a drone to survey land so that we can devise informed solutions. Drones have become a popular tool in capturing accurate measures and data about wetlands, farming areas, and forest conditions.

Our ancestors left us an abundant planet, and we have the same responsibility to our children and to the progeny of all animals and plants. With modern, advanced tools, we can be the link to the wise ways of our ancestors for the survival and success of our future generations by living our lives more mindfully. Below are some examples.

- Live minimally, and acquire only what is needed.
- Do not be wasteful with money, even if you have too much of it, and do not perpetuate the circular anxiety economy I talked about in chapter 13, MLOL 12
- Work in nature. To easily feel content, get out and dig in the dirt. Maybe plant something that feeds birds, bees, butterflies, or even yourself
- Appreciate insects. When you see a bug, repeat in your mind, *Thank you for being here and doing your part.*

When you see and care for nature, you'll discover that it is fulfilling and restorative for your mind and body. When you reconnect with the practices of ancestors who were in alignment with nature, you reap the fruits of their wisdom. It can provide peace of mind that comes with knowing you're acting responsibly and handing down a planet well on its way to recovery, one that will sustain stability and abundance for our children and all generations to come. If you believe in rebirth, you will want to come back to a planet that is not desolate but green and alive.

Let us leave the legacy of ancestors who safeguarded their children's future.

MLOL 26: MINDFUL MANUFACTURING: REGENERATIVE INTEGRATION MANAGEMENT SYSTEM (RIMS)

We are here, living in this era and sharing life experiences with varying generations. Some of us still value traditional, minimalist living based on contentment, but keeping those values is difficult due to the millions of products that flood the market, which we are constantly told we need.

I tried to find out how many products are bought, sold, or made in the United States and around the world. The exact information wasn't available, but the scope is mind-boggling. Amazon alone lists and sells millions of products on a weekly basis. The younger generations are immersed in digitalization, creating and selling products with faster results. It's not possible to live minimally as a society — may be as a small group or an individual but not as a society, at least not with the same mindset and systems. But there is a way to live a satisfying life and produce necessary products effectively and efficiently.

RIMS: A Solution for Entrepreneurs, Leaders, and Management

If you are an entrepreneur, whatever generation you may identify yourself with, you can mindfully optimize your work, management system, and innovation processes by learning to mimic nature's regenerative design. Remember, regenerative simply means everything that is produced in nature either is food or becomes food; it is used and reused, integrated and disintegrated. No waste or toxic products are left behind. Regeneration is the epitome of minimalism and efficiency.

Let's look at a holistic solution I call RIMS (regenerative integration management system), a model I designed based on biomimicry and the way nature manages life efficiently and masterfully. RIMS provides the necessary structure to create an interdependent chain with clear, strong links that makes any management system efficient in productivity, profitability, and planetary action and transforms harmful greed to systemic prosperity — a perfect economic model.

Nature's Regenerative Design

When we think of nature, we must include all that our planet relies on to create and maintain life, including needed elements and energy from the sun and the solar system.

Without getting too scientific, we can find some parallels with systems we create. As I see it, there are four components that make up nature's regenerative system:

1. Nature's Objective: Creating, maintaining, and continuing life
2. Regenerative Function: Processing energy and elements and generating food, medicine, and other necessities for life to continue
3. Nature's Resources: Natural elements and energy
4. Nature's Implementation Strategy: Engaging and assigning roles and responsibilities to each link in a chain of ecosystems and automating this process through preprogramming those roles and characteristics

While RIMS is an example of how to deploy a circular economy to produce zero waste, it is also a zero-anxiety and prosperity model. It promotes putting in place a system and processes through conscious and intentional choices and strategies. This system creates new livelihood opportunities for a community of handlers who will facilitate the wasteless results we're looking for. Handlers include anyone who manages to process the products to ensure they end up back in the regenerative system of nature. These handlers include consumers and organizations who aid in cleaning up not only after products have been consumed but also during each stage — converting raw materials to product, packaging, shipping, and so on.

To see my regenerative integration management system (RIMS)

zero-waste, zero-anxiety prosperity model, go to drmanijehmotaghy. com/sustainable-business-model.

Some factories have found ways to mimic these regenerative and efficiency systems in at least some of their production stages. A good example of this is Toyota, which, aside from recovering, recycling, and refurbishing their parts, also managed to figure out how to reduce their energy consumption by adjusting the temperature and humidity needed to paint their cars and reducing their CO2 emissions.

The Prius, Toyota's line of hybrid automobiles, is built with recyclable components. Their third-generation models are 85 percent recyclable and 95 percent recoverable. Even the hybrid battery is recyclable, and it can also be refurbished for use in other electric vehicles. Here is Toyota's statement about avoiding waste:

> To keep waste to an absolute minimum, we try to recover as much as we can from our manufacturing operations. We work with specialist partners to create the best possible disposal processes for our vehicles. Even the finest waste residues can be recovered and used, for example as an alternative fuel source for industry. We also conserve water by using as little as possible and recycling wastewater generated by our production processes. Our attention to detail means that we even make sure the boxes in which our parts are supplied are designed for purpose and can be reused again and again.

Toyota's example of understanding the imperative of living regeneratively to preserve our planet and taking initiatives toward doing so is a great model of conscious leadership. But anybody can lead his or her life consciously with improved perspectives and innovative solutions. You can do so in your own kitchen. Our society is filled with ordinary leaders who have a hand in the systems we utilize, including businesses, governance, public infrastructure, and education. We can all have an impact. We can research and support corporations that align with higher values and conduct.

Managing the Impact of AI

When innovating with artificial intelligence, whether we utilize it to run our businesses or enjoy our hobbies, we can be curious, remaining present and cognizant of negative impacts, such as excessive power consumption. We can reduce these activities or look into measures that offset, mitigate, or eliminate such impacts. By applying the RIMS strategy in business and management systems, we can become better stewards of our planet.

To read our white paper about how RIMS works, go to https:// drmanijehmotaghy.com/ regenerative-integration-management-system- white-paper/ .

Next comes the domain of human experience, conduct, and happiness.

PART IV

THE THIRD DOMAIN:

HUMAN EXPERIENCE, CONDUCT, AND HAPPINESS

The next six chapters provide MLOLs for the final domain, includes seven main topics: the brain, the mind and suffering, wisdom and resolve, heart intelligence, mental development, healing wounds, and gaining MLOLs as a human right. Included is a case study that describes how these MLOLs help to improve mental health and relationships. We will begin with the human brain, as it plays a central role in human programming and conduct.

JOIN

THE MAKING IT EASY TO BE HUMAN CLUB & COMMUNITY

Scan to Register Your Book to Meet the Author.

Get Support on Your Transformation Journey.

CHAPTER 16

HUMAN BRAIN

The human brain is considered the most sophisticated of all animal brains, one that scientists are still discovering. It is said the human brain is so complex and capable that no computer can match it—though with the skyrocketing growth in robotics and AI, the human brain may not be the most capable for long. We also have sub brains in our bodies, such as in our guts. The gut has been thought of as the second brain, with its own set of neurons that manage our emotions and experiences. There is much to know and learn about the brain. I will cover only what I believe can save humanity from itself. Many of these points I have already covered in earlier chapters, but they deserve to be given their own MLOLs, and reviewing them can help you to see their role and importance. I encourage you to read *Seven and a Half Lessons About the Brain* by Lisa Feldman Barrett to learn these and other pertinent lessons in more depth.

DOMAIN III:

HUMAN EXPERIENCE, CONDUCT AND HAPPINESS

PERTINENT TO KNOW ABOUT THE BRAIN

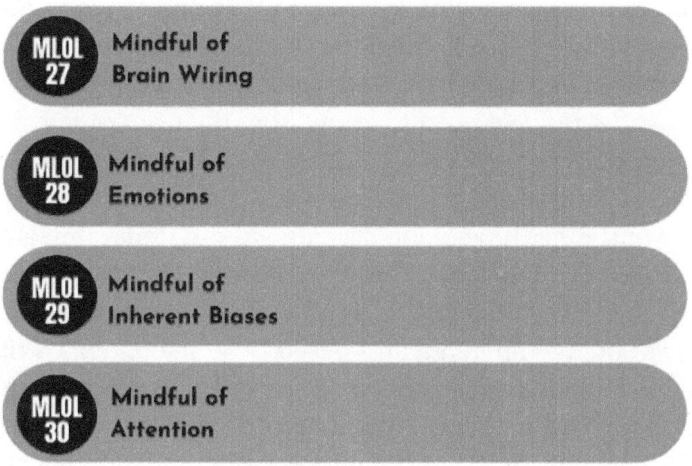

Figure 12

MLOL 27: MINDFUL OF BRAIN WIRING, LACKING AN INHERENT MANUAL

According to Barrett, we are not born with all the self-sustaining knowledge and skills we need to become happy, functional human beings. As our brains grow into adulthood (and after), our beliefs and perspectives are created and influenced by other humans. One theory for why humans need one another this way is because the human brain's evolution has made it so. We cannot survive without the help of other humans to complete the wiring of our brains and help us to discern how we feel, what we experience, and how to be human.

Like anything else, these perspectives and beliefs are subject to change and reform. But we lose sight of that change phenomenon I talked about under natural systems, and instead, we take perspectives and beliefs as unchanging facts and realities. In *Seven and a Half Lessons*

About the Brain, Barrett tells us it is the job of our brains to set these realities for a very important reason: to use energy most efficiently. The brain is not designed to be concerned about the accuracy of our realities. Rather, it takes our perception sat face value, oblivious that humans who transfer learning to us may not be fully developed. When we don't know the full picture, we make things up in our heads to fill in the blanks, and we are coded to conclude that those things are true.

Our subliminal interdependence requires us to know our place in the human world. We need to know how to be a woman, a man, a sister, a specific gender, a parent, a boss, and all the other human roles we play. Without other humans to wire our brains and create our template and inner navigation system, we can doubt ourselves and feel confused and less than. This innate need to belong is beautifully depicted in the Netflix series *This Is Us*. In it, an African American child is adopted as an infant and raised by white parents. With their genuine love for him, his adoptive parents are active participants in making things equal for him in public and in places where he might feel different, to the point of sometimes ignoring their other children. But somewhere along the line, through the expression of other kids and adults in the community, he becomes aware that he's different and maybe not as regarded. Their wiring and programming influence his perception of himself, seeding confusion and unhappiness about who he is. He feels lost at times, and his adoptive parents look for understanding about what to do.

A friend of his parents explains that he could use the presence of a male role model who looks like him and suggests that the boy train with an African American karate teacher. Jack, the white father, seeing other fathers at the session lift their children onto their backs, is instantly inspired (influenced by those parents' brain wiring) to stretch on the floor and replicate their action to indicate to his son that he's got him—that he's there for him. But it isn't about Jack's being there or not. He has always been there. It is about the boy identifying with someone so he can feel he belongs.

Jack questions his parenting methods and doubts his role as a father, but it turns out he is the most important anchor in all his children's lives. We see how strongly Jack has wired his family when his adult kids, after losing their father at a young age, feel they have lost their support system, the one who regulated their emotions and psychological needs. As they become adults, as a family in various circumstances, they think of their dad as a model for their own lives. Jack was the perfect romantic husband, a present father, a kind and compassionate being, a hard worker, and an understanding friend. His model and wiring are set and automatic; they cannot get away from comparing themselves to their father's perfection.

Our wiring process continues in life. Anybody can wire or rewire our thinking and change our trajectory. This happens through what we say and write, our tone, and what we do. This invisible wiring mechanism is how a charismatic leader can get others to trust and follow him or her. It can also become painful. Our interconnection with others can be so powerful and neurologically bound that when we find out someone close to us has kept a secret, it can be disorienting and painful—as if a tube that feeds us our sense of identity or role stability has been punctured. Our sense of safety and support and even our immune system weaken. Keeping our agreements is an intrinsic mechanism of our brains to keep energy usage efficient and ensure there is enough support from other humans to survive. When we break such intrinsic needs, we lose that feeling of being whole and integrated.

You can see why people like to associate with like-minded people who do the same things, have the same beliefs, speak the same language, and participate in the same rituals. There is a larger assurance that they can trust one another and feel peaceful and safe.

There is a Persian saying I heard while growing up: "Pigeons with pigeons, doves with doves, flying together with the same kind." I always thought that saying was a bit disconnected and limiting. But I have heard many express that associating with like-minded people is pleasant and comfortable. However, it can potentially result in getting stuck in rigid views and conflict and being unable to grow. This one innate system (wiring and programming) alone is why I decided to write and tell the world why it's not easy to be human.

Knowing that our human brains unconsciously and by design wire and program one another, we can become discerning about those we associate with and be mindful of protecting ourselves from picking up social norms and realities that are not aligned with truths of life. We can observe and understand how we or others may feel protective and become exclusive. While doing so with discernment, we can make continual efforts to consciously rise above our automatic programming and connect with the heart and shared humanity. In chapter 17, I will show you how to go about seeing and undoing the rigidity of the mind and false wirings that cause suffering.

MLOL 28: MINDFUL OF EMOTIONS

The problem with emotions is that we think they relay the facts, are unavoidable, and are felt by everyone in the same way or intensity. The fact is, the presence of emotions doesn't make our stories true. Also, we are not obligated to feel negative emotions, such as anger or sadness, just because it is customary to do so. Emotions are energies in motion that run through our minds and bodies. We can learn better ways of experiencing and expressing them and respond to situations more objectively, wisely, and peacefully.

When the concept of emotional intelligence (EQ) was first introduced by Daniel Goleman, a renowned psychologist and researcher out of Harvard University, it claimed that facial expressions could reveal what a person was feeling and that understanding this could improve communication and work environments. Billions of dollars then went into training managers and employees globally (this is still going on) to help them understand what coworkers or customers were feeling, create a more connected and compassionate workforce, and provide better customer experience.

Since then, this aspect of emotional intelligence theory has been debunked. Lisa Feldman Barrett explains in How Emotions Are Made: *The Secret Life of the Brain* that emotions are not inherent at birth. We actually learn how to feel and how to express our feelings as we grow up. As a result of cultural differences, people around the world feel and express emotions differently. Barrett's research verified that facial expressions cannot tell what a person really feels and that it isn't reasonable to think all facial expressions mean the same thing to all people. People can frown while thinking joyful thoughts or seem to others as if they're in pain while enjoying a delicious meal.

Another concept that can weaken us by creating false beliefs about the nature of our emotions is the idea of the triune brain and the amygdala. The amygdala is supposed to be an old reptilian brain, all about instincts and reactions to fear and threat. It was (and is) believed that with evolution, this reptilian brain was covered by two other layers: the emotional and the cognitive logical brains. However, according to Barrett in *Seven and a Half Lessons About the Brain*, there is no amygdala, and the human brain does not have different sections. Rather, it is a network of interconnected clusters of neuropathways with various roles and responsibilities. One of these responsibilities is to predict and meet the body's needs by releasing an energy in motion—emotion. The goal in releasing an emotion is to create unpleasant feelings to get humans to do what they need to balance their budget—eat, sleep, drink water, and so on. The rest of the emotions we humans feel, label, and express are all learned, which means they can also be unlearned or transformed.

To deal with this imaginary amygdala, a presenter may try to convince people to believe in something, such as the idea that we are light and love and flawless, as a remedy to overcome or evolve from the imaginary amygdala. Well, if that thinking can rewire you to not feel hateful or hostile when things don't go your way, more power to you. But if those beliefs don't do the job, it's because you may need to develop other inner skills, and without them, you can't blame yourself or others for not simply coming from light and love all the time.

I encourage everyone, especially those who are in the mental health field or train humans to manage their emotions, fears, and anxieties, to read *Seven and a Half Lessons About the Brain* as well as look up courses on the wisdom of emotions and healthy immune systems at perfectlyhere.org. There is more to rewiring and optimizing our internal world, which we will continue to explore next.

You can also take this MLOL to chapters 7 and 8 to mindfully authenticate and develop the necessary skills to improve your reactions to difficult situations and create ease and well-being in your life.

Next, we'll look at inherent biases.

MLOL 29: MINDFUL OF INHERENT BIASES

When I was thirteen and had that traumatic experience at a gynecologist's office (see chapter 4), I assumed the doctor's question meant I had lost my virginity, and that caused shame and confusion. There was no evidence for this conclusion, but not knowing what was going on, I filled in the blanks with a guess. This guess sprang from concepts I had adopted from society, which produced learned feelings of disgrace and danger of being an outcast. Notice that my believing the assumption as the truth came from my mind. I felt shame (a learned emotion), which David R. Hawkins describes in *Power vs. Force* as the lowest energetic feeling one can have. This false truth caused me immense sadness and disconnect for more than twenty-five years before I had the chance to learn that I was wrong. Even then, I wasn't free of it. This one false truth had given birth to countless others that affected how I felt about myself and related to others through habitual perceiving and reacting.

But why do we so easily accept so much of what we think and hear? This is due to biased thinking. *Psychology Today* describes a bias as "a tendency, inclination, or prejudice toward or against something or someone." It's an unreasoned judgment or tendency to think in a certain way. There may be countless biases, and three of these inherent biases are key to this chapter.

Neuroscientist Amishi Jha indicates that our brains come with novelty, truth, and confirmation biases, all built in. Here are what they mean.

Novelty bias causes anything that's new and different to grab our attention. By its nature, novelty means we either have no previous association with the thing or idea or have little to compare it to. Our brains pay attention to things that are novel, whether we like it or dislike it.

Truth bias is an even more instrumental default mechanism built into our brains that makes us believe whatever occurs to us or whatever someone tells us. I already covered the ramifications of truth bias in chapter 2. From the start of our brains' wiring, when we are just learning to act human, our brains have to capture data and build the model of how we should think and behave. The brain does so bit by bit, with no mechanism for fact-checking. This function helps our brains to conserve energy and resources by putting trust in others from our species (our family and community) to provide the knowledge we need.

Confirmation bias is there to protect our mental models and build on what our brains perceive as true by only noticing or accepting new information that confirms these prior supposed truths. Even something novel may be rejected if it contradicts a person's existing beliefs. But information will be easily accepted as truth if it backs up even one aspect of what we believe or desire to believe. People who are good at consciously twisting things can take great advantage of the innate confirmation bias. They can build a whole story around just a little bit of truth. Even if you realize that the story itself is false, it can be confusing and hard to rebut, because parts of it are true.

Confirmation bias helps us to feel more at ease and confident that our truths—the stories we believe in—are reliable. As these biased truths pile up, they form the foundations of how we think of life. Our realities, more often than not, are just suppositions, assumptions, interpretations, and storyized experiences, yet if others' viewpoints are different, then we think they must be wrong. Anything that confirms our perceived truths is more convenient to accept and build our lives around. Because no one is immune to false beliefs, it makes good sense to have some higher doctrines, such as human rights, and rules and regulations to guide our lives.

Many of our social realities are built on false truths, which perpetuate all kinds of prejudices, harmful choices, and horrible acts. They could become as bad as capturing and selling children for their labor, treating them as slaves and commodities, with no regard for their freedom and suffering. Extreme maladaptation too can result from bias glitches in the human brain.

However, when we understand that what we perceive and conclude is not necessarily accurate, we can examine our beliefs more closely and become aware of how we may have been led astray by innate biases. This provides inspiration and motivation to develop wisdom (a quality the brain is not prewired for) and compassion (a quality we may not have adopted fully) to offset the harmful effects of truth and confirmation biases.

For all of this to happen, we need to understand and develop attention.

MLOL 30: MINDFUL OF ATTENTION

Attention is one of the most important resources and functions of the human mind and brain that needs development. Attention needs to be developed simply because all the other essential qualities and skills we need to learn depend on how attentive we can be. In the book *The Mind of the Leader*, authors Rasmus Hougaard and Jacqueline Carter assert that attention is the most important asset for a leader and that those who are high achievers in life have a higher ability to manage and utilize their attention well. To develop attention, it is helpful to know what attention consists of.

According to Jha, the neuroscientist who talked about inherent biases, attention has three systems: orienting, alerting, and executive.

Orienting works like pointing a flashlight onto something to see it. It's directing attention to a particular thing, which usually means excluding other things from our view so that we can recognize, understand, and make a choice about the object of our attention. For example, think of the game pool, or billiards (played on a rectangular table with cloth covering, where players use long sticks called cues to hit balls against one another and into pockets at the edges of the table). Directing attention to a ball by using this orienting system helps a player with seeing the best direction to hit the ball.

Alerting, the second system and function of attention, allows us to pay specific attention to situations that might be alarming — for example, if the black ball is in line with a basket and could be hit and fall in by mistake (the black ball is the last ball to sink and determines the winner, and if a player hits the black ball too soon, he or she loses). The alerting system does not guarantee the win; it just reminds the player to be aware of the dangers ahead.

The *executive*, the third system of attention, is there to make sure our actions are aligned with our goals and priorities. The billiard player's goal is to win the game. The priority is to hit all of the opponent's balls into the pockets first and then the black ball. For this to happen, the player must pay close attention and study the ball to be hit and the ball he or she is aiming it toward, hold the cue in the right direction, touch each ball at the perfect spot, and hit it with the exact right power to knock the opponent's ball into a pocket without hitting the black ball. Orienting, alerting, and executive goals of each experience are vital attention systems and skills that need to be learned straight from birth and honed throughout life. If caretakers don't teach an infant how to zoom in, direct, shift, alert, and manage attention, the infant may struggle to discern differences between objects, concepts, meanings, and other factors of life. When our brains run on autopilot, we automatically conduct a function as well (or poorly) as we've learned it.

Many people who come to one of my MLO courses are astounded to realize how inattentive they are in their lives. With low attentiveness come low self-awareness and all kinds of stress and conflicts with the world. These include low levels of self-care and self-love, which are other reasons for being depleted and stuck in unhappiness. But with understanding and some practice, attention and attentiveness can improve greatly.

You can gain tremendous benefits from using mindfulness meditation and mindfulness practices to learn to focus and manage your attention. With better self-awareness, you can become capable of helpful skills, like seeing your biases, being in touch with your physical needs, and recognize what causes you disharmony. By strengthening your attentiveness, you can be present in your relationships and enjoy life much more fully. For guided meditations and to develop your attention and wisdom, visit my YouTube channel https://youtube.com/@DrMotaghy

The next chapter will talk about the mind and its role in our happiness and suffering.

CHAPTER 17

MIND AND SUFFERING

"How do I love thee? Let me count the ways," wrote Elizabeth Barrett Browning. For any number of ways we love, we may count a hundred times over the ways we hate and suffer in life, most of which are due to an untrained mind. The mind can be fickle. One minute, it can be happy; the next, it might be angry, sad, or confused. The next, if someone says something that confirms our reality, we feel confident again. But this fickleness also represents malleability, changeability, and opportunity for great development and growth. First, we need to understand that our minds create our world, and they cause the unhappiness we experience.

But how do we know it when our minds cause us suffering? How do we discern between a real difficulty and agony caused by our untrained minds?

FINDING RELEASE IN TRUTH

For each of us, this knowing is a journey that begins somewhere. Mine began during the Asian Thoughts course I took in my undergraduate studies, which awakened the hero in me when I heard of Siddhartha's leaving home to find the answer to suffering. We were assigned to read an article that had a black-and-white picture of a monk sweeping the ground. Underneath it was a caption that said something like "For this Buddhist monk, sweeping the ground is like praying." As soon as I finished reading that line, I heard a resolute voice that said, "I am a Buddhist." I still remember looking around fearfully to see if anyone had heard me. I wasn't yet familiar with Buddhism and did not want to be associated with anything unusual or not widely accepted.

For days after, feeling connected to Siddhartha, I kept feeling drawn inward. Images of my childhood passed through my mind. I recalled being named Shakespeare by my father's intellectual relatives and remembered myself as a little girl searching to understand what a rock was, what ants did, and why people thought the way they did. There was something about my search for truth that matched the Buddha's search to end all suffering. After that, it took me some time to find the opportunity and resources to learn more about this journey. But this success in finding life's veracities and learning about them never left my heart.

It was a new chance for me to learn the truths, inner qualities, and skills I had missed or needed to relearn. His teachings were logical, to be investigated for myself (which had been natural to the five-year- old me), with practices that enabled me to gain the highest potential of my humanity. I remembered Professor Volkin saying that one can learn the Buddha's teachings to be better at one's own religion and that converting to Buddhism is not necessary to apply its principles to one's life. It appealed to me that I wasn't required to blindly accept or follow a religion or perspective. As time passed, I saw for myself that his teachings are compelling and transformative.

So what made the Buddha's teachings so compelling and transformative? The key lies in his journey to enlightenment, during which he became aware of the root causes of human suffering. Ending the suffering of all humanity became his hero's journey and the driving force behind his decision to give up his right to the throne and leave the palace and everything he loved behind. Asa prince, he had been protected from knowing about the mundane and shared sufferings of life. Once he left and encountered them, his mission became to understand the origins of human suffering and find ways to eradicate them. He had been well trained in all the skills a prince needed to rule a country, Including language and communication, matters of war and strength, poetry, culture, debate, and, most importantly, the skills of attentiveness and investigating the truth for himself. Possessing singular focus and an extraordinary determination, the Buddha discovered, created, and offered a path that has empowered individuals to take control of their own happiness for two and a half millennia.

His viewpoint was revolutionary for his time: It suggested that one need not rely on beliefs, prayer, sacrifice, or spiritual rituals in the hope of achieving favorable outcomes. He recognized that those beliefs and rituals often led to disappointment and helplessness, as they reinforced reliance on external forces, rather than encouraging people to learn not to cause the issues to begin with. He taught that suffering originates in the mind, and therefore, it can be eradicated from the mind. He taught that one could gain optimal happiness by developing oneself in the lessons and skills that he organized as the Four Noble Truths and the Noble Eightfold Path.

DOMAIN III:
HUMAN EXPERIENCE, CONDUCT, AND HAPPINESS
THE MIND AND SUFFERING

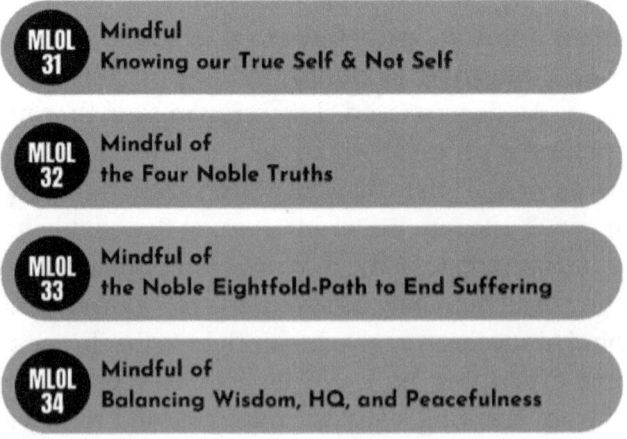

Figure 13

But if the Four Noble Truths and the Noble Eightfold Path elicit engagement and investigation, how do we decipher them from sayings and affirmations?

THEY'RE NOT SIMPLE AFFIRMATIONS

The Buddha acquired great reputation for the precision and effectiveness of his teachings, and the internet is filled with spiritual sayings, affirmations, and feel-good advice attributed to him. However, many of these sayings are not his and often are not effective. For example, statements like "You have a choice to be happy." When one is not trained to make choices with awareness and intention, one may end up feeling stuck and unable to make the choice to be happy.

Noticing this issue, I asked my teacher Ajahn Pasanno, "With all the sayings, affirmations, and other spiritual teachings out there, how do we know if the Buddha said them or not?" He explained that the best way to know if what is being taught is a Buddhist teaching is to analyze whether its core aligns with the Four Noble Truths and the Noble Eightfold Path. If it doesn't, then that teaching is not Buddhist. If, in any way, it does not acknowledge that there is suffering, that suffering has a cause that can be eliminated, and that the way to eliminate it is the Eightfold Path, then the saying or lesson is not Buddhist.

It is said that the Buddha's knowledge of the universe was vast, but he saw no benefit in teaching random truths. He discerned that suffering and happiness are the concerns of humanity. He didn't harp on happiness much either. His insight revealed that when people can understand how suffering is created in their minds and learn to relieve it, happiness will be an automatic outcome. So he kept his teachings focused on that goal.

In *The Island: An Anthology of the Buddha's Teachings on Nibbana*, Ajahn Pasanno and Ajahn Amaro explain, "It's a feature of the Buddha's teaching, particularly in the Theravada scriptures, that the Truth and the way leading to it are often indicated talking about what they are not rather than what they are." This is a rather scientific outlook: by eliminating what something is not, we are left with the truth.

Let's look at MLOLs about how suffering is caused by the mind. But before we get to the suffering and its cause, it might be helpful to look at the idea of self and who within us might be the one who suffers.

MLOL 31: MINDFULLY KNOWING OUR TRUE SELF AND NOT-SELF

When people are asked, close to the end of life, to share the most important experiences of their lives, they often talk about having connected with another person, having lived with meaning and purpose, and having felt love and care for and from others. When asked about their regrets, a painful one that shows up is having done what others expected of them instead of being true to their true selves.

Let's look at this true self. How do we know what or who the true self is and how to treat it? In early chapters, we looked at some of the reasons why it's NOT EASY to be human. While learning how to be a human, in order to function as a person, as a family member, and as part of the greater society, one ends up getting programmed or habituated to be and do these roles. The question is, then, where are our true selves amid all that programs us, such as social realities, norms, labels, meanings, and assumptions? How can there be a true self, when we are wired to copy others' mindsets, values, and behaviors—to follow common practices that may be acceptable yet cause disharmony within us?

For example, we learn to tell white lies as a quick strategy to avoid being judged, to get someone to do something, or to boost our egos. No matter how small or how necessary they may seem, we know white lies are, at best, distortions of truths, and we present them as real events because they are convenient. They are, in fact, convenient false truths. Most people believe that the little distorted stories they tell don't count as lies and are inconsequential. For example, they may think, *It's OK to make up a false story about heavy traffic to justify being late; everyone gets it or does it.* The problem is that all our mental activities contribute to the building blocks of our programming (the true or false self we operate

187

from), and when we create false truths, deep inside, our self-confidence and sense of authenticity are damaged; it happens a little bit at a time.

This type of programming is what happens in the first three stages of the SMADE mental model (chapter 3) that continues throughout life and gets one stuck in anxiety and dissatisfaction. These distorted realities, especially as solutions to day-to-day affairs, eventually become our adaptations, habits, and automatic responses. Without truthfulness and integrity, how can there be a true self or even a peaceful self?

The interesting thing is that truth, once you see it and engage in it, is peaceful no matter the context. Even if you don't like the truth of something or are afraid of it, facing it, though it may be difficult, can unburden the mind. Once we stop concocting reality and see things as they are, obsessive thoughts stop, which allows us the space to find useful solutions or work on accepting the situation. Lies, on the other hand, including white ones and lying to ourselves, undermine our inner peace. To test this, go back to chapter 7, and use the step-by-step process to mindfully authenticate the experience for yourself.

Let's go back to the concern about not being true to our true selves. Other than our programming, which makes up our habits and default mechanisms, there are other concerns to understand about the self itself. One of the Buddha's profound insights and teachings about humans' sense of self is called *not-self*. Its aim is to help us become free from the complexities and suffering we create by believing in a solid self or identity.

The Buddha taught not-self to explain how the five things humans see as indications of a consistent self cannot be relied on, and therefore, they are not-self. He expounded that this thing we refer to as *I, me, and myself* is actually composed of five aggregates: form or body; mind or mental formations; feelings, including emotions and physical sensations; sense consciousness, which recognizes anything that catches our attention; and perceptions, which are meanings and interpretations. All of these five aggregates are inconstant and subject to change from moment to moment or context to context. The body changes, thoughts change, feelings change, sense consciousness changes, and perceptions change.

Think about it: When the very thing that makes you feel like you changes, it is disheartening. For example, you identify yourself (a combination of mind, body, feelings, perceptions, and consciousness) as an employee at a company, and this identity changes by your getting promoted or laid off. Changes you don't like make you feel uneasy, upset, worried, and anxious. Changes you like you may welcome, but those good changes can turn too. It's like constantly feeling abandoned by oneself. People particularly agonize when they assume they shouldn't or don't want to age, get sick, die, or lose something they cherish.

For this reason, the Buddha indicated that looking for a true self, or who we really are, is a waste of time, as there are only these five aggregates we can find, and they are continually changing. There's no use in clinging to them, or we will suffer.

You might be thinking, *That's a fascinating idea, but what about having to live in the real world and having to relate to and present myself as myself?* When you are getting educated to excel in life or working hard to differentiate yourself from others who provide the same services, thinking about yourself as the five aggregates of not-self may not seem relevant or useful. The point is not that you shouldn't have an identity — we need our identities to live in human society. Rather, the point is to help you see that this identity, or self, is bound to change for good and bad, so do not expect it not to and do not cling to it.

Though the Buddha was not concerned about getting caught up with identifying the true self, it is useful to allow for the conventional uses of self that people share with other humans and that many yearn to be in touch with. In order to connect with the true self and make the teaching of not-self practical and applicable, I teach my students and clients to pay attention to their internal self. The one who experience their lives — the one who feels the sadness, the joy, and the bewilderment and who is aware sometimes and confused other times; to tune in and connect with how they navigate life through their changing perceptions. You can practice and develop the skill to recognize your changing perceptions. As you go inward to connect with the one who experiences your life, notice the flow of change in different levels of experiences. As you become more mindful and operate on autopilot less, you will spot that everyone's body, thoughts, understandings, insights, and intentions are subject to change. Eventually, everything about us becomes otherwise and altered. Also, what we own, including our knowledge, changes; evolves; grows; or gets debunked, lost, or broken, as with the recent Los Angeles fires that burned through thousands of homes and billions of belongings. Even what feels like a definite ending changes too. Destroyed homes will be replaced in no time, belongings will be renewed, and lives will continue their new cycles. With awareness and mindful life intelligence, what can stay constant is not that solid sense of *I, me, and mine* but an uninterrupted knowing of the truths of life, such as the reality that everything is in constant transformation. With this deep understanding, you can be adaptive and flexible, not reactive and miserable. Otherwise, anytime you try to create or maintain a permanent self, your attempt will fail.

So learn to be connected to your inner experience (the only present moment true self), and work on bringing yourself back to peace and joy. This way, at the end of life, you will have less to be regretful about. Review MLOL 50 in chapter 20 to develop these skills.

Note that this teaching about not-self applies to and explains MLOL 16, about the falsehood of ownership and preventing agony over financial and material loss.

Next, we move to the Buddha's Four Noble Truths.

the Four Noble Truths & the Eightfold Path
The Buddha's Core Teaching

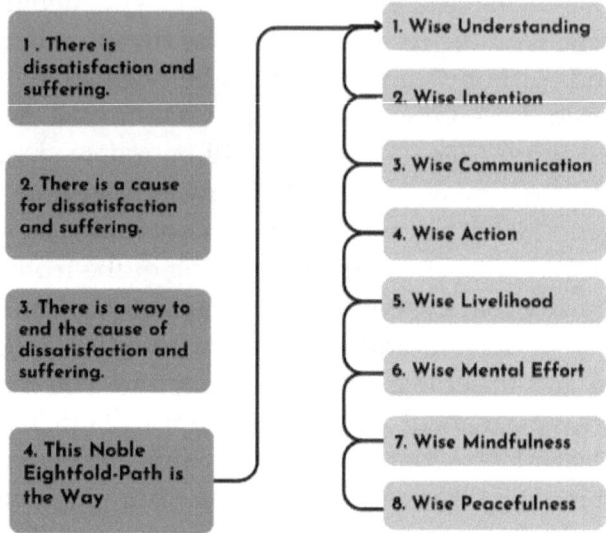

Figure 14

MLOL 32: MINDFUL OF THE FOUR NOBLE TRUTHS

The Four Noble Truths teach us how to recognize and diagnose various forms of dis-ease, stress, anxiety, irritation, agitation, fear, judgment, and any form of unhappiness, which are collectively referred to as *suffering*. They also explain the conditions that fuel this suffering and the means to eliminate the fuel and cool the internal flames of pain. As a note, this diagnostic tool and prescription are the foundational basis for my five stages of Human Software Optimization and the three domains of life intelligence.

In his master's thesis, "Mindful Leadership and Climate Action," Matthew Law points out that the Four Noble Truths are a tool not only to diagnose and cure the causes of dissatisfaction and suffering for individuals but also to diagnose the collective human perspective and conduct that have led to significant suffering in the global and environmental domains.

When the mind is riddled with false notions that are misaligned with the natural patterns that govern life, it looks for happiness in all the wrong places. False notions create useless or damaging thoughts. These faulty perspectives lead to actions that result in all kinds of avoidable issues. The Four Noble Truths can help us to recognize this and offer a remedy to end both the causes and the experiences of suffering.

The First Noble Truth: We Experience Dis-ease and Suffering

The first Noble Truth is about recognizing the presence of dis-ease and suffering. As a brilliant teacher who could teach both linearly (for those who are analytical) and nonlinearly (for those who connect the dots through creativity and intuition), the Buddha realized he had to teach us first to acknowledge that while there are natural pains, there are sufferings that can be avoided. This is both a compassionate first step to ease a person's pain by validating that there is suffering and a way to make a person's suffering apparent to him or her. But often, we miss this first compassionate step in our communication or attempts to assist someone in agony. Others may not even know they're experiencing agony. They may think the appropriate response is to feel upset because something has gone wrong. Seeing or admitting that the anger, resentment, or sense of failure one is feeling is an added suffering is the first Noble Truth. And why is this noble? Because it is a truth worth paying attention to, investigating, and penetrating.

The Feeling of Suffering

The word suffering is an overarching umbrella that covers all kinds of unhappiness and complaints in life. It ranges from the smallest irritations to sorrow, lamentation, grief, anxiety, stress, judgment, jealousy, conceit, despair, hatred, and so on. The Pali word for suffering is dukkha, which refers to getting stuck or losing balance or having a bad fit. During the

Buddha's time, people rode horses with wooden carts, and the carts sometimes got jammed. A stick could get caught in a wheel and prevent it from turning with ease, or an uneven road could cause the cart to rattle and throw the things and people in the cart all around, creating disharmony. They called whatever stopped the free movement of the wheel or didn't fit right *dukkha*, or suffering. The metaphor aims to recognize the stick that jammed the wheel and the unevenness of the road as the causes and conditions, as well as describing how suffering feels in the mind and body when events in life don't fit or flow well. The mind wants everything to fit favorably and to happen promptly, and it feels disharmony when that's not the case. This mindset becomes the stick that jams your life, and you can see it manifest as irritation. The idea is that if you see the causes and conditions that has jammed your life, you can stop and tend to it. When you don't see that the causes and conditions that jam your life are in your mind, you continue in disharmony and easily swing from happiness to unhappiness. So what are these sticks or causes and conditions that cause disharmony and suffering? The answer is in the second Noble Truth.

The Second Noble Truth: There is a Cause to Dis-ease and Suffering

The second Noble Truth claims that humans' never-ending dissatisfaction and suffering have causes. These are states of mind. The Buddha emphasized that no state of mind arises on its own; causes are influenced by conditions.

The root cause of discontentment and agony, the Buddha discovered, is delusion, reinforced by clinging and aversion. These are the sticks that stop the wheels of our lives from turning smoothly. The *delusion* is in believing conditions won't or shouldn't change and being oblivious or living in denial. *Clinging* is attachment to the desires our minds conjure up as the source of happiness. *Aversion* is the tension we create around the changes or situations we don't like. These three mental conditions are always there to make us suffer — unless we recognize, prevent, and eliminate them.

This brings us to the third and fourth Noble Truths.

193

The Third Noble Truth: There is a Way to End the Causes of Suffering

The third Noble Truth teaches that the cessation of suffering is attainable by eliminating delusion, craving and attachment, and aversion. By relinquishing these, one can experience a state of ultimate peace and liberation from the cycles of unhappiness. It's an encouragement to know we are not stuck with our conditions, our faulty programming, and the ways in which our minds cause our suffering. By developing certain qualities and skills, we can live with ease, discernment, and fulfillment. This is when the fourth Noble Truth comes in to guide us.

The Fourth Noble Truth: There Noble Eightfold Path is The Way

The fourth Noble Truth offers a prescription that includes a list of truths, qualities, and skills that return us to well-being. It's like getting the perfect medicine after being diagnosed with a disease. The medicine for the suffering of the human mind is the Noble Eightfold Path, and its fruit, or result, is successful, lasting happiness. Each fold in the path is a seed of happiness that comes with instructions on how to prepare, plant, nourish, grow, and harvest the fruits to sustain our well-being and fulfillment.

To know you have accomplished each of these Four Noble Truths, you must acquire three levels of insights.

Three Insights

These insights are penetrating, becoming free of the causes of suffering, and knowing that one has accomplished the goal. These insights recognize the beginning, the middle, and the end results. They emphasize that merely learning these teachings conceptually, memorizing them, and even articulating them won't really help us in becoming free from the three causes of delusion, clinging, and aversion. We can read and memorize all kinds of great teachings, sayings, and affirmations, but if they have not become part of us, they are not beneficial to us. You can read more detailed explanations of these twelve insights in *Dancing with Life* by Phillip Moffitt.

MLOL 33: MINDFULLY EMPLOYING THE NOBLE EIGHTFOLD PATH

The third Noble Truth tells us there is a way to end delusion, clinging, and aversion—a prescription to cure suffering. The fourth Noble Truth identifies the Noble Eightfold Path as the part of practice and cultivation the Buddha promised would free us. This path, or prescription, that can end human suffering consists of wise view, wise intention, wise speech, wise action, livelihood, wise effort, wise mindfulness, and wise concentration. *Wise*, in these folds, is a translation of the Pali word panna, which refers to discernment of the true nature of each fold and its benefits. For example, wise view means seeing the logic and inner workings of the Four Noble Truths. *Panna* is also translated as "right," which means the same. They are called *eightfold* because the assembled qualities and skills in these eight folds are inseparable, like folds of a piece of fabric. It is fine to work on a fold out of order; eventually, you'll be working on other folds, because they are all linked. At some point into enjoying the fruits of your practice, you may realize that the order in which they are given makes good sense. It's important to note that wise view, wise effort, and wise mindfulness should always be present, because they support the understanding and accomplishment of all the other folds. The Noble Eightfold Path also provides balance among three overarching essential skills and qualities: wisdom, heart intelligence, and peacefulness.

MLOL 34: MINDFULLY BALANCING WISDOM, HEART INTELLIGENCE, AND PEACEFULNESS

The Eightfold Path provided a map that made possible my hero's journey and mission to become as pure as I could. To become as pure as I could, I needed to develop wisdom, heart intelligence, and peacefulness through mind and heart development. These three qualities were necessary for me to become free from my programming and have consistent control over my happiness. Let's look at these three characteristics.

Wisdom: Folds one (wise view) and two (wise intention) aim to develop our cognition, logic, and rationality into the capability for discernment, which our brains were not originally wired for. We have to develop this.

Heart Intelligence (HQ): Folds three (wise speech), four (wise action), and five (wise livelihood) aim to develop the heart through virtuous conduct and integrity. The goal of these three folds is to develop and incorporate the heart as a strong voice in partnering with our thoughts and intentions to guide our choices and actions so that we avoid doing harm and being harmed. It is not always easy to do, which the next category can assist with.

Peacefulness or clarity: Folds six (wise effort), seven (wise mindfulness), and eight (wise concentration) emphasize the necessity of a clear mind, which is peacefully engaged, present, emotionally stable, and kind. Some call this "the meditation section" because the folds work as mental development through meditation. But clarity and peacefulness can be accomplished during daily tasks as well as through formal meditation and contemplation. The purpose of these three folds is to clear the mind from false notions, judgments, and attachments and replace them with wisdom and heart intelligence.

These qualities seem to be noble and fine — why would we need to have balance for them? This is because if one has too much wisdom (logic) and not enough compassion, one can make choices and actions that seem rational but are also rigid, one-sided, and inconsiderate. A good example of this is found in religious rules, which may intend, for example, to protect women from being violated or taken advantage of but instead end up isolating or demeaning them. On the other hand, if people have too much compassion and not enough wisdom, they may be indecisive, give too much, do too much, deplete themselves, or unwisely suffer for the suffering of others. Similarly, if people have too much peace and not enough wisdom and compassion, they may be too relaxed and complacent. They may not see the cause of an issue, not attempt to resolve it, or fall into indifference or ignorance about the problem. Such is not true peacefulness and won't last long. Indifference, in fact, is the near enemy of peacefulness. But it can be remedied through wisdom and heart intelligence.

Balance in developing the categories of wisdom, heart intelligence, and peace is particularly important for heads of families, leaders of organizations, heads of states, and anyone else others depend on for guidance or decisions. Those who have acquired these three qualities often become irreplaceable assets as founders, leaders, spouses, parents, teachers, and guides of society.

Next, we'll look at wisdom and the role of superior resolve in our path to eliminating suffering from our lives.

CHAPTER 18

WISDOM AND SUPERIOR RESOLVE

This chapter is about transforming reason into wisdom and creating superior and intentional resolve to live consciously and enjoy the benefits that come with it.

DOMAIN III:

HUMAN EXPERIENCE, CONDUCT, AND HAPPINESS

WISDOM AND RESOLVE

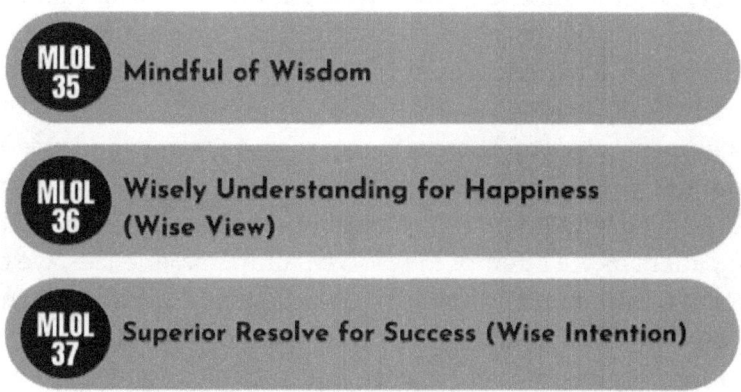

MLOL 35 — Mindful of Wisdom

MLOL 36 — Wisely Understanding for Happiness (Wise View)

MLOL 37 — Superior Resolve for Success (Wise Intention)

Figure 15

MLOL 35: MINDFUL OF WISDOM

Reason plays a key role in our lives because it can withstand unfounded conjectures and unskillful or bad intentions. Wisdom is an added component, a knowing that urges us to pay attention to reason and facts to produce proper actions or make the necessary changes to set things right. It empowers the rational mind that values truth and accepts the logic of how things work. Wisdom may be explained from various perspectives. From the Buddhist perspective, Ajahn Pasanno explained wisdom as a cluster of qualities, including clearly knowing and being able to apply this clarity in practical ways. It's about knowing the truth of something and relying on that truth to guide and shape our values and actions. Acting wisely is beneficial for us.

We benefit from this clear knowing and the ability to have the truth guide our choices, not only in everyday life but also, especially in our later years. Studies show that having more wisdom later in life helps elders to enjoy more well-being than having wealth and living in better environments. As we previously learned, the human brain is not designed to be wise, and we have to cultivate wisdom in ourselves and our children. While wisdom can be learned through educational systems, parents, and society, it is most often gained through personal experience and deep, genuine exploration and observation of how things work.

Sometimes wisdom develops because we've experienced a particular difficulty or challenge in life. It's often not obvious during our life challenges that we will gain helpful insights as a result. But if we're patient as we attempt to resolve painful experiences, we can look at our situations, our thoughts, and our actions differently and can expand our knowledge and grow. One study found that big life changes for women in their thirties had a positive effect on their development of wisdom. As they faced challenges and found ways to resolve them, they gained insights. Other studies indicate, however, that while stressful living might make us stronger or teach us something, when negative experiences outweigh the positive ones, the overwhelming stress may block us from gaining wisdom.

Scientifically, wisdom, according to *Psychology Today*, can be viewed as components that can be measured. Those components include

> Cognitive components, such as knowledge and experience; reflective components, or the ability to examine situations and oneself; and prosocial components, meaning benevolence and compassion, and abilities such as perspective-taking, open-mindedness, and intellectual humility.

By these scientifically measurable components, a wise person is dedicated to the truths of life and is not cruel, egotistical, or driven to achieve his or her own agenda at any cost. The wise understand that the universe has its own rules, laws, and processes, and they're fine with that.

Wisdom does not belong to any particular segment of society, such as gurus, philosophers, or scientists, nor should it be accessible only to a few. It's a foundational building block of an optimal inner navigation system every human being can benefit from. We learn to become wise not only through the rational mind and heart and our life experiences but also through presence with our inner world, our bodily sensations and emotions, and attentiveness to the results of our actions. Wisdom also involves seeing the relationship between cause and effect and creating conditions that benefit all living beings, including oneself. This ability requires a collaboration between the rational mind and the intelligence of the heart to ensure the mind is not acting alone. As Blaise Pascal is famously quoted, "The heart has its reason, which reason does not know." In fact, the heart can often save us from unnecessary pain and suffering.

For example, on one of my editing days, I stopped editing this part and went to make myself a milkshake. As I poured fruits and milk into the mixer, I felt sorrow welling up in my heart. I recognized that I was triggered by seeing the mixer, which belonged to my son, whom I lost. For a short moment, I felt a combination of emotions: sadness that he wasn't there, gratitude for the machine he left behind and the fact that

I was actually using it, and the quick realization of what might follow. I was headed toward feeling some really painful emotions if I didn't stop my mind from going down that rabbit hole. The intelligence I had developed through my own heart and compassion reminded me of the pain that was coming and guided me to avoid it. I was fully present when my body went from neutral to uncomfortable and tight and then back to neutral, but I was peaceful. By being present, observing all of this in real time, and actively engaging in a wise direction, I learned once again how the second and third stages of Human Software Optimization are truly effective and, with practice, lead to the fourth stage, which is transformation. I easily came back to editing to make sure every sentence was clear and valuable to you, my beloved reader.

Developing wisdom will make life easier and greatly affect your degree of happiness, with benefits for all your relationships, including those with children, spouses, parents, neighbors, and all others you encounter. Implementing wise strategies will also result in incredible levels of well-being for your business (employees, direct reports, vendors, profit) and for our planet and all forms of life on Earth that contribute to food ecosystems and other planetary systems.

Next, we'll get into the folds of the Noble Eightfold Path, beginning with wise view.

MLDL 36: WISE UNDERSTANDING FOR HAPPINESS (WISE VIEW)

Wise view, also called wise understanding, is about understanding the Four Noble Truths, the reality of not-self, and the laws of nature. For example, it involves understanding that anything breakable is bound to break and, thus, not agonizing over a broken thing. When we have wise understanding, we don't storyize situations, which only tricks the mind and leads to dissatisfaction. One might think, *That's easy, not such profound teaching*. But it is profound because our minds are programmed with expectations and attachments (second Noble Truth, the cause of suffering) we've picked up or developed throughout our lives. One of these expectations is for something that we love not to break or be lost. Such attachments make it difficult to have wise understanding about the nature of change. As we cultivate the first three Noble Truths and other MLOLs offered here, we can develop a wise understanding or view of life by decoding our programming one thought or perception at a time and recognizing one faulty code at a time until we have decoded every false notion.

The teaching the Buddha gave to Rāhula necessitates wise view, the understanding that discontentment, disharmony, and ineffectiveness (a.k.a. suffering) exist and that something causes them. The first step of the Buddha's lesson to Rāhula (and others, including us) is to stop and investigate: *Is there anything about this thought or idea that could create suffering for anyone?* If the answer is yes, avoid it, as wisdom would have it.

To complete the development of wisdom, we must also work on superior resolve, which comes in the second fold as wise intention.

MLOL 37: SUPERIOR RESOLVE FOR SUCCESS (WISE INTENTION)

Intention is the underlying force behind our thoughts and actions. Wise intention, also known as wise volition, is about the wish for and exhibition of appropriate types of intention, or will, and agenda in response to wise understanding. Since wise understanding is about knowing suffering and its causes and relieving oneself of them, it's logical and wise that our intentions be harmonious, effective, and beneficial to all involved to avoid the causes of suffering. In every step of the Buddha's guidance to Rāhula, he was to connect with his underlying intention and exhibit intentions that were beneficial to all and to himself.

There are three qualities, or types, that make up wise intention:

1. *Unconditional goodwill (or loving-kindness)* means we intend unconditional goodwill for all living beings, without bias, including those we don't approve of or are hurt by ourselves. Often, staying kind and friendly when someone is pushing your buttons is not easy. However, practicing unconditional goodwill, whether someone deserves it or not, results in peace

and harmony within oneself. This is a fruit of the eightfold path; one can experience and benefit from. When one feels in harmony, one can act objectively and more successfully.

2. *Nonharming* means not wishing harm on or acting in any harmful way toward oneself or any living being, including those we don't like. This too isn't always easy to achieve either. It takes understanding what it feels like to experience pain and suffering, as well as knowing that keeping ill will alive in one's heart increases that suffering. Seeing this clearly, one becomes less willing to engage in thoughts and actions that are harmful. To be clear, neither this quality nor unconditional goodwill promotes weakness. On the contrary, one can be fierce by acting wisely (without harming and with kindness) and gaining the trust of others.

3. *Letting go (or generosity)* is about the ability to let go of anything that could cause us suffering. It could be a material belonging, an opinion, a harsh judgment, or a negative action. Letting go is not always easy and needs to be developed. Once, a few of my students and I visited some of Ajahn Chah's monasteries in Thailand. On that trip, one of my students, who is a psychologist, said to a senior monk, "It's so hard to let go—how do we let go?" The monk responded, "Letting go comes from understanding." He explained that when you experience suffering that comes from hanging on to something, you naturally let it go. It's like picking up a hot rod: your hand burns, and you immediately drop it. When you feel tension and suffering in your mind and recognize that it is due to clinging to some judgment, your mind will naturally let go because it would rather enjoy life without pain and peacefully.

Next, we'll look at mindful heart intelligence qualities.

CHAPTER 19

HEART INTELLIGENCE (HQ): A SUPERIOR INNER GUIDANCE

In any circumstance, one can benefit from a better-developed, sharper inner guidance. We are faced with internal and external turmoil on a daily basis. Some shifts in employment or laws and governance can bring relief and release; others can lead to feelings of fear and the erosion of security and rights. Sometimes the uncertainty of what lies ahead can create a sense of isolation and helplessness. Hence, developing resilience and a superior level of inner guidance is essential to discerning and overcoming these painful experiences. At the core of this resilience lies a mindful heart intelligence that empowers us to stand for the rights and principles we believe in without suffering as we hold those principles.

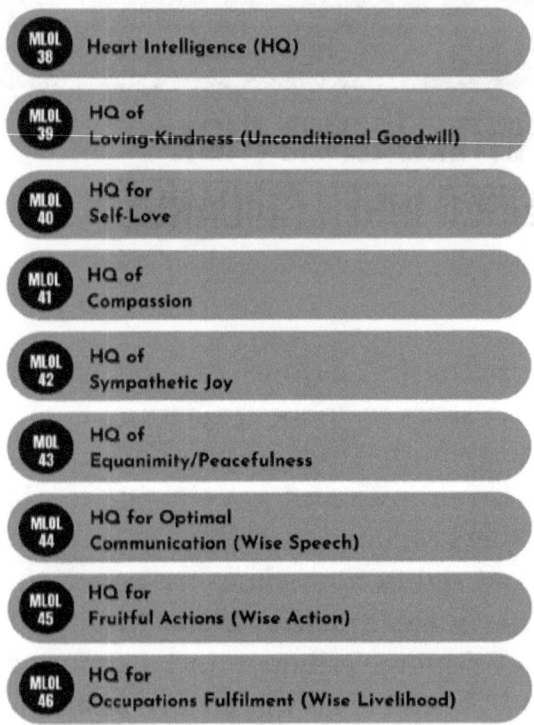

DOMAIN III:

HUMAN EXPERIENCE, CONDUCT, AND HAPPINESS

HEART INTELLIGENCE: A SUPERIOR INNER GUIDANCE

- **MLOL 38** — Heart Intelligence (HQ)
- **MLOL 39** — HQ of Loving-Kindness (Unconditional Goodwill)
- **MLOL 40** — HQ for Self-Love
- **MLOL 41** — HQ of Compassion
- **MLOL 42** — HQ of Sympathetic Joy
- **MOL 43** — HQ of Equanimity/Peacefulness
- **MLOL 44** — HQ for Optimal Communication (Wise Speech)
- **MLOL 45** — HQ for Fruitful Actions (Wise Action)
- **MLOL 46** — HQ for Occupations Fulfilment (Wise Livelihood)

Figure 16

MLOL 38: INTEGRITY, HEART INTELLIGENCE (HQ)

There is a type of HQ that is about the heart as a vital organ that manages many functions in the body, including the nervous system, and affects our emotions and perceptions. The Heart Math Institute defines this type of heart intelligence as "the flow of awareness, understanding, and intuition we experience when the mind and emotions are brought into coherent alignment with the heart organ." This is somewhat aligned with the first three foundations or doorways to mindfulness: body, feeling, and mind awareness.

The type of HQ I would like to focus on is an intelligence in integrity and benevolence, in which the light of hope and goodwill shines through and in which pure love, the highest good in humanity, prevails. For many of us, our hearts are like dusted jewels that need polishing and cleansing in order to become HQ. Some push the idea that we already are love and light and don't need anything else. That enthusiastic idea may work for boosting a person's confidence or beliefs, but when he or she is confronted with difficult experiences, the love and light may give way to fear, worry, anxiety, hostility, and cruelty. It is true that we are all precious and were born precious. But the highest goodness of humanity, or HQ, is not inherent in us from birth. It's another aspect we learn from others.

We acquire some level of HQ through our experiences and social grooming and conditioning, which are constructed by other humans and are not consistent in meaning across cultures. Each one of us has certainly developed the heart's goodness in some capacity, and we all have the potential to achieve or become and experience the highest love and light. So it's not necessarily about specific codes of conduct, but about internalizing the intention behind them in a more generalized way. When our HQ is fully developed, transformed, and optimized, it becomes an abundant resource for healing, happiness, and success, a powerful ally to wisdom. It becomes a potent intelligence of its own kind, with nourishing qualities that can become a reliable source for self-confidence and resilience.

There are some qualities, such as gratitude (expressing the benefit of receiving) and generosity (letting go), that feel like heart qualities, but they are really mental activities and are developed in other sections. There are four superior heart qualities we can develop and increase HQ: loving-kindness, or goodwill; compassion, or nonharming; sympathetic joy, or joy for the joy of another; and equanimity, or peacefulness. The Buddha called these the four jewels of the heart and claimed they have the power to protect us against fear, anxiety, self-doubt, and ignorance— and, I believe, from the SMADE program and feeling stuck. They increase our chances of success and enjoyment in any relationship by optimizing our emotional, mental, and spiritual maturity.

Let's look at the first HQ quality, loving-kindness.

MLOL 39: HQ OF LOVING-KINDNESS (UNCONDITIONAL GOODWILL)

As one of the heart's intelligent qualities, which I also covered under the first quality in superior resolve, or wise intention, loving-kindness is about unconditional goodwill toward oneself and all beings. It's an experience that can calm and balance the nervous system. To benefit us at an optimal level, it cannot be conditional or circumstantial, and it's not just a feeling—it also includes mental attitudes, intentions, and actions. To develop loving-kindness and unconditional goodwill, we have to understand what it is and why and how it should and can be unconditional.

The Benefits of Loving-Kindness Practice

On my journey to freedom from the sufferings my mind created, I came across a meditation practice that promotes cultivating an unconditional loving regard for myself and all beings. I cringed—not because I hated being kind but because I couldn't handle being any kinder. I avoided it, thinking I was already too kind and loving and didn't need to grow in that department. I was the sacrificing type and had made more than my share of sacrifices in my life. So I set it aside, thinking loving-kindness was for others—cold people—and not me. Nonetheless, I couldn't avoid hearing about it regularly during retreats and while being guided to meditate with mindfulness. The process of cultivating loving-kindness is simple: send goodwill first to people you care about, then to those you feel neutral about, then to those you've had difficulty with, and finally to yourself. When it came up, I usually distracted myself, and unfortunately, I didn't get the core of its intention, nor did I enjoy its benefit.

After a year of constantly hearing about its benefits, one day, when I sat to meditate, I spontaneously decided to consciously practice loving- kindness. Oddly enough, I skipped the first two easy parts and jumped right to the challenge of sending loving thoughts and well-wishes to all those who had harmed me throughout my life. I don't know about you, but my brain thrives on a topic of interest, especially when it's coupled with a challenge, which is probably why I went right to the difficult people. I sat down, and Oreo, my little shih tzu, sat next to me as I meditated. I closed my eyes and opened my mind to my past. I chose three phrases to wish for people as I thought of them: "May you be safe and protected," "May you be healthy and strong," and "May you be peaceful and at ease."

I was stunned by how many people rushed through my mind, as if I were offering them gold: the shoemaker who'd touched my thighs when I was five; the tall father of a neighborhood friend, who'd slapped me for saying a curse word to his daughter when I was seven; the mean relative who'd falsely accused me when I was thirteen; my father, who sometimes had yelled and embarrassed me in front of my friends as a teen; the manager who'd made a pass at me when I was nineteen; and the lawyer who'd offered to help me in exchange for *something else* when I was thirty-five. My ex-husband, bless him, emerged among all of them. So many people came to my mind I could barely track them all.

I didn't even have time to finish saying the three phrases before a new person popped into my vision. With every person who appeared in my mind came a painful feeling. I felt a yucky, hot feeling in my stomach, but I kept at it. With a genuine desire for their well-being, I focused on sending them loving-kindness wishes. All of this took about forty-five minutes and organically stopped. I opened my eyes, looked at Oreo, and said, "Let's go, Oreo." We went into the bathroom, I washed my hands and then took Oreo for a walk, and I continued with my day. The next day, while on a hike, I shared my meditation experience with an old friend with whom I had graduated, who had become a therapist. When I told her about washing my hands afterward, she stopped us and asked if I did that after every meditation. I said no. She looked at me with a peaceful gaze, smiling, and said, "You washed your hands of all those people. What a beautiful, symbolic gesture. You are free of them."

From that day, I felt lighter. The emotional suffering my psyche had carried with each of those memories reduced considerably. I finally understood the point of unconditional love and its benefits. Through my own personal experience, I understood why the Buddha had categorized loving-kindness as one of the four jewels of the heart that needs cultivation. I recognized an inner intelligence that first and foremost worked for our own healing and benefit. It was an incredible aha moment, one that became my motivation to continue with loving- kindness as my main mindfulness practice for the years to come.

Later, as I taught loving-kindness in my mindfulness classes, I described it as a pure intention in one's mind and heart to wish well-being for all beings, including those we may hate or have issues with. It's free of the notions of whether someone deserves love or not. It's an inclusive way of kindly loving. You may know love and know kindness, yet even when you love someone, there may be times when you are not kind to him or her. Consider a loving mother: A mother can be loving and kind when her kids behave properly but become angry with them when they do things improperly. While she loves them, she can justify being angry and unfriendly when they make her upset. She feels justified to punish them or treat them with unfriendliness to teach them the right way to behave and to protect them from harm. Naturally, deep inside, she often feels upset that she has to feel angry and regretful, and she feels helpless about getting upset. Aside from not having fully developed the skills related to HQ, we also get confused about what love is because of all the mixed messages we receive as parents, such as the importance of tough love: "If you love your children, you have to scold them, so they won't hurt themselves."

Love is also often misunderstood as only an emotion or feeling, but love is an action and is made up of several components. Experiencing an emotion is optional, but making connection is necessary. It also includes wise intention and making choices and actions that lead to the well-being and happiness of the one we love. We can always find ways to do a tough act with kindness. That means considering how the other person might experience your tough choice and act and including him or her in the process to ease discomfort.

A lot can be said about love and its various manifestations as well as the predicaments one might find oneself in. A good book I recommend is *On Love* by Ajahn Jayasaro, a Buddhist monk, who goes into the details of the ways we need love, the drawbacks of love, and unconditional love. You can find a link to a free copy of this book at forestsangha.org. The point is, being loving in a kind manner is an undertaking that's inclusive of everyone and everything. It's about having a mind that is clear from judgment, anger, expectations, and negative emotions that make one unhappy and reactive. Therefore, practicing sending loving thoughts and intentions to anyone will not only help to establish inner peace and happiness for oneself but also create the habit of engaging in more useful mental activities that can transform obsessive thoughts into calming, beneficial thoughts.

Give it a try, and see for yourself. Choose three loving phrases, and wish them in your mind for anyone you encounter. Don't forget yourself. Do this for a few days, and see the results.

Let's look at self-love and how it can improve our happiness, health, and well-being.

MLOL 40: HQ FOR SELF-LOVE

There is a sweet story about a king who went to the Buddha with his queen, asking for advice to reconcile a dispute between them. The king said to the Buddha that when he had asked his wife, the queen, whom she loved the most in the world, she had responded that she loved herself the most. The king was baffled, as he was supposed to be loved the most In all his kingdom. He wanted the Buddha to set her straight, as they both respected and followed the Buddha's teachings.

The Buddha responded that she was correct: If one searches the entire universe to find another who is more precious than oneself, one is unable to find such a person. When a person is able to love him- or herself fully, which is a skill, then she can love another fully as well. The king realized the benefits of this truth. He was happy the queen loved herself so much, and he began to think of the ways he could love himself so he did not have to rely on others as much and could love others equally well.

Among the most important skills we need to learn are self-love and self-care. People usually know how to care for their physical needs, such as food, water, sleep, and cleanliness, and they know they need money to do all that. But our well-being also depends heavily on how comfortably we experience life mentally, emotionally, and energetically and how we care for ourselves consistently and lovingly. Often, we don't know how or don't pay enough attention to ourselves, and we suffer for it. To reduce these sufferings, we must learn to have self-love and increase our self-care so we can live with more ease and fulfillment.

In my MLO courses, under "Essentials to Self-Love, Self-Care, and Healing," I teach four aspects that help us to go beyond basic survival needs and ensure our happiness. The first HQ essential to self- love is **self-awareness**: being aware of our thoughts and where they lead us; being aware of our feelings and not dismissing, suppressing, or overly expressing them; being aware of our choices and which ones deplete our energy; and being aware of tension and tightness in our bodies so we can adjust and prevent further damage to ourselves. This list can go on and on; add what you need to be aware of that impacts your internal experiences — that self I talked about in MLOL 31, Ch. 17, who is always with you. Self-love also includes being aware of our actions and how they result in harmony or disharmony.

The second essential to self-love includes **loving-kindness** and **self-compassion**, which manifest in having a positive relationship with oneself; having an unconditional sense of goodwill for oneself; having warm understanding when one messes up or fails, instead of judging and criticizing oneself; and being one's own best friend and holding one's difficulties like a real friend who cares and treats any shortcomings with love and care. This HQ essential is about taking initiative to fulfill one's sense of happiness and not waiting for another to do it for one.

The third essential to self-care is **emotional stability**: creating the means to stay calm and peaceful during challenging times; being receptive to change; looking into resolving issues objectively; learning to listen and connect with others to reduce conflicts or their intensity; cultivating the HQ qualities mentioned in this chapter to strengthen the self-soothing inner resources; communicating one's needs and not just assuming others should know about them; asking for space when one needs it; asking to discuss things to clarify intentions and best ways going forward, not assuming; and preventing end-of-life regrets by listening to oneself and acting on what's really important now.

The fourth essential of self-love is **action**. This includes taking care of basic needs well, such as eating healthy food and getting enough sleep and exercise; tending to one's emotional needs, such as affection, attention, and appreciation; tending to one's social needs by initiating time spent with those who are kind and wise; avoiding those who are unskilled at being wise and kind; creating relationships in which one can be authentic, feel understood, and grow; forming a reliable support system; engaging in humor and laughter as well as relaxation and space to spend time and connect with oneself; and, most importantly, creating routines for the aforementioned and other beneficial self-care acts to become habitual.

Moreover, the offering of love, care, and compassion to us as adults helps us to heal past trauma, prevent future traumas, and feel happier and more content in the present. Then we can extend what we learn about loving ourselves more deeply to love others more effectively and genuinely.

I had always thought I was a good and caring person, but that meant I would easily give up on what made me happy and fulfilled my needs. I learned to let go of half measures and instead give myself full self-love and care. I hope this helps you to do the same. To learn more and cultivate these skills, please check perfectlyhere.org, where you can also subscribe to get MLO lessons and be notified about upcoming MLO courses.

Next, we'll look at the second of the four heart intelligence qualities: compassion.

MLOL 41: HQ OF COMPASSION

The HQ of compassion (nonharming) facilitates the second quality in superior resolve, or wise intention. It's a sincere understanding of failure and pain, and it includes feeling moved to relieve such pain when one encounters it. Compassion can manifest in acts of generosity (the third quality in superior resolve, or wise intention). When we relinquish harsh criticism and ill will toward someone, we've practiced an act of generosity, or letting go. From the law of karma and intentional actions, we know that a person acting unskillfully is connected to and inherits the results and consequences of those intentional actions. Likewise, if we root for others to have negative consequences, we connect ourselves to their karma and intentions. It is smart not to be part of someone else's negative consequences. Heart Intelligence guides us to remain merciful and wish others well. Take this lesson to the five stages of Human Software Optimization in chapters 5-7 to check it out and develop it.

Next comes sympathetic joy.

MLOL 42: HQ OF SYMPATHETIC JOY

Sympathetic joy, also known as appreciative or empathetic joy, means feeling joy when thinking of or witnessing others feeling joy. This HQ has two positive effects: It resolves the negative feelings that come from envy and jealousy and increases inner joy manyfold. Our joy often depends on circumstances, such as when a child is born, when you laugh at a joke, or when you get a gift. Imagine how exponentially joyful you can become by tapping into everyone else's happiness and feeling others' joy within yourself. The amount of joy you can feel becomes unlimited. This may be smart and at times difficult to do.

If you find that you cannot feel others' joy because their joy results in your feeling pain and suffering, then you can fall back on feeling compassion for the whole situation, yourself, and everyone involved. You can practice sending loving thoughts to yourself to calm your mind. Practicing sympathetic joy is not particularly easy in competitive societies, sports, or work and family environments. Losing the game or what matters to you means there is usually no reason to be happy about it. It's a dead end. But if you were to open to the joy of the other side and how they feel with their winning, you can feel their joy and realize that gain or loss is all part of the same process. You may have lost the game, but you can gain an inner joy, by feeling their joy, which you were after to begin with! Give it a try.

The last HQ is equanimity or peacefulness.

MLOL 43: HQ OF EQUANIMITY AND PEACEFULNESS

Equanimity means having a peaceful mind, heart, and body; experiencing oneness; and being connected and content. This feeling can be momentary or be developed to have a long-lasting, natural flow during your day-to-day experiences. Equanimity is not passive peacefulness. It does not mean ignoring things that bother you; it means allowing for change and for difficulties and being active in resolving them calmly. Being equanimous results in clear thinking, which leads to practical solutions and resolution of those internal obstacles. It is a state of being that can be developed through meditation as well as daily mindfulness practices. To feel this peaceful state, you work on resolving the five inner obstacles of aversion, clinginess, restlessness, fogginess, and doubt, which I will cover in chapter 20, MLOL 51. Without these obstacles present, the mind, heart, soul, and body are unburdened and feel rested.

Although we all know of these four heart qualities and most of us have felt all of them to one degree or another, it might come as something of a revelation that through various practices to develop their deeper intelligence, all of these qualities can become richer and more fulfilling and can serve as remedies to heal pain and suffering for both individuals and societies. These are inner skills that, when fully learned, lead to a life of ease, joy, and harmony.

Next comes what it means to apply HQ to our speech and communication.

MLOL 44: HQ FOR OPTIMAL COMMUNICATION (WISE SPEECH)

Wise speech is the third fold of the Noble Eightfold Path. Before getting into the benefits of HQ in communication and wise speech, let's talk about the role of communication, speech, and language in our lives and interactions. Development in written and spoken language has been an important priority for humans. Through words and language, humans communicate their needs, their ideas, their offerings, their likes and dislikes, accounts of historical events, rules and regulations, and everything else communities share with one another. According to UNESCO, the world peace organization that launched the World Atlas of Languages, there are 8,324 languages around the world.

The variety of languages and meanings makes communication and connection complicated for us. In some ways, it separates us. But humans have enough issues with understanding others who speak their own language. People are raised in different family dynamics and have different amounts or degrees of schooling or life experiences. Some families place great importance on the formalities of language, while others may place more value on virtues, such as helpfulness and self- expression. As adults, we've had to learn how to communicate effectively to get the results we want. But we're not always successful at it.

In addition to 8,324 languages, we have to deal with perceptions that can be clouded by how we associate with things: by false information, misunderstandings, conflicting values, and hidden or self-serving intentions. If the words we use are negative or ambiguous or if they are untimely and inconsiderate, they can cause confusion, mistrust, struggle, and loops of suffering for all involved. With increased HQ in loving-kindness, compassion, sympathetic joy, and equanimity, these negative effects can be reduced and eliminated.

It's important to note here that every word we use or phrase we compose leaves an imprint on the listener, the reader, and even the environment, either positive or negative, and we won't be separate from its results. The Buddha taught that we can improve our lives by developing wise speech. With wise view, we see clearly the causes of suffering. With wise intention, or superior resolve, we cultivate goodwill, nonharming, and letting go. Wise speech, then, is used to improve the results of our interactions. In addition to using it with others, we can apply wise speech to words and phrases we use in our heads to prevent disharmony within ourselves.

There are four aspects to wise speech and creating harmonious, effective communication. These are things to avoid.

The Four Things to Avoid In Wise Speech

1. **Avoid false speech.** Why? Aside from the obvious reason that it's a good idea to be truthful, this goes further to completely avoiding any and all false statements. At first, this was a bit hard for me to swallow. "Aren't there times when it's harmful to tell the truth? When bending it a little could save a lot of pain?" I asked my Buddhist teachers. They responded that it's never beneficial to bend the truth. The remedy to this is to not share something that is true when it's not beneficial, is harmful, or is not timely. When you commit to not telling any lies, even white lies, you find opportunities and ways to convey messages that are not false at all. You learn to explain what the truth is by using wiser, more thoughtful words. If the situation is unpleasant and you can see that telling the truth may get someone rattled or create more issues, you may find it helpful to calm yourself first and then use more neutral, encouraging, nonjudgmental, and solution-oriented statements.

2. **Avoid harsh or harmful speech.** This one is easy to understand but sometimes not easy to do. When we use harsh or harmful language, we give reason for the receivers to retaliate. It's like throwing a dart at them — they feel hurt and might react in kind. Or maybe they don't react outwardly, but internally, they hate us for what we have said. In the end, it'll come back to bite us. This was the case for Salizar (name changed), a client of mine, who was remorseful after his partner left him due to his outbursts and demeaning language. Salizar was in pain and couldn't understand why his partner had left. I worked with him to recognize how it felt to be demeaned and degraded and the pain one feels internally when using harsh or harmful language, whether toward oneself or toward others. He came to realize that aside from the pain he caused his partner, he was the one who had to first experience the intense effects of negativity that it took to conjure up anger and ill will to act meanly. Cultivating self-composure, he determined, can save

him from the pains of regret and remorse. But sometimes you may not even be using harmful or demeaning phrases. You may be using phrases that are completely normal to you, but the receivers, due to their past experiences, are triggered and become offended. Pay close attention to this, because if they are emotional and reactive, continuing to be logical may not be the right channel. It may make them even more reactive because they may perceive that you don't feel their pain; you don't get it. And you may genuinely not get it, because your words and statements were not intended to hurt them. In this case, you may pause and ask them to explain their pain and the reasons behind it. Listen carefully to understand so that you may have the most effective response. To learn more about this process, go to MLOL 58.

3. **Avoid divisive speech.** Why? Well, no one likes to be singled out, separated, cast out, or divided from what he or she holds dear. "Divide and conquer" is a strategy Winston Churchill is famous for, which he used to weaken bonds between people for the purpose of playing them against each other. Divisive speech can be productive in this way, but it causes harm; people who have been exploited or manipulated will retaliate and harbor ill will, and it can potentially cause more conflict and unhappiness. For this reason, divisive speech is unwise speech.

4. **Avoid idle chatter.** Idle chatter is prevalent in human society. Sometimes people call it small talk or, in negative cases, gossip. Idle chatter involves elaborating on things that are unimportant, not useful, or not relevant to the conversation. It wastes time, and it increases the chance of making up false truths and causing issues. As purpose and intention play an important role in our communication and should be evaluated carefully, idle chatter has no real purpose, and it robs the mind of being peaceful. You may be trying to impress others by saying more and more, but they may be bored or not impressed at all, which will have a negative effect on you and them. Idle chatter can also consist of internal monologues that preoccupy you and tire you out.

> To avoid idle chatter, ask yourself, *What is the use of speaking or thinking about this topic? What is the benefit? How does it add value to the conversation or to my life?* If there is no real value, then you can let that one go.

Most importantly, aside from truthfulness, what we communicate must be beneficial to everyone involved and be delivered at the right time and in the right place for it to be effective.

Next is HQ for fruitful or wise action.

MLOL 45: HQ FOR FRUITFUL ACTIONS (WISE ACTION)

Action is usually thought to be physical, but actions can also be thoughts, intentions, and words. Even when we leave things alone or disengage, we're acting (by not acting). With wise action, one can take beneficial, intelligent actions. It requires wise understanding about the causes of suffering and how to avoid them, and it takes wise intention to have a superior resolve for nonharming, bearing goodwill, and acting with generosity. It's about integrating wisdom with HQ to acquire the most-effective, least-harmful results.

When dealing with actions that would have a systemic impact, we need to ask how to best implement them to avoid creating wicked problems that fight the flow of the natural systems that govern our lives. But wise action can be developed individually first. There are four types of actions.

Four Types of Actions

1. **Actions that we like to do and that are good for us.** They are beneficial, and we do them, such as going for a walk every day. There is no problem there.
2. **Actions that we don't like to do and that are bad for us.** They are harmful or useless to us, such as smoking cigarettes or overeating. They are bad for us, and we don't like doing them anyway, so we don't do them. No problem there either.

1. **Actions that are good for us but that we do not do.** Even though we know that something is good for us to do, we procrastinate, ignore it, or avoid it. We may not be motivated enough, we may lack sufficient knowledge to do it, or there may be other obstacles in the way.

2. **Actions that are bad for us but that we do anyway.** These are things that cause disharmony and have negative consequences for our health, our relationships, our finances, or other aspects of our lives. We seem to be unable to stop doing these actions, or we don't have the desire to stop doing them. These things could include, for example, spending more money than we earn each month and causing stress and anxiety.

The last two types of actions are the ones that need our attention and care.

MLOL 46: HQ FOR OCCUPATION FULFILLMENT (WISE LIVELIHOOD)

Heart intelligence (HQ) in occupation, wise livelihood, can reduce stress and anxiety and ensure prosperity and well-being. It's about conscious work and leadership—choosing our ideas, choices, and actions with awareness to equally benefit people and the planet and create prosperity; conducting our work and business with compassion; and caring for everyone's well-being and experience.

This category also includes the work we do voluntarily and other concerted efforts toward accomplishing greater goals—for example, planning cities, innovating new ideas, and developing any strategy that affects large numbers of people. Cultivating HQ will assist us in taming the part of the rational mind that can deceive itself to believe that getting or creating more at any cost will guarantee happiness.

To understand this better, we can look at wrong livelihoods. Obvious examples of wrong livelihoods include selling tobacco and other substances that cause cancer or knowingly selling cars with defective parts that endanger people. In recent years, new types of wrong livelihoods have rapidly sprung up. With the supercharged power of AI in reach and proliferation, deceptive advertising is off the charts. Identity theft and cybersecurity concerns have risen exponentially. Banks, government, and law enforcement agencies send out warning messages to guide people on how not to fall for scammers and digital bots. The LA County Department of Consumer and Business Affairs has laid out descriptions of what constitutes false, misleading, and outright illegal advertising. You might want to check out their link in the bibliography section at the end of this book. It's useful to learn how unscrupulous people are able to deceive others easily and even nudge people to make a decision they otherwise might not have made. Nudging is a subtle act that can be structured to create big results.

Richard Thaler and Cass Sunstein, in their book *Nudge: Improving Decisions About Money, Health, and the Environment*, describe how companies have found ways to push consumers to make choices that automatically benefit the company. *Nudging* refers to designing a choice for people that makes it easy to choose what the nudger wants them to choose. Nudging, in and of itself, is not illegal or necessarily deceptive. It's an effective tool to architect the desired outcome by getting your attention and putting you on autopilot. One example is the way fast-food companies bundle packages: Menu item number one includes a cheeseburger, fries, and a soda; number two includes a double cheeseburger with large fries and a shake; and so on. By setting up these options that make choosing easier, the company sells more of their products.

Choice architecture is prevalent in the health-care, banking, investment, and cybersecurity industries and in almost any business that can afford to build a website and content to nudge people to make a certain choice. For example, when you're asked to click to agree to privacy statements or terms and conditions as soon as you open a website, the legal format and presentation of these choices tend to make people trust that they won't be taken advantage of, so they just click *Agree*. Nudges do not involve incentives or rewards—they just make a choice easy to see and make.

We can use nudging skillfully to create conscious and wise

livelihoods or unwisely, as in deceptive advertising. Using any kind of deceptive method is not intelligent because it is tainted by actions that aim to take that which is not freely offered. In the end, deceptive tactics will create stress, anxiety, and loss of self-worth and self-confidence for those taken advantage of as well as for those who implement such strategies.

Wise speech, wise action, and wise livelihood are the folds in the Noble Eightfold Path that strengthen the heart so it can have a stronger voice at the table of our inner committees and boardrooms. When the mind is making wrong choices, the heart sounds the bells of goodwill, compassion, joy for the joy of others, and peacefulness to point the mind to change direction.

Next, we'll look into factors that help in developing your mind.

CHAPTER 20

FREEING THE MIND BY DEVELOPING IT

The last three folds of the Noble Eightfold Path focus on mental development to allow wisdom and heart intelligence to bring us home to the peace and ease we all crave and deserve to enjoy. The process of mental development begins with wise effort. Then come the MLOLs about awareness, self-awareness, and wise mindfulness; inner obstacles in the way of peace and happiness; the pleasure trick and the selfish gene; and, finally, ultimate peacefulness, or wise concentration.

DOMAIN III:
HUMAN EXPERIENCE, CONDUCT, AND HAPPINESS
FREEING THE MIND BY DEVELOPING IT

MLOL 47	Intelligent Mental Action (Wise Effort)
MLOL 48	Mindful of Awareness
MLOL 49	Mindfully Self-Aware
MLOL 50	Skilled in Mindfulness (Wise Mindfulness)
MOL 51	Mindful of Inner Obstacles in the Way of Peace and Happiness
MLOL 52	Mindful of the Pleasure Trick and Selfish Gene
MLOL 53	The Ultimate Peacefulness (Wise Concentration)

Figure 17

MLOL 47: INTELLIGENT MENTAL ACTION (WISE EFFORT)

We humans make all kinds of efforts. Wise effort, though, specifically refers to our mental efforts. It is the sixth factor of the Noble Eightfold Path and comes before wise mindfulness. That is because to become mindful and present to accomplish happiness and live stress-free, one needs to develop other mental skills that wise effort offers.

I think of wise effort as intelligent mental actions. In *Buddha dhamma: The Laws of Nature and Their Benefit to Life*, a comprehensive collection of Buddhist teachings, P. A. Payutto describes wise effort as "the arousing of energy in the mind; progress, perseverance, determination, effort, exertion, persistence, steadfastness, constancy, steady progress, not forsaking enthusiasm, not neglecting work, and shouldering responsibility." As you can see, these are intelligent, decisive, and engaging mental qualities and actions, compared to those that are frivolous or harmful.

Indeed, this is my favorite of the folds because through the guidelines in wise effort, we can investigate all our mental formations and their underlying intentions and take back control of our minds. It is also where we can cultivate and nourish the goodness of HQ. Here the Buddha offers the mechanism to develop the mind and remove inner obstacles created by the fabricated self or ego. This can be done by going inward, observing thoughts and qualities and states of the mind that hinder happiness, and skillfully eliminating their negative impact.

These intelligent mental actions, or wise effort, offer four types of mental actions as the mechanism for cleansing the biases, agitations, ignorance, attachments, and mindsets that cloud our judgment and prevent us from living easy, content lives, as well as aiding to strengthen HQ:

1. **Guarding** the mind from polluting or agitating thoughts that taint our moods and perspectives, as well as protecting our minds from external influences. For example, watching negative news excessively can have a negative impact on our minds, so

being discerning about the amount of news we take in and its sources is an example of guarding and protecting the mind, an intelligent mental action.

2. **Weeding** out negative states of mind that have become habitual. When we notice judgmental attitudes, envy, jealousy, hatred, clinging, restlessness, fogginess, obsessive thinking, or doubt and confusion, we passionately work on uprooting them to make room for peace and wisdom.

3. **Planting** seeds of HQ that bear the fruits of kindness, care, prosperity, and joy for all. Through meditation or other acts of generosity and kindness, we plant seeds of happiness.

4. **Nourishing** those seeds of kindness, care, prosperity, and joy to maintain and grow them.

The Buddha's teaching his son, Rāhula, to examine his thoughts and to abandon them if they would lead to a painful result for himself or anyone else is an example of using the first and second steps in wise effort: protecting his mind against harmful thoughts and mind states that influence his choices negatively. When he abandons those harmful thoughts, he is weeding out old, harmful states of mind. The Buddha instructed Rāhula that when the results of his actions were painful, he should feel them fully before letting them go. This way, using the third and fourth steps of wise effort, he would naturally engage and nourish his heart by consciously making wiser choices.

However, to make choices consciously and wisely, we need to develop awareness, which I will cover next.

Note: *Buddhadhamma: The Laws of Nature and Its Benefits to Life* is a priceless book accessible for free download as a PDF. See the link in the bibliography, under the books section.

MLDL 48: MINDFUL OF AWARENESS

Awareness is another essential inner navigation ability we must understand and develop. It's part of our mental development. Without a well-developed sense of awareness, we can get lost in our own made-up world and be inattentive to things that might be critical. Awareness, attention, and sense consciousness are closely tied.

I covered attention in chapter 16, MLOL 30. We're usually good at being aware through our five senses because they are basic functions. For example, when we see an object—say, a pen sitting on a table—our eye sense consciousness arises, the eye organ catches it, and we become aware of the pen. We may or may not have oriented our attention toward the pen, but when our eyes catch the pen, we become aware of it.

Becoming aware of something is also influenced by our perceptions, related associations, and motivation to connect to that thing. We may see the pen on the desk but ignore it because we don't need it at the moment. Often, though, we are unaware that we've ignored the pen, unless we've consciously made a note of it for later use. When we get lost in a cascade of thoughts and stimuli that occupy our attention, especially with all the distractions of social media, we can be unaware of the passage of time, unaware of how something has created a feeling in us, or unaware of our judgments and unskillful actions. Knowing that you ignored the pen, a feeling, or the negative outcome of a choice is the type of awareness that strengthens all your faculties and capabilities.

The Four Types of Awareness

Diana Winston, the director of mindfulness education at UCLA Mindful, teaches about four types of awareness we can cultivate, develop, and benefit from. In her book *The Little Book of Being: Practices and Guidance for Uncovering Your Natural Awareness*, Winston categorizes awareness into focused awareness, investigative awareness, choiceless awareness, and natural awareness.

1. **Focused awareness** is when we are concentrating on an object in meditation or while doing a task in daily life. Sometimes we can become hyperfocused and tune other things out. Recognizing this type of awareness, when we are mindful of our attention, we can pull back if necessary to include what's happening in

the environment. (See chapter 16, MLOL 30, about attention's three systems.)

2. **Investigative awareness** is when you are observing an experience; identifying it; and seeing its impact on your mood, body, or mind. This can be done in meditation as well as during daily tasks to regulate your feelings and responses. For example, try to conjure up a thought, and see how it makes you feel. Does it make you feel excited, angry, depressed, ashamed, or any other feeling? Or nothing? Through investigative awareness, you gain insight and the option to make conscious choices, as opposed to being on autopilot.

3. **Choiceless awareness** is when your thoughts move with objects that catch your attention, again both in meditation and during an activity. For example, you're sitting in meditation, and a sound arises: the lawnmower. It may be too loud and distracting. Not liking it or trying to force yourself not to be distracted by it can cause agitation. When you get caught up in an opinion about the sound of the lawnmower or get irritated because you don't love it, you are no longer simply aware, choiceless or not. You are in aversion to it—and, most likely, unaware that you have moved from awareness of sound to thinking about the sound. Choiceless awareness has its usefulness in helping you to stay present to witness the passing of all phenomena. By witnessing the passing of all phenomena, we can understand that attaching to anything we might lose can cause us considerable pain. By not attaching to anything, we learn to remain calm.

4. **Natural awareness** is about being at peace, in a restful state, content, steady, and empty of any agenda that is not about the moment.

The first time I became aware of experiencing this peaceful and present mind was a few years back, during a Mother's Day luncheon. There were nine of us around a round table in a beautiful restaurant with lots of candy for the senses: colorful flower bouquets thoughtfully placed around the room and the smell of food permeating as waiters and waitresses passed by with trays of elegantly designed dishes. The smells of saffron, cinnamon, sautéed raisins, onions, and rose petals and the sound of happy Persian music all contributed to make a delightful experience.

Just sitting there, savoring all that was going on around me, I became aware of people at every table chattering away. This was choiceless awareness. Then I looked at the people around my table. They were either on their phones or lost in thought. Their eyes were open but not seeing; their ears could hear but were not really connected. I could see they were lost in thoughts and feelings and realized in contrast my mind was empty. That was natural awareness — peacefully being without any opinions or mental activities.

I turned to my daughter-in-law, Esther, who was sitting next to me, and said, "Esther, my mind is empty!"

She responded with surprise, "You are lucky."

I smiled with joy and said, "It is no luck, my dear. I have worked hard to develop this."

As I took another look at the others, I felt sadness. They were missing out on the presence of abundance, beauty, and joy. Our kids had coordinated for their mothers to have this meaningful experience, to feel appreciated, and to enjoy a meal they didn't have to prepare. The interesting thing about it was that while I recognized the others' lack of presence and felt compassion for them, my mind remained peaceful, content, and well. That's the state of being fully integrated, which I will talk about in MLOL 53, the ultimate peacefulness.

Next, let's look more closely at self-awareness, which is an important aspect of awareness and other pertinent inner skills we need to develop to live good lives.

MLOL 49: MINDFULLY SELF-AWARE

With so much complexity to deal with in modern society, self-awareness is more essential than ever. Without it, our inner navigation system can malfunction and send us in the wrong direction. Self-awareness is a skill that many of us miss out on while growing up. We usually think of ourselves From the perspective of our bodies; our feelings; our thoughts, wishes, or desires; our beliefs; status; the people we associate with; and a whole host of other defining characteristics. But self-awareness comes down to being aware of our internal experience as it changes from moment to moment and situation to situation. It goes back to the experience of authentic self some people yearn to be loyal to.

With established self-awareness, we also get to see that what we are experiencing is happening in the present moment and not some past or future time. We can discern that something we're thinking is about the past or the future and learn to manage the negative effects of those thoughts in the present moment. By being aware of our thoughts, our actions, and the results of our actions, we can regulate and control all our internal and external reactions. We can reduce stress and anxiety, make better choices, and produce better outcomes.

In the next MLOL, we will learn how to become self-aware through skillful mindfulness and the four doorways to establish mindfulness.

MLOL 50: SKILLED IN MINDFULNESS (WISE MINDFULNESS)

Mindfulness is one of the most important inner navigation qualities and skills one can develop. It makes all our other skills work better for us. There are tons of books about and descriptions of what mindfulness is and how to achieve it, including definitions and guidelines from both the secular movement that started in the United States about forty-five years ago and Buddhist sources that date back 2,500 years to the Buddha himself. Some authors in the secular movement interpret mindfulness as pure awareness—observing the present moment without any preconceived notions, with curiosity, and without judgment. Some call mindfulness a tool, which can be misinterpreted as something to use when you need it and put down when you're done, like a hammer.

As I have practiced, verified for myself, and understand it, mindfulness consists of both an engaged state of mind and as practices (not tools) that help to develop and maintain this state. It includes several components.

As a state of mind, mindfulness involves being calm, alert, present, engaged, and kind. It means being in touch with and aware of what goes on in your mind, how your body feels, and any changes in these. It also includes having an interest and will to consistently create harmony within oneself and the world. For this to happen, one must use intelligent mental actions or wise effort, which I described in MLOL 47, to actively cleanse wrong notions that arise in the mind and to nourish HQ of goodwill, compassion, generosity, and peace. In this way, one can be calm, alert, present, and kind. This is being mindful. As you can see, wise effort must always be active for mindfulness to fully be achieved. So it is not just being present; it is being actively and wisely engaged and responsive in the present.

The venerable Ajahn Thānissaro Bhikkhu, a highly venerated scholar and practitioner of the Theravada tradition, explains in his book *Right Mindfulness* the three necessary components that create mindfulness:

1. **Alertness:** Being attentive, awake, and present
2. **Ardency:** Being interested and passionate about the goal and mission of mindfulness
3. **Function of memory:** Keeping the goal of mindfulness, as well as the content of the present moment, in mind so one can determine an appropriate response and how to go about it

The Goal of Mindfulness

It is of utmost importance to know and uphold the goal of mindfulness. The inherent goal, Ajahn Thānissaro emphasizes, is to experience well- being, which ultimately comes through integrity and conduct that harm no one. When people are alert and ardent, they are also authentic and care about themselves and others. It's a goal of inner peace, which is what most people are looking for when they come to mindfulness: to relieve their stress and anxieties.

However, managing one's internal nervous system purely by calming oneself and having nonjudgmental awareness isn't sustainable.

Aside from wise effort to consistently sort out our mental biases and distortions, the factors before wise effort and wise mindfulness explain how to live through wisdom and integrity to maintain a peaceful nervous system. Otherwise, you can keep cleansing your mind and become peaceful but still do things that cause suffering and find yourself back at square one, anxious and stressed out. This is why mindfulness isolated from the rest of the Eightfold Path provides limited effects; one needs to complete the development of the whole path.

Four Doorways to Establish Mindfulness and Self-Awareness

Our brains are designed to work for energy efficiency. Hence, we go through our day habitually and automatically. This mechanism conserves energy and keeps us alive. Being on autopilot makes it hard to be present, attentive, alert, and focused on well-being. You may be lost in thoughts and tasks and forget to eat when you should, work long hours without a break, and make choices that cause conflict in your relationships.

So how do we override the mindlessness of autopilot mode to become mindful and self-aware? There are four ways to do so: body, feelings, mind, and dharma. We establish mindfulness by using our attention in the present moment to experience the body, our feelings, and our mental activities and by penetrating the nature of life, or being with things and situations as they are, not as we wish them to be.

Body: Our bodies are made up of parts, some of which are solid and some of which are fluid. Some are about function and movement, and others are about energy and temperature. It's all happening in the present moment. By turning inward, we can become mindful by sensing the changing conditions of the body.

For this, it is not necessary to experience all our bodily functions. Can you imagine if we could hear the pumping of blood and feel the movement of the kidneys, liver, intestines, and other organs? We wouldn't be able to attend to anything else, which is why it's all designed to be hidden from our attention. But we need something that's happening in the moment to bring our attention back to when thoughts pull us away. So we can pick an aspect of the body and try to experience it. For example, the breath can be easily felt. We can put our attention on the breath, follow its journey, and experience its impact on the body, such as the rib cage expanding and the chest rising when we inhale and the opposite happening when we exhale. We can also manipulate the flow of the breath for different purposes—for example, to help the body relax and release tightness or to help settle the mind.

Another anchor of attention can be the solid aspects of the body, sensations, or temperature in the body. To explore the solid, we can feel some muscles, such as the thighs or the arms, or feel the sensation of touch. We can explore differences in temperature in various parts of the body. This is mindfulness of the body.

Feelings: You can also become mindfully aware through experiencing your feelings in the present moment. This includes emotions, which are energies in motion, and their physical experience, called feelings. For example, you may become mindfully aware of experiencing intense emotions of anger or rage. Mentally, it's unpleasant because of the stories and reasons we attach to the experience of rage. Physically, it's unpleasant because of the powerful surge of emotional activity within. Feeling this might mean noticing heat in the face, tightness of muscles, and so on. When you become aware of the feelings in your body, something can shift when you learn not to identify with a passing emotion, as it is not you. Staying attentive and engaged, remembering the inherent goal of calmness and well-being, and bringing yourself back to it help the anger to pass or subside more easily. That's mindfulness through feelings.

Mind: The mind is its own sense and doorway to mindfulness. Any mental activity—such as images, videos, memories, fantasies, desires, to-do lists, or planning—can be a catalyst to become present in the moment. When you are lost in a story or mental activity, you are the actor, creator, and director of that story; there is no mindfulness present. You're not aware that this is just a mental activity. You're fully experiencing that scenario.

But as soon as you become aware that you're caught up in those thoughts and mental activities, you enter mindfulness. You can clearly see the content of the mind, engaged with your goal of peace and well-being, and you can discern what is going on in the moment. This is where wise view can reveal if there is suffering present and if it has a cause you should eliminate. You can become curious about how these thoughts are affecting your present-moment experience. Do they make you excited and motivated, or do they just make you sad or bored and waste your time? With mindful awareness of mental activities, you can activate wise effort to abandon the negative thoughts and change the course of your thinking.

Dharma, or nature of life: The last doorway to enter a mindful state is through investigating or recognizing the nature of life. These are life-intelligence lessons about how life works, the systems that govern us, and an objective experience of life. From the Buddha's perspective, the human experience of life has three characteristics:

1. **Dukkha, or dissatisfaction and suffering:** Humans can experience and create pain and suffering.
2. **Anicca, or impermanence:** Everything changes by cycles of beginning, changing, and transforming.
3. **Anata, or not-self:** There is no inherent self or identity in anything in life. When you look closer and see this as impersonal, your mind becomes quiet and relaxed. You are in a state of mindfulness.

This is how you enter a mindful state through penetrating the dharma, or the nature of life. It can cause something to shift in your perspective and unburden you of stressful thoughts. It might be subtle, but it can release you from some tension.

The doorways of mindfulness are all interconnected. They are parts of a process, rather than separate doors. For example, when you tune in to a sensation in the body, such as an itch, a feeling tone is associated with it that can be unpleasant and form the perception that you don't like it. Your brain forms a reaction to it. If you try to pin down only physical sensations, for example, and isolate them without their impact, the process might feel robotic, tense, and even impossible.

This happened to me one day during walking meditation during a ten-day retreat. As I tried to be present with and aware of the feelings in my body and paid attention to various inner experiences, my mind became steady and calm. After I spent a while paying attention to movements and physical sensations and feeling pleasant, unpleasant, or neutral tones, I realized the feelings weren't separate from the physical sensations. As my mind slowed down, my consciousness picked up a feeling tone and then a physical sensation and a mental activity. I couldn't pin myself to one of these experiences. They were transient, like a stream of water. Finally, I realized they were all interconnected and changing processes, rather than separate events or parts. So give these four doorways a try, but keep it light.

Next, we will talk about obstacles that block our ability to be mindful, peaceful, and happy.

MLOL 51: MINDFUL OF INNER OBSTACLES TO PEACE AND HAPPINESS

Obstacles, by nature, prevent us from flowing or progressing in life or in some aspect. There are five obstacles to happiness and peace that most people experience within themselves. These are inner hurdles we developed while growing up. Think of them as interrelated codes and glitches in our programming. Some have them at a lower level; others have them more prominently and are unable to be present and happy. These inner obstacles bias our thoughts, choices, and actions. They cause suffering.

1. **Craving**, fantasy, wanting, attachment, clinging, desire
2. **Aversion**, hate, resistance, anger, and judgment
3. **Restlessness**, high energy, fidgetiness, and impulsiveness, both mental and physical
4. **Drowsiness**, laziness, lethargy, fogginess, and disconnection

1.   **Doubt** that causes confusion and blocks progress

Almost everyone who tries to learn mindfulness and how to stay present, aware, alert, and focused through meditation encounters these obstacles. We practice mindfulness meditation to be able to see these inner obstacles for what they are and work on releasing them, because you have to first see them, then understand them, and then learn how to become free of them.

These five obstacles make it difficult to be peaceful, clear, or objective about what is going on in the moment. All our perceptions become subjective, one-sided, and deluded. They show up in our daily affairs. When left unattended, they can overshadow the moment and keep us from having effective and fulfilling interactions with others.

For example, while sitting in meditation, you might start fantasizing about (craving) your favorite food. While this is going on, you cannot concentrate; your mind is not at rest. Or you may read an email with an unexpected response from a coworker and feel agitated (aversion). This agitation may cause you to write something back that you might regret or have difficulty justifying. Aversion makes the mind reactive, unkind, and unwise. In another scenario, you may try to sleep but feel too much energy in your body or mind (restlessness) and be unable to settle down and fall asleep. You toss and turn and think and think, and you cannot become peaceful. This hinders your well-being and rest. Or you may need to take care of something important, but you don't get to it, because you feel bored, lazy, or sleepy (drowsiness). This is the opposite of restlessness. Drowsiness is low energy. It can fog the mind, making you inactive and tuned out, in meditation or in life.

With doubt, you may sit in meditation and wonder whether you're even doing it right or doubt if you can ever do this. Or you may think that may be meditation isn't effective anyway or that the teacher doesn't know what he or she is talking about. In this case, confusion, loss of enthusiasm, and lack of trust hinder you from progressing. These examples of doubt aren't the same as healthy questioning to find the answer. They hinder progress and happiness.

While experiencing any of these mental obstacles, you can get stuck and be unable to resolve an issue properly. The trick is to get to know these inner obstacles and recognize them for what they are (not-self). They are energies that are passing through you. To eliminate them, go back to MLOL 47, intelligent mental action (wise effort). This corresponds to the HSO stage 3: Development.

Understanding the five inner obstacles to happiness (craving, aversion, restlessness, drowsiness, and doubt), you can become more mindful of your daily connections and respond to life's experiences and challenges with more wisdom, happiness, ease, and appropriately. Each one of these obstacles can be overcome through penetration and the use of its own antidote. However, craving or clinging to desire
is found to be the most difficult for most people to overcome.

Next, let's go a bit deeper into why it's so difficult to give up clinging and craving or attachment, which are all desire-based and promise pleasure.

MLOL 52: MINDFUL OF THE PLEASURE TRICK, THE SELFISH GENE

Desire is the main obstacle that prevents us from peace and happiness. It is the mother of them all. We usually think of pleasure as something that comes from fulfilling our desires. We desire to eat something delicious; to enjoy entertainment; to have love, sex, fame, wealth, or status; or to wear an amazing outfit. This desire is designed with the mechanism to trick us pursue with the promise of pleasure. We become deluded to believe, *If I get what I want, I will get pleasure out of it.* This is not untrue, but the trick is that having had such pleasure or fallen for the promise of it, our minds come to believe we can reproduce it in the same amount and the same intensity or, even better, have it forever. We cling to it. Another mechanism of pleasure and craving for anything is that once desire attaches itself to that thing, it creates an uncomfortable feeling in us to push us to fulfill it. This discomfort can come in degrees, and when it is intense, the drive to get what we want can be overwhelming.

This drive can make us feel restless, agitated, impatient, and off-balance. It does so to motivate us to seek contentment (peace) by fulfilling the object of our desire. We believe that it will, and we pursue it, or we go through painful experiences to deny ourselves. It's an added layer of clinging to those thoughts, which only results in unhappiness, fear, worry, and irrational, harmful behavior. Throughout the history of humanity, wars have been fought to fulfill human desires. Think about it: Those who run a nation can cling to the thought that they must have such-and-such land and that only when they have it and have enough power, or whatever it is that owning such lands provides for them, can they be content. With their innate truth bias, they believe this theory, and their discomfort due to clinging to this notion can rise to the point of intolerance. Nothing anyone might suggest to deter them from killing and invading will work.

But what fuels pleasure so powerfully that it can trick the most earnest of us?

The Selfish Gene

In my research to understand more about clinging and the remedy to it, I stumbled on the evolutionary theory of the selfish gene, which gave me some insight into where the power behind desire comes from. In *The Selfish Gene*, Richard Dawkins discusses evolution from a gene-centered perspective, as opposed to focusing on how populations' actions and environments contributed to evolution. Selfishness in genes means that they push us in any way they can to keep their own kind alive. The theory is that the more people have the same genes, the better the chances of collaboration and continuation.

In the case of pleasure aimed at ensuring the survival of the species, the selfish gene is what controls our drive for reproduction — which can take over our perceptions, choices, and actions. Nature created an unwavering goal encoded in that selfish gene: ensuring there will always be enough sexual and reproductive activity among members of any species to create the next generation. Toward this goal, nature rewards us with substantial pleasure and induces agitation and impatience to keep us seeking. This powerful force overcomes people's willpower, causing many broken vows, divorces, and other heartaches and leading to all kinds of related costs for families and societies.

As Dawkins claims, genes are immortal, and the information encoded in them is forever. There is no changing it by mere resistance or will power. Until we really understand how nature works and become able to neutralize the drives in our minds that negatively influence our choices and actions, it'll be difficult to find happiness, no matter what rules and agreements societies create.

Let's look at monogamy, for example, as Dawkins explains the evolution behind it. When mothers were left caring for too many offspring alone, and to combat the pain and suffering that come from acting freely to fulfill sexual desire, humans created rules and emotional conditions: religious doctrines that define sin, shame, monogamy, and abstinence. To create stability in the community and help identify responsibility and care for children came marriage, including consequences for breaking marital vows.

Like the brain, the selfish gene is not coded for wisdom or to consider these societal rules or fear the consequences. It doesn't even consider reproductive limitations or that a person who is seventy years old, for example, cannot have or easily care for an offspring. It has two narcissistic (from the human perspective) goals: self-preservation and proliferation of its species. To offset the gene's superpower of getting us to hurt ourselves or others, we rely on the heart, specifically on romantic love and making commitment.

Studies about love indicate that falling in love is associated with keeping the immune system healthy and that romantic love is also designed by nature (our genes) to ensure couples stay together and care for offspring until those offsprings can have their own. American psychologist Robert Sternberg explains that romantic love includes three components that must be experienced consistently and with enough strength to be effective:

1. **Intimacy:** Feelings of closeness, connectedness, and bondedness
2. **Passion:** The drive and actions that lead to romance, physical attraction, and sexual consummation

3. **Commitment:** The decision that one loves another and will maintain that love

Though this can vary across cultures and genders, when one of these three components loses strength or is lacking, the relationship suffers. From the selfish gene's perspective, passion cannot be the one to go missing in a relationship. Without it, often, people end up separating or breaking their vows, or if they stay, they find themselves unfulfilled. So, it keeps producing the desire for passionate exchanges.

Moreover, my theory is that the selfish gene's pleasure trick to create desire and clinging expands beyond ensuring the continuity of the species. After all, our survival doesn't end by our being born; we must also achieve social realities, which include relationship and financial security, advancement, and achievement. When shared by billions of people, the internal force to get what one wants creates an unbeatable delusion that we can fulfill all our desires and live forever. The selfish gene could very well be the most powerful invisible force behind innovation and progress. Unfortunately, the quest to fulfill desire has caused all sorts of problems for humans and the planet. So no judgment here—it is not easy to be human. My hope is that raising awareness about primary conditions that may affect our judgment and conduct can give humanity more agency to live wisely and be less troubled by expectations that create suffering.

I encourage you to reflect on the power behind truth and confirmation biases and how you may be run by this dominating selfish gene, which cares about nothing except for its own proliferation at any cost. By developing self-awareness, mindfulness, and heart intelligence, you can relieve the tension around wanting and let go of some of the painful habits of the desirous mind, which can cause dire consequences.

To understand and experience an ultimate peacefulness, we'll explore the last fold in the Buddha's Noble Eightfold Path.

MLDL 53: THE ULTIMATE PEACEFULNESS (WISE CONCENTRATION)

It's not a coincidence that wise concentration, or the ultimate peacefulness, is the last fold, or factor, of the Noble Eightfold Path. You can think of it as the result of having developed all the other folds in the path. Having cultivated the other folds and resolved the causes of suffering, the mind becomes steady, calm, peaceful, and free from the inner obstacles that cause stress and unhappiness. In the absence of stress and unhappiness, there is nothing but peace and contentment. That is the goal of the path: not to pursue happiness but to eliminate what prevents it.

Concentration is usually thought of as single-pointed, focused attention. Wise concentration has more to do with one's overall feeling of peace and comfort. The mind is bright, and without the conditions that make it unhappy, it can easily focus on an object of choice and remain attentive to it. The body too is comfortable, at ease, and settled. This feeling of ease and wakefulness can be experienced in meditation or during daily activities.

With wise concentration, one does not become agitated by difficult people or difficult situations. This doesn't mean being cold, tuning out, or not caring; on the contrary, one is filled with awareness, compassion, and peaceful wisdom. This peacefulness can be experienced momentarily or developed into a constant stream of experience. There are various degrees of absorption and steadiness one can acquire through deeper levels of meditation and contemplation practices. As always, having wise guidance and models we can learn from is of utmost value.

There are also ninth and tenth folds, which are not mentioned much. I never ran into them or heard any teachings on my journey of cultivating the Four Noble Truths, until I sat with my teacher Ajahn Pasanno to verify the Buddhist lessons I've brought to you in this book. I was shocked when I heard there were ninth and tenth folds. I guess lessons come to us when we are ready for them. The ninth fold is the recognition that one has accomplished the eightfold path and is enjoying the fruits of it in a great degree and consistently, not circumstantially. The tenth fold is about continuing to practice and develop, going even deeper, and maintaining a reliable and consistent sense of peace and joy. So I wish for you, my dear reader, to successfully accomplish the Four Noble Truths and the Noble Eightfold Path and experience a high level of peace and happiness.

As a part of decoding, healing and reprogramming your life, the next and final chapter in this book offers other necessary inner skills that can help to heal the emotional wounds that prevent you from accomplishing Mindful Life Optimization.

CHAPTER 21

HEALING OUR WOUNDS

This chapter covers inner resources that help to heal our wounds and ways to prevent future perception-based traumas and maintain emotional well-being.

DOMAIN III:
HUMAN EXPERIENCE, CONDUCT, AND HAPPINESS
HEALING OUR WOUNDS

MLOL 54 Mindful of the Vulnerable Self (Anger Management)

MLOL 55 Mindful Emotions Strengthen the Immune System

MLOL 56 Mindfully Healing Perception-Based Traumas

MLOL 57 Mindfully Minimizing Hurt Feelings

MOL 58 Optimizing the Effects of Healthy Boundaries

MLOL 59 Mindfully Resolving the Pain of Grief and Loss

MLOL 60 Mindful Life Optimization Make It a Human Right

Figure 18

Copyright by Dr. Manijeh Motaghy

MLOL 54: MINDFUL OF THE VULNERABLE SELF (ANGER MANAGEMENT)

We've been learning about self-awareness, self-care, self-love, and self- compassion. But it's sometimes hard to know whom we're loving, caring, and compassionate toward. This can be experienced with anger or rage. Sometimes we may not be able to control our emotions — for example, having angry outbursts, even when we know it's not logical or beneficial. There may be different reasons for this. One of the less obvious reasons is our neglect of ourselves and our own cries for attention. When we don't pay attention to that inner voice — the one who becomes (or has been) threatened by others or by our own thoughts, choices, and actions — rage can build up.

Rage is not always about protesting a situation outside us. It can also be the voice of the vulnerable self, screaming for our attention, care, and love. I've seen this with clients who were logical and knew that their rage was out of proportion but still couldn't calm themselves down. For example, Jeff (name changed) expressed that he couldn't get over his rage at an unhoused man who had scraped his car with a grocery cart filled with his possessions. Jeff drove beside the man, who was pushing his cart, and screamed at him to turn around and look at the car to see what he had done. Jeff was horror-struck at himself and heartbroken for the man and his situation, yet he couldn't stop shouting to get the man's attention. It was astonishing to him that even days later, he discussed this situation with wrath. He couldn't understand why he couldn't just let it go.

As Jeff described the incident, I read something deeper in his words — the words of a vulnerable person within him who felt helpless against the madman (himself). That was when I had him stop and reflect. I saw two sources of anger. One was the grown-up, confident Jeff; the other was the meek, vulnerable Jeff. We recounted the incident, which made him irritated and snap. If he'd recognized that pursuing and threatening the man was most likely reckless and fruitless, Jeff could have quickly left the scene to eliminate further hardship for all parties involved. But he didn't. That was when the secondary anger showed up, his vulnerable self. We all have vulnerable selves we should pay attention to and care for. The ongoing anger that wouldn't let go was the voice of the vulnerable Jeff to get his attention.

In this scenario, it's as if a five-year-old is sitting next to him in the car and witnessing the grown-up Jeff recklessly pursuing this disheveled person and jeopardizing both their safeties. Little Jeff feels frightened and helpless, pleading, "Dad, please stop. I'm scared," but the grown-up Jeff carries on.

Someone has to wake the grown-up Jeff to see that what he's doing is not wise. The continued rage is not against the unhoused man but against the ego within himself, who ignores rational fear at that moment of vulnerability. If he stopped and felt the fear of the potential additional danger, his ego would have to admit its wrongness, and it's not willing to do that. So little Jeff screams louder to make the big Jeff feel that fear and learn from the results of those actions. Once Jeff opens to himself compassionately, he can truly hear his vulnerable self, and the compassionate, warm, and understanding heart within can hold his little vulnerable self with kindness and nonjudgment.

As Jeff gave this practice a try, he was able to let go of the situation, and the rage subsided. In these cases, often, with a little love, kindness, and assurance to oneself, the anger fades away. Self-love and attentiveness and caring for one's fears are great ways to manage rage.

MLOL 55: MINDFUL EMOTIONS STRENGTHEN THE IMMUNE SYSTEM

By keeping our emotional experiences and expressions healthy and balanced, we not only enjoy happy lives but also can benefit from stronger immune systems and enjoy long lives. As I explained in chapter 16, MLOL 28, our brains produce emotions to alert us to balance our bodies' budgets. Some of these emotional experiences are cries for help or the need to be seen and heard by others. These are our emotional budgets, which are usually balanced through others' affection and attention and by having opportunities and the ability to be authentic about those emotions. For example, when grief over the loss of my son used to hit me hard, I'd call a person who could handle it and would cry to that person as hard as I could. Doing that calmed me down completely. It's because someone else witnessed my pain. That pain is too much for anyone to feel it alone. Likewise, when I feel joy from the smallest encounter, I like to share it with someone close to me. When I do that, I feel a deeper bond with that person. Sharing our joys and sorrows with another person balance sour emotional budget.

As it turns out, emotional expression plays a key role in our health and well-being. Ignoring, suppressing, or neglecting our emotions can lead to weakening of the immune system. Trauma expert Dr. Gabor Maté talks about a study of two thousand married women in the United States over a ten-year period, which found that women who were unhappily married, were programmed not to say no, and did not express their emotions had mortality rates four times higher than those of women who were unhappy in their marriages but said no and expressed their emotions. The issue Maté underlines isn't unhappiness; rather, the issue is not being authentic and not expressing one's emotions (good or bad), which suppresses the immune system. Self-expression is a way of feeling free to be as we are.

In his book "When the Body Says No: Understanding the Stress- Disease Connection," Maté explains how stress and repressed emotions can contribute to the development of chronic illnesses, such as multiple sclerosis, rheumatoid arthritis, and breast cancer. He urges medical professionals to consider conditions that relate to the social aspects of a person's life in order to understand the causes of illnesses and formulate the best treatments. You may think, *Are those who are dramatic and overwhelm others by expressing their feelings healthier than others? It sounds a bit selfish.* No. In fact, overexpression can become stressful to the body. The key is balance.

Balancing Emotional Expression

As seen in stage three of the SMADE stuck model, our emotional meanings and expressions become adaptations and habitual. In the stuck model, we either overly express negative emotions or do not express them at all. Not saying no when we need to or harshly reacting to life challenges can result in our losing our jobs, our marriages, or other things that matter to us. Likewise, our not expressing our emotions makes our vulnerable selves feel ignored, unimportant, and helpless. Repressed emotions silence the inner voice, which may show up as rage, dissociation, self-isolation, self-inflicting, depression, high anxiety, and early death. The more we ignore this vulnerable inner voice, the worse it is for the immune system. I taught about emotions in the UCLA Mindful MAPs 1 course. Through a mindfulness approach, I explained that neither suppressing nor overly expressing emotions is conducive to one's health and well-being. Rather, expressing emotions and needs calmly, in a timely manner, and effectively can help the immune system to function as it should.

Other studies have shown that in the same way negative emotions are related to higher inflammatory and lower antiviral gene expression, positive emotions are associated with lower inflammatory and higher antiviral gene expression. In other words, engaging in negativity increases inflammation in the body, and experiencing positive emotions reduces it.

By mindfully observing persisting negative emotions—for example, anger—you may realize you need attention, love, connection, and care; humor; or rest so that you can feel peaceful and happy. Take some time to go inward and reflect on yourself as a little child you're responsible for. As the grown-up you, you can seek out tools, such as meditation, to bring you to a state of balance and objectivity. You will also benefit from developing MLOL 44, HQ in communication (wise speech), to help you express your emotions as needed objectively, with kindness toward yourself and others. This will improve your overall mental health and help to reduce inflammation in your body.

MLOL 56: MINDFULLY HEALING PERCEPTION-BASED TRAUMAS

One of the most important MLOLs in this book is knowing how to reframe past experiences to heal their trauma effects. The same skill—properly framing present-moment experiences with objectivity and warm heartedness—can prevent future traumas. This is one of my most potent discoveries and personal accomplishments. It has enabled me heal from past traumas; to live fully and express what I need wisely and compassionately.

In chapter 2, I spoke of trauma as one cause of becoming stuck in unhappiness. In some cases, what makes an event traumatic is our interpretation. Knowing what I know about inherent biases — such as truth and confirmation biases, which make us believe that what we think is true — I am willing to bet that if we looked everywhere on this planet to find a human who has never suffered from a perception-based traumatic experience, we probably wouldn't find one. Although trauma is usually associated with past events and experiences, unfortunately, it's not limited to the past — we can be traumatized at any time, now and in the future. Fortunately, we can not only heal our past traumas but also prevent future traumas. Hence, this is an important subject for training.

Unresolved traumas tend to keep people locked in reactivity to or avoiding what might resemble the painful events they experienced. I am not a clinical psychologist or an expert in trauma work, but I have gained personal insight into a good understanding of trauma. Dr. Maté, the world-renowned psychologist I've mentioned before, classifies traumas according to two types: little-t trauma and big-T Trauma. Little-t trauma is caused by not receiving the care and attention children need. Big-T Trauma is caused by big stuff, such as wars, abuse, and other painful major events.

What I found fascinating about Maté's characterization of trauma and Trauma is that our internal experiences of an event — our unique perceptions and interpretations — are what cause us pain and suffering. So it's not necessarily the event itself but our relationship to it. Throughout my journey of healing and developing inner resources, I organically saw and understood Maté's perception-based traumas before I even read his perspective. This first-hand insight was hugely important in resolving much of my past traumas.

The Three Factors in Healing Perception-Based Traumas

There were three factors in my healing and recovery from traumatic events. First, developing wise view allowed me to skillfully reframe traumatic past events (for example, the experience with my mother in the gynecologist's office when I was thirteen and others related to my relationship with my mother). Second, optimizing my HQ and my love and compassion for myself and others allowed me to be the warm, understanding, and present mother for myself that I was seeking in every relationship but couldn't find. Third, by developing wise effort and wise mindfulness, I learned to manage my internal reactions to triggers by protecting my mind from creating horror stories about an event.

Most significantly, these inner resources have allowed me to recode and redesign several aspects of my programming that were wired through those traumatic experiences and resulted in, for example, a lack of self-worth. The new programming has made me my own best friend and freed me from being stuck in wanting, expecting, and suffering. The transformation and optimization have empowered me to protect myself from becoming traumatized in any given present moment.

How To Prevent Experiencing Trauma

Here is an example of how I've done this (preventing trauma in the present moment). One afternoon, I was hiking upward on a narrow, uneven path near my home, when I heard a dog and its owner coming from below. At first, I didn't pay much attention, trusting the owner had the dog on a leash and under control. The dog, a German shepherd, restlessly barked as they moved up toward me. At that point, the pathway became pretty narrow, about four feet wide. On my right were bushy rocks and hillside, and on the other side were bushy rocks and a downhill drop. So I was kind of stuck and just kept moving forward.

There was no one on the path except for me and the old man and his dog. As they got closer, the dog's aggression intensified; it began barking and growling and charged toward me. It was so strong and animated that it pulled its owner, and he tripped, still hanging on to the leash. To protect myself from the dog's jaws, I started running around in circles. The road was uneven and hard to manage, and the man was struggling to hold the dog back. It was like a wolf, barely an inch away from my thighs at all times, determined to get to me. It became more and more triggered and barked louder and more viciously. I thought for sure it was going to bite me. Finally, I realized that nothing either of us did helped.

With that realization, I turned inward and calmed my breath. I stopped moving around, folded my arms over my chest, stood on one side, and looked down. I breathed slowly and calmly and stayed still. That pause helped me realize the dog must have been as scared as I was, if not more. I began sending thoughts of goodwill to the dog and its owner: *May you be calm. May you feel safe. May you be happy and at ease.* I repeated this in my mind as I tuned out the dog's thunderous noise, its owner's shouting, and the physical threat: *May you be calm. May you feel safe. May you be happy and at ease.*

I felt an energy shifting. Still barking, the dog slowly stepped back, moving a couple of inches away from me—enough for its owner to drop his entire body onto the dog and hold it down.

I noticed how calm I was. The old man was almost having a heart attack. He was shaking and stuttering. I tried to calm him down, but he couldn't hear me. I slowly knelt so he could see my eyes and hear my words: "Please don't worry; nothing has happened. It's fine. I'm not hurt. Nothing has happened."

The poor man was worried I would sue him. Drowning in guilt for what could have happened, in a plea for my understanding, he explained that the German shepherd was a formerly abused rescue dog, and he had taken her out to reintroduce her to nature and socialize her. I reassured him that I was fine and would not press any charges. As he took her down the path, I continued my hike. I can say with confidence that becoming present and mindful with goodwill in my heart at that moment prevented a scary situation from escalating— and from becoming long-term trauma in my brain to trigger fear and anxiety whenever I saw a dog.

Since then, I've had two other unpleasant encounters with dogs. Another German shepherd, which belonged to one of my best friends, did bite me unexpectedly. My friend explained that she had just had puppies, was overly sensitive, and had snapped at me out of protectiveness when I got up to go to the bathroom. I was hurt physically but not so much emotionally. I was able to remain calm and understanding.

My third encounter was with an even more ginormous dog—I had never seen one that big. I think he was an English mastiff or something like that. I found out after that he was the neighbors' worker's dog. One day this giant snuck up on me from behind on my front porch. You have to understand—I'm a five-foot-two, petite woman, and this dog was like a bulldozer. Or at least he seemed like it to me. I screamed several times as loudly as I could, frankly because I was scared to death, though also to scare him off. His owner eventually got him and came over to apologize and explain that he was friendly and harmless. Well, they all bark. As I reflected on the situation afterward, I felt compassion toward the dog for my having screamed at him so loudly. I thought that to make up for it and to keep the experience from being recorded in my brain as a traumatic event, I should make friends with the dog, which I did. I also suggested to his owner that whenever he brought the dog into a new neighborhood for a long period, he might take the initiative to introduce him to the neighbors.

Given that there is a direct correlation between dramatizing an experience and long-lasting trauma, mental hygiene practices are necessary to keep the nervous system calm so that the mind can remain objective. This allows us to find solutions more effectively and keep love and kindness alive in our hearts.

Next, let's look at how we can manage our perception so minimize hurt feelings.

MLOL 57: MINDFULLY MINIMIZING HURT FEELINGS

Misinterpretations are common, as learned from the second stage of the SMADE stuck model. When we don't have enough information, don't understand something, or are biased, we fill in the blanks with our own associations and come up with a conclusion. This is often the most prevalent issue for couples I work with. Both sides complain that the other doesn't get them or that they misunderstand or assume something that isn't true. Another important need and skill is to be able to hear others fully to understand their intentions and the core of their message.

Mindful Listening Exercise

I often have everyone who comes to me, whether in a private session or at a retreat or workshop, do an exercise to practice mindful listening. It's about being present and aware of the other; listening with interest, curiosity, and a kind attitude; and not tuning out to think up one's own responses. This is NOT EASY for most who don't have this training, but when developed it is really effective.

For the exercise, I ask two people in a workshop or a private setting to sit across from each other and take turns asking a question I have prepared. I tell them to think of the person sitting across from them as the most important person in their lives. For these moments, I emphasize the fact that no one else is in front of them but their partner: "This is the person who matters the most in your life, until the next person shows up." This is to shift their minds from providing divided attention to giving their attention openly and generously and being fully present. I also give instructions on grounding themselves in their bodies, letting go of their thoughts, and not interrupting their partner for a short time, until I ring the bell, when they switch roles. The question I have them ask their partner is "What brings you joy?" The whole thing takes about four and a half minutes, and I observe them as they go through the exercise.

During debrief, I ask them how listening with curiosity and care (mindfully) felt. I ask how it felt for the speaker to be listened to as the most important person in his or her partner's life. Their responses always include a profound sense of feeling loved and cared for, peacefulness, and oneness—and most of these people have just met in these classes for the first time. I then give them time to ask their partner any follow-up questions they have. This is to let them practice asking questions that are pertinent to their interests and connection and clarify misunderstandings. Try it for yourself. See what effects you'll experience.

Mindful Questioning

Most people who haven't learned how to listen intently are also not skilled at asking relevant questions to avoid misinterpretations. It's important for each of us to learn to ask clarifying questions and to do so without judgment or implications. The point is to make sure we are clear about what others are thinking and the purpose of their actions before concluding that what we surmise is absolutely true. For example, before asking a clarifying question, I usually observe how I feel about what someone has done or said that made me feel uncomfortable or what I said or did that made another person uncomfortable. I try to breathe and neutralize those feelings so I can have compassion and openness. Knowing that it's not easy to be human, I try to understand where others are coming from. This does not mean I keep relationships that are toxic or harmful to me. But I will not hate the other person for it, as hating or resenting will only disturb me.

In case of trauma and how to prevent it, asking clarifying questions can do wonders. Trauma pains and confusion don't disappear by being ignored and numbed. Even worse, they don't get resolved if we cling to the story that supposedly explains them.

For example, my traumatic experience at the gynecologist's office could have easily been prevented had I stopped to ask questions or had my mother been wise or skilled enough to explain what she was trying to accomplish and to treat me with kindness and friendliness rather than coldness. The oddest thing about that experience was that she was given a perfect negative result. My purity and integrity were intact, and she didn't even bother to tell me. I just didn't exist. That was the real trauma.

In chapter 1, we looked at how we don't have many independent choices in life, due to being programmed by culture, religion, peer pressure, and other conditions. My mother certainly didn't have a choice. She was a product of her culture, which she had courageously defied by even taking me for examination. Any discussion about sex and sexual body parts was taboo. It was better just to ignore those topics and carry on.

251

That's why understanding trauma and triggers is particularly important for coaches and group facilitators who work with people to improve their lives. This allows us to become more sensitive and better equipped to remedy clients' or group participants' discomfort and help them move through it. Learning to pose questions to clarify prevents our minds from believing all our perceptions and thoughts as facts.

Next, we'll look at how to make your boundaries more effective.

MLDL 58: MINDFULLY OPTIMIZING THE EFFECTS OF PERSONAL BOUNDARIES

In Western societies, the concept of setting emotional and psychological boundaries became popular in the 1980s and 1990s as a way to prevent oneself from being hurt, taken advantage of, or manipulated. These boundaries include saying no to what makes you uncomfortable or to unfair expectations.

Boundaries help us to function in life and relationships without feeling overwhelmed or run by others. They're meant to allow you to distinguish yourself from others and to feel whole and safe. A simple example is asking others to knock on your bedroom door before entering or not to share something that's private to you. Other boundaries are not as clear or simple. They also can be disrespected and broken. It happens in families and homes more than we know. You may have experienced a time when someone didn't respect a boundary you set or did something you asked him or her not to. The violation results in tension, irritation, and disharmony in the relationship.

As with everything else, we have to learn how to create boundaries, how to communicate them, and how to be fine with them. When created clearly and thoughtfully, boundaries can work well. But when they are not clear or strong, they can be broken. They can sometimes be interpreted more as personal requests. People may not recognize them, because they are subjective lines drawn by the one who sets them. People commonly believe that they are entitled to create boundaries and impose them whether others agree or not. This, however, is not always effective.

When boundaries are held rigidly and without agreement, people can experience resistance and end up ignoring the boundaries or feel rejected and rebel against the boundary setter. They may also lack the inner ability to respect them. It's just another way people get stuck in tumultuous relationships. A better way is to create authentic agreements.

Authentic Agreements

Setting boundaries through authentic agreements can resolve some of the issues with boundaries being broken. When a client complains that someone doesn't respect his or her boundaries, I explain the limitations of the concept of boundaries and why they don't work. For example, Alabina (name changed), a young woman with long-term issues with her mother about feeling judged and not accepted, announced to her siblings that when she was in town, she didn't want to see her mother. Her siblings, who didn't have the same relationship with their mother, had a difficult time in abiding by Alabina's request. They invited the mother to their parties when she was in town. Alabina then felt not only anxious about seeing her mother but also deeply disappointed that her siblings didn't understand her pain or respect her boundaries.

In working with her therapist, Alabina had learned that by setting some boundaries with her mother and her family, she could regain control of her space and emotional safety and exercise her right not to be subjected to irritating comments from her mother. Great! Except holding onto those boundaries did not solve the issues—it made things worse by making everyone uncomfortable. The mother felt rejected and reacted even more dramatically, which Alabina did not want.

To help her understand why her boundaries were not respected and to give her a more effective and holistic option, I had Alabina think of the boundaries of her house. I discussed how the walls around our houses are boundaries to keep us safe from intruders and other harmful elements. We have walls so we can call our space ours and do as we wish without having to explain anything to others. Those who are outside these walls are deemed strangers, and they are not allowed in unless we invite them and open the door to them. Similarly, psychological boundaries can relay the same message. The message is "This is the line I am drawing between you and me, and you must stay outside it." This might make the recipient of such boundaries feel like a stranger or an outsider and feel rejected, especially a mother. In other words, we have to take into account the more fundamental impact on the recipients of the boundary to understand why they resist or break it.

A boundary that is interpreted as "You are not accepted, so stay out" can produce ambiguity or fear that the door may never open and that they will never be part of the inner circle, which is difficult for families and close relationships to cope with. Hence, the boundary itself becomes a separate problem one has to resolve. Here you can see how the natural patterns in cause and effect and intentionality govern the outcomes.

An effective way to reduce the chance of boundaries being broken is to create them through authentic agreements between the parties.

Four Stages of Creating Boundaries through Authentic Agreements

The four stages of creating authentic agreements, in my experience, are much more effective in setting boundaries, at least with those who have the mental capacity to understand and keep them. These agreements would benefit from continual refinement, and in the long run, all sides grow in understanding and honoring others' wishes, which leads to more harmonious and fulfilling relationships. With the mindful listening and questioning I described above, you can use these four stages to create authentic agreements without judging the other, hence creating connection and understanding.

1. **Authentically Expressing Perceptions and Feelings**
   Here we practice the concept and quality of authenticity. With authenticity, people can state what they feel and what they need but also make an effort to gain others' understanding and even compassion. With understanding and compassion, both or all parties can discuss behavior possibilities and come to an agreement. Let's take Alabina's case. To help reduce or end her

mother's criticisms, which was what she wanted to begin with, I suggested that Alabina express her thoughts and emotions to her mother, using words and statements that would not make her mother feel attacked and criticized. That way, her mother could be more open and receptive.

For example, Alabina could say, "Mom, I'd love to have dinner with you and spend a few hours with all of us together. I am resisting that idea because I think you will most likely say something that makes me feel less than or ashamed. That is really painful for me, and I'm trying to protect myself by not accepting your invitation to dinner with the family. So what do you think? Will you be saying things that might jab me or belittle me? For example, in regard to my kids, can you be conscious and try not to teach me something that makes me feel I'm not a good mother?"

In this scenario, chances are, the mother would plead that she's never done that, loves her, only wants her children to be happy, and so on.

2. **Creating Understanding and Agreement**
   In response, instead of arguing and trying to prove her mother wrong, which would go nowhere and dig deeper into the same hostile and unhappy place, Alabina could acknowledge her mother and say, "Well, in that case, will you be able to notice your words before saying them to me and refrain from saying anything blaming or judgmental? Can you pay attention and try?" The mother likely would say yes, wanting her daughter's approval.

3. **Clearly Stating the Benefits for All Parties Involved** and preventing to be ghosted or going no-contact as it's become customary these days to deal with an unpleasant relationships.

4. Here Alabina could soften and express the benefits of feeling safe in her mother's presence—for example, that the family could enjoy one another peacefully—and her mother could enjoy her gatherings with all her children and grandchildren present. There would be more love and respect for everyone to benefit from.

5. **Agreeing on a Signal**

Because this new behavior or boundary is not automatic yet and could be broken unconsciously, the next step would be to agree on a signal. When the mother habitually or purposely made a negative comment, Alabina could use the signal to bring it to her attention without making a scene in front of others. The signal could be something simple, such as drinking a glass of water and raising it toward her mom as an agreed-upon message that she was out of line. This example is clever because drinking water can cool down the nervous system and calm emotional reactivity. It may actually reduce the effects of being triggered by previous assumptions and traumas!

These four stages may not occur in order, as we are dealing with emotions and triggers that can flood the mind and derail the intention to be peaceful and communicate authentically. You may, for example, jump back to reiterate the agreement and forget the signal. It's fine. These things need to become programmed in you and the person you're setting authentic agreements with. Be patient with both yourself and others, and be willing to get imperfect results. As you stay with it, these qualities and skills improve, and so do your relationships.

MLOL 59: MINDFULLY RESOLVING THE PAIN OF GRIEF AND LOSS

Grief is deeply personal. Each of us reacts to loss differently, and the further we are from the nature of life, the more we suffer from losing people and things we own. Generally, when we realize that our desires for safety, certainty, and ownership will eventually be unfulfilled, we can learn to let go of our preconceived notions that life should be a certain way, with certain people, or for a certain amount of time. By penetrating the insight that all events are in the flow of change, we experience a joyful freedom. Of course, it is easier said than done.

The grief of losing a loved one through death or separation can overwhelm the mind as well as the body and heart. It can affect the whole being at a cellular level. Grief can lock us in a dark prison of sadness, hopelessness, and loneliness. Being in that state disconnects us from our own hearts and from others present in our lives. It can make it hard to see the key to freedom from the suffering which is laid right in front of us.

Not seeing the key to freedom, people try to escape in many ways, some of which are conducive to more imprisonment, such as consuming drugs or alcohol, raging, avoiding facing those feelings or clinging to something or someone for relief. These ways only create the illusion of relief from the pain. I have gone through many losses, including by death and by relationship separation, most of which have been painful, some much more than others. I've found that the best way to find relief from grief is by mindfully experiencing the waves of suffering as the shadows of memories pass through my mind and break my heart over and over. I've learned to be with my own suffering with a present and kind heart.

The intelligent heart with all those great qualities reduces the anguish of losing someone and having no possibility of rejoining him or her in this life. It can help us to see how our minds create more of that suffering and throw us back into the darkness, as I experienced each time. The compassionate heart is the fierce hero within that, if you let it, will rebel against more suffering, as mine did for me. It will say, "No, I will not suffer anymore. I will find a way to enjoy life."

Mine was no ordinary loss. It was a pain that every fiber of my being had to endure, as if my brain had lost a part of itself. My eyes, my eyelashes, and every bone and organ in my body had lost a part of themselves. The pain of losing my son was so powerful that I felt flashes of insanity move through my brain. I fainted every day for thirty-five days in a row, as my brain could not handle the tsunamis of emotions that shattered my heart, body, mind, soul, and life. If I compared this grief to having never-ending COVID-19 symptoms and feeling near death, it would understate the pain his death caused and how dramatically it affected my being. Day after day, I felt lost, drowned in dark emotions, while having to tend to life's duties. Sometimes, while I was driving around, getting tasks done, grief would hit me so hard that for fear of doing something dangerous, I'd call a friend or family member, sobbing for help. They'd be afraid for my life and plead for me

257

to stop, but they would realize there was no stopping the hurricanes of tears. So they'd listen, cry with me, and try to calm me down.

Slowly, I realized there was nothing anyone could do to bring him back. So what was the point of suffering? Just now, writing this, I felt a deep sorrow, and tears flowed. I took a breath and allowed myself to feel the sorrow, realizing again that loss is a natural condition. When I protest it, I lose every time. This inner resilient resource is the result of developing all three qualities of wisdom, heart intelligence, and peacefulness in balance, which I explained in chapter 17, MLOL 34.

Through an authentic look at cause and effect, I gained the insight that hanging on to the wrong view of life can lead to tremendous suffering and that adjusting my view to the realities of life diminishes my suffering. When I think of the person who came into this world through my body as my son who passed away, unbearable grief takes over. My entire being feels the loss and obligation to suffer. But when I think of him as nature and belonging to nature—as a collection of the same elements that exist in everything, without that particular human-made identity—I can see him present in a flower, in a rock at the bottom of the river, In a tree standing tall, in the moon, and in the energy of the sun. He is everywhere, within me and around me. He, like anything else, cannot belong to me, as none of us belong to anyone. With this realistic view, there is nothing to suffer for. I didn't own him, so I didn't lose him either. All that's left is to feel joy and togetherness with all of life, which includes him. There actually is no him or me, just nature. This perspective is not only philosophical but also practical and truthful. You can use the second stage of Human Software Optimization from chapter 7 to verify this MLOL for yourself.

Even with that wise way of thinking, emotional pain hits, so having the inner resources to deal with it is paramount. That's when the second quality of HQ, specifically self-compassion, can help to sustain this truth and pull us out of the darkness. Like a good navigator in the sea, I learned to avoid thoughts, stories, and memories that could intensify the waves of grief and tear me apart in an instant. Through developing the HQ of peacefulness, I could remain calm and observe the passing of all these experiences. I became skilled in protecting my mind so I wouldn't exacerbate the storms of grief. As I calmed my mind and engaged my heart, those pains gradually subsided. This grief ultimately transformed my heart into knowing a deeper compassion for the pain of all beings.

This transformation and freedom from suffering are the fruits of all my practice efforts during all those years: attending silent retreats, listening to wisdom teachings about how life works, practicing meditation to clear my mind of any story it conjures up, and developing my heart of goodwill and compassion for all living beings (including myself). With mindful awareness and the desire to experience life authentically, I could see the truth and the flow of life: My child's body had to dissolve like those of all other humans before and after us, just as all other particles in the universe move through their own cycles. I saw that death and loss are impersonal events—part of the grand scheme of nature that keeps the wheels of life turning.

Even with this acceptance, from time to time, the storm hits, usually around his birthday and his passing day. So I go with it; I allow those emotions to emerge and pass. I have this one life to live—the current life I know of, and the most loyal friend we can count on is change. It is not personal. But it is your right to know what to do with grief. Please give it a try; work on those qualities to see their immense benefits in your life.

MLOL 60: MAKING MINDFUL LIFE OPTIMIZATION A HUMAN RIGHT

After reviewing a draft of this book, young scientist and human rights speaker Vincent McNeeley said, "These MLOLs should be a human right." I loved his insight. It's been what I had been rooting for and making these fundamental skills our human rights is exactly right. Everyone should have the right to grow up and live without traumas and not have to endure so much agony and unhappiness—the right to know what to do with intense emotions and painful experiences; the human right to understand and develop in these fundamental truths and enjoy life with inner qualities and skills that can help in navigating the human realm and its complexities with ease and fulfillment.

Recently, I've come to realize that the human realm is one of the most magnificent and mysterious realms of all, one that even we humans can't fully figure out.

Given that nature left the development of our kind to our kind, we have a responsibility to reduce human suffering by passing these lessons to the next generations. In fact, being fully developed with mindful life intelligence should be recognized as a natural human right. Passing on such MLOLs might be one of the greatest contributions to humanity, giving our future generations tools to maintain well-being and happiness and to keep our natural systems effective, efficient, abundant, and supportive of life on our planet. Passing these MLOLs would also support organizations, scientists, and others to ensure a regenerative and dependable lifeline for the future.

Keeping MLOLs Optimized

As you decode, recode, and reprogram your own life template and optimize your inner resources, you may find better ways of practicing or expressing these MLOLs. Please feel free to adjust them to suit your process. In the end, you will pass these new traits to others through your new and optimized outlook, actions, explanations, and responses, as well as how you live your life.

As you model better behaviors, set realistic goals, instill right intentions, provide appropriate care, and reduce perception-based traumas, you'll teach your children and others how to experience life authentically, think intelligently, conclude without biases, understand life's inevitabilities, acquire lasting internal resources for happiness, and intend success and well-being for all others. For these MLOLs to be optimally effective it may require adapting to cultural and language shifts. It is important to do so. So that together, we create a world that everyone can live in with joy, respect, and ease.

We are the ancestors of the future generations, and if you believe in rebirth, we may even be setting the stage for our return to a better life. I hope you are inspired to help our younger generations fulfill their human rights to learn these Mindful Life Optimization lessons well, so they may lead fulfilling lives and pass the lessons on to all generations to come.

A CASE STUDY: THE POSITIVE EFFECTS
OF MLO LESSONS & METHODOLOGY FOR MENTAL HEALTH

As an organizational psychologist, I am trained to work with cognitive and behavioral improvement in the corporate business world. My other certifications, training, and deep exploration of the human psyche enable me not only to help teams and executives but also to see individual clients. My holistic approach to addressing and resolving problems in life applies to a variety of personal development and relationship issues. Some come to find themselves and set out on a spiritual path to better understand and function in the world. Others want to fine-tune their roles in life, such as communicating with their spouses or teens more effectively. Some come with a victim mentality: their troubles are always someone else's fault, yet they can't free themselves from that person. Some people are more challenging to retrain, as their programming includes sensitive triggers that were created by attachment traumas and other unfortunate life experiences. This programming can make people so reactive that they run every time they feel uncomfortable. So I have learned to be even more thoughtful and individualize my work for each client.

There are those so deluded in how they perceive themselves that they won't even entertain the idea that they need to change anything. They continue creating suffering for others and are not able or willing to see their part in it. They seek help just to appease someone else. An example of this might be someone who suffers from a narcissistic personality disorder. For this type (with a true sense of compassion and not judgment, knowing that it's not easy to be human and that everyone is the result of his or her programming), I've learned how to get in and work with their minds with ease and gentle intelligence. Here is an example, which uses my general approach.

George (name changed), upon walking into our first session,

announced that he had been diagnosed as a narcissist and that nothing I could say would change that. That was interesting. I said, "OK, then we have nothing to talk about."

He laughed and said he had to get help, or he'd lose his beautiful wife. I announced that I was not a clinical psychologist— I couldn't diagnose him, nor would my methods follow traditional therapy or clinical treatments. He was delighted to hear that and responded that he was there not for therapy but because I was highly recommended for my method.

I had some knowledge that people with narcissistic personality disorders have excessive admiration for and interest in themselves, and their every choice or action is to benefit themselves and to preserve the image of being exceptional. For this image to be guarded and upheld, they choose relationships with people who are codependents or people who have what Ross Rosenberg, author of *The Human Magnet Syndrome, calls self-love deficit disorder (SLDD).* Technically there are several types of Narcissistic Personality Disorders (NPDs). Generally, I knew several characteristics to watch out for: narcissists believe that every relationship's purpose is to cater and benefit them. They know how to lure a person of interest with praise, kindness, giving, or whatever the person needs. They don't take criticism well. In conflict, they wholeheartedly believe they have no faults. They become skilled in defending their actions and convincing the person with self-love deficit disorder that his or her complaint is invalid and that he or she is the one at fault.

Some therapists claim it is almost impossible for narcissists to change, but I believe there are a few lessons they can learn to help alleviate their relationship issues. Having sought education about this for my own personal relationship issues, I've learned that their self-image codes are linked to their survival codes. A challenge to their self-image of perfection seems like an attempt to take them down. If you tell them they are wrong or that their actions are harmful, you will get nowhere. That idea would be the death of their egos, and they will not entertain it. That is their nonnegotiable code, which has trapped them in the SMADE stuck model. From this perspective, people with a narcissistic personality disorder suffer from being deeply stuck in delusion, clinging, and aversion. The pain of being wrong is unbearable, and with any attempt to criticize or correct them, they will see you as the enemy or as dumb, useless, and to be discarded. They'll easily abandon you.

In the safety of our sessions, George explained that when someone challenged him, the shame of mattering less to the world filled him with anxiety, rage, and defensiveness, triggering his nervous system to fight back. He would snap and be impatient. This was to reclaim the self-worth he perceived he had lost or never formed as a child. I saw that helping George to develop his HQ was the key to authentic self-worth and compassion for his wife. But it had to happen indirectly. So I teased out his thoughts about other people he spoke of in his stories. For example, when he mentioned a colleague who had issues with her partner, I casually asked what he thought of his colleague's sadness due to her partner's hurtful behavior. When he felt sympathetic, he was able to draw an insight into his similar behaviors toward his wife. This indirect style nourished his understanding for his wife without making him feel blamed or targeted.

Then I moved even further from topics that defended his wife or could otherwise have triggered a threat to his self-image. I transitioned to a different topic from the two other domains of mindful life intelligence. After all, most people were missing some of these MLOLs. To develop his HQ, I described the example of bugs and how they run away at the slightest inkling of danger. I emphasized that their lives matter to them and that they were born not to annoy or disturb us but to live their lives and do their duty in life—which is important in keeping our ecosystems healthy so we can grow food and eat. He didn't expect these topics and was intrigued.

I talked about natural laws, such as how dependent and interdependent we all are with one another and everything around us and how harming anything causes disruption in our systems, including our family and work systems. For example, I said, "Think of the different roles and responsibilities your wife plays in your marriage. If she were to feel threatened or dismissed, she couldn't fulfill her roles properly, and it would negatively impact everyone and everything in the ecosystem that you live in." He listened to this, from the bugs being responsible for our food to his wife showing up for her role in their marriage with ease and safety, as if listening to a loving aunt tell him a story.

What transpired were incremental refinements in his overall outlook and engagement with life in general. As I brought in different MLOLs, he became less self-centered and defensive. (In addition, a side benefit emerged: Though I never directly asked him not to kill a bug, he came back and reported that he had more respect for bugs, let them be, and didn't kill or hate them as much.) He reported that when he became upset or felt selfish, he thought of his family's ecosystem and how he didn't want to disrupt things. He felt proud of himself for doing so.

George also needed some skills to self-regulate his emotions and understand a different way of loving himself that didn't harm others. So I taught him how to be mindful. I gave him short meditations to connect with himself through his breath and other senses. What I had to teach him never threatened his ego. We never talked about narcissism or anything that would single him or his wife out. He was surprised that he wanted to come back to learn more and even heal more. He began talking about his father, who was never happy with him. Unpacking those thoughts and feelings, he felt the confidence to approach his father with less anticipation and more care.

Gradually, George recognized that he could be treated with more respect and harmony when he was more considerate. Being nasty to others took a lot out of his health too. At a relatively young age, he had high blood pressure and was at risk of a heart attack. His blood pressure gradually stabilized over the course of our sessions as he learned how to calm himself and not react as intensely.

I've had other cases in which participants gauged their blood pressure during their time in my mindfulness classes and saw a drastic balancing, just from adjusting their perception of life and doing some light meditation and mindful-living practices.

Some of the Mindful Life Optimization trainings I did with George also included his becoming mindful of his body, his breath, and his moods and thoughts, meditating in various postures, such as while sitting and while walking; noticing how he planted his feet as he walked; being mindful of the foods he ate and reflecting on how the food was prepared and where the resources came from; and imagining the universe (a chain of interdependence) that served him. Once, he reported that hangry (hungry and angry) George wasn't there at the restaurant where he'd eaten the previous night. He explained that the food had been delayed, and everyone had been anxious that he would say something rude to the waiter, but George had sat there enjoying a kind conversation with the waiter and even had expressed his appreciation. He laughed as he recounted a friend's comment: "Who is this, and what have you done with George?"

Simultaneously, I taught his wife how to increase her self-love and decrease her tendency to be judgmental, and I encouraged her to honor her husband's strengths and gifts (while I worked on building more noble qualities in her husband). Over the course of a year, the three of us gently and deliberately decoded and redesigned a healthier sense of self for both of them. Mindfully optimizing their lives by infusing these and many other MLOLs and skills proved transformational, even for a person with NPD. It became a conduit for reducing the suffering in their lives and those they affected.

FINAL THOUGHTS

WHAT ABOUT THE ORPHANS?

As far back as I can remember, I have seen children in my dreams, sometimes several nights in a row. They come in all ages, from a day old to ten or eleven years old. I always thought they represented my own children, especially after I lost my youngest one to fentanyl. I asked a therapist friend about the significance of these dreams. She said that a child in dreams may signify a sense of responsibility. They kept occurring, and I really wanted to know why.

On one of my yearly silent retreats, I had two vivid dreams of children. One child was wrapped in a blanket, burning up with fever, and her mother wasn't concerned. The other was a boy with a long black ponytail, who woke me up by imitating the sound of the 4:30 a.m. bell for meditation. This time, I became even more curious. It seemed like a wakeup call to something.

I asked myself, *What am I supposed to wake up to?*

The retreat was a perfect place to clear all distractions, connect deeply, and ask the universe — or the spirits of these children — what they wanted me to do. Maybe I had abandoned a child in a past life, and these children showed up with a request for me to make amends or save some child. But they never asked me for anything or created any uncomfortable feelings. It was more as if I were watching them, and I deeply felt them.

I had nothing but peace, open space, and time to reflect. During walking meditation time, I walked, deeply absorbed in meditation, with my mind empty and well connected to my body. All of my senses were awake and receptive. As I walked mindfully, a thought occurred to me about this book and what I'm asking people to do: *I do all this meditation on retreat after retreat. I clear my mind and heart and develop compassion and wisdom so I can do what I'm asking them to do. But how will others transform without making such efforts? By just reading this book?*

Concerned and filled with compassion, not even thinking about children, I walked. I found myself under a massive maple tree as a sudden, tsunami-sized feeling overtook my mind and heart. I had an instant insight: *The MLO school I'm trying to build should be an orphanage!*

It all made sense. Thoughts went through my mind like a strategic plan with a clear vision: *Orphans' lives are open to better chances than those of children who learn an MLOL at school but have home environments that don't accommodate the right conditions for them to grow and develop in mindful life intelligence. At an orphanage where the conditions are right, they can excel in understanding life, its flow, its challenges, and their own emotions. They can learn how to navigate natural systems, be authentic, and remain connected to the world without getting confused by contradictory choices and behaviors they see at home. We can teach them from day one how to trust life and be part of it, not fear it or exploit it. We can teach them how to be kind, understand inherent biases, be supportive to others, and, most importantly, be loving toward themselves. They'll learn to be in tune with nature and Mother Earth.*

My mind couldn't stop seeing all the possibilities and the ways they could learn to live with ease. Those thoughts flowed like a waterfall into stillness.

As I shared this vision with others, many felt touched and loved the idea. Some warned me about the difficulties of managing orphans, who come with complex psychological issues, such as being abandoned by mothers whose addictions have adversely affected them. However, I see only a new generation highly skilled in life intelligence and optimally wired in all three life intelligent domains. Even those with mental illnesses can be transformed and given a chance to thrive in reality. It will be a new day for anyone born and released into the universe through this care. They, like the rest of us, come into this world without prior knowledge of how to be human. It is their right to receive an optimized operating manual right from the beginning.

This is the core of human rights we are advocating for: When first learning to stand, infants are gently guided to place their feet on the ground, to breathe, and to feel the ground's solidity and stability — to build trust that the earth will hold them. The adult caretaker breathes softly and looks into their eyes, smiling and showing them how to stand firmly. As the little humans stand, the caretaker touches the ground: "Earth. Earth is here to hold you. Wherever you go, the earth is there. You can count on it! Here — feel it with your foot. It's firm. It's strong." The little ones can feel the earth's solidness for themselves by taking one step and then the next and the next, feeling held not only by humans but also by nature. Instead of developing insecure attachment and mistrust and anxiety or clinging to parents who may not always be there, they learn to become reliant on what they can always count on, nature.

They will be taught that they are nature and made of all that is natural and that the water that becomes the clouds, rains to form rivers, flows into oceans, and moves into the sky as clouds again is the water in their urine and saliva. They'll learn they have the right to consume the earth's water, which is freely offered by Mother Earth. Food is provided by Mother Earth, and we have the privilege and right to eat it; there is an abundance of it, and each of us plays an important role in supporting one another. They'll learn what ecosystems are and how they feed us and how humans create systems to get our food and other necessities to us. They'll understand that we must strive not to exploit these resources, both natural and constructed systems, so the earth can replenish itself. They'll learn about their emotions and innate biases and how to question and verify what they can for themselves. And while living a modern life among other humans, using digitalization and other advancements, they'll do so with care, confidence, and respect.

Research indicates that by the year 2050, the human population will reach ten billion, making it very difficult to feed and sustain healthy lives. This generation will learn to be self-sufficient and not wasteful, needless stuff, and plant and forage safe foods and medicinal plants for their consumption, reducing their burden on governing systems.

With MLO lessons such as these, we can increase the sense of secure attachment and happiness in children so they can grow up trusting that all is well.

You, my dear reader, can be part of this wholesome intention, approach, and legacy. I would love to know your thoughts about opening a Mindful Life Optimization orphanage or at least bringing these lessons to existing places to help children grow up without stress and anxiety and learn to live with compassion, joy, and contentment. Of course, all children should learn these lessons. Please send your ideas and interests for collaboration by writing to http://drmotaghy.com.

Thank you for reading and for your dedication to your well-being and that of others in our world.

SMADE Self-Assessment

Use the following questions to rate yourself.

#	Stuck Statements	Never 0	Sometimes 3	Often 6	Always 9
1	When I feel anxious, worried, sad, or angry, I get caught up in thinking about all the things others have done to make me				
2	When someone offers to help me, I refuse or ignore the offer, and later, I feel no one cares				
3	When others say something I don't believe in or don't like, I argue with them or resist seeing				
4	I don't like conflict and avoid it at any cost.				
5	I feel I don't get enough love—I feel lonely.				
6	I believe I am the way I am and will not change. Others have to accept me the way I am.				
7	When others wrong me, I react harshly or stop speaking with them to show them how it				
8	I prefer to pretend I am doing great than to show that I need				
9	I yearn for or fantasize about someone doing something fantastic for me.				
10	No matter how much I try or do, I don't feel I'm good				
11	I feel like a failure, either in general or in some specific				
	Please add up your score under each value.				

Answer Key

Total Possible	0–25	26–50	51–75	76–99
Degree of Being Stuck	Stuck in minor ways	Stuck in more obvious ways	Stuck in major ways	Severely stuck in multiple ways

GLOSSARY OF TERMS

Accountability: The ability to account for one's own thoughts, feelings, choices, actions, and results, as well as the impact of those results on oneself and all others. It extends to the ability to make things right. It requires learning self-awareness, mindfulness, and the other folds in the Noble Eightfold Path.

Authentic Agreements: The four steps of making boundaries effective.

awareness: Having knowledge or consciousness of the presence of either internal experiences or external events.

clinging: Holding on to the desire for an idea to be true. Attachment to objects, money, relationships, feelings, fantasies, or anything else too tightly. It causes tension within the mind, muddies our intentions, and can lead to unskillful actions.

compassion: Not only being able to feel the pain of another or oneself but also being moved to alleviate that pain. It's a warm understanding of failure, based on the knowledge that all human beings are products of their learning and growing. It's an antidote to harsh judgments.

Compassion Intelligence: Knowing that compassion is an appropriate attitude and that lacking compassion in interactions and relationships leads to conflict, disharmony, and separation. It results in increased patience, goodwill, care, peacefulness, and resolution.

Confirmation Bias: The brain and mind's tendency to validate whatever information would confirm the person's existing

beliefs. It keeps people rigid and lacking in interest toward alternative views.

debugging, or decoding: Teasing out false mental views and faulty programming to reveal the thoughts, beliefs, and responses that are misaligned and create suffering.

delusion: An inability to see reality and the causes of suffering (the opposite of wise view).

doubt: When thought is rooted in confusion and doubting oneself, one's ability, the teachings, the process, the goal, or the direction.

Dependency: The concept, or reality, that explains interdependence (i.e., every experience or event in life depends on another experience or event, and no one is truly independent).

dukkha: A Pali term that points to all forms of mental suffering, agony, agitation, harsh judgment, jealousy, envy, sorrow, nagging, and so on—anything that is a result of not accepting the nature of truth, clinging to something, resisting, or hating. It is the discontent that arises from not seeing things clearly as they are.

ecosystem: A community of plants, animals, and other beings that live within a specific environment and support one another as a unit. One ecosystem is the food chain, wherein one creature becomes food for another, no resources are wasted, and life continues naturally.

equanimity: A Buddhist term that describes mental stability even in the face of difficulty. It's a peacefulness that comes from accepting change and impermanence, not reacting to unpleasant and painful situations, and understanding the impersonal nature of natural laws and patterns. It leads to and from living wisely and not harmful.

focused awareness: Being concentrated on an object in meditation or while doing a task in daily life.

Four Noble Truths: The Buddha's teachings on how to recognize suffering, the causes of suffering and how to end them, and the path and practice to live a fulfilling life.

generosity: Aside from giving gifts, it's letting go of anything one has been clinging to, especially one's opinions and views of oneself, others, and the world. Generosity defuses truth bias.

Heart Intelligence (HQ): A set of mature, cultivated, superior emotions that help humans to resolve discontentment and integrate with life fully and completely. It is synonymous with the Buddha's teachings of the four Bramaviharas (loving- kindness, compassion, sympathetic joy, and equanimity). Through practice and implementation, HQ and the Noble Eightfold Path are mega powers that will create beneficial results for humanity and our planet.

happiness: A state of peaceful contentment, steadiness, and joy that arises in the absence of suffering (aversion, greed, and delusion).

Human Software: A combination of unique codes, or programming, that represents a person's unique perspectives, qualities, and skills that become his or her personality. It's the inner blueprint used to navigate both mundane daily routines and complex functions of analysis, choice-making, creativity, visioning, and so forth.

Human Software Optimization (HSO): The five stages of training to optimize one's template of life or human software: (1) Mindful Life Optimization lessons (MLOLs), (2) mindful authentication, (3) development, (4) transformation, and (5) optimization.

ignorance: A misunderstanding, mildly put. It's an obscuration, the root cause of all suffering—a deep-seated misconception about what is real. Ignorance arises from gaps in learning, false information, wrong perspectives, ego fabrications created by need for survival, and the five obstacles to inner peace and happiness. Ignorance is the same as delusion.

inner development: Cultivating and embodying essential principles, qualities, and inner resources that help us to become more resilient, emotionally, and spiritually mature, and effective beings.

Inner Development Goals (IDGs): Areas of inner development determined by scientists to be necessary qualities and skills for humanity to develop (via each individual human) so that we can live sustainably and change the planet's route to destruction. The five categories of IDGs are being, thinking, relating, collaborating, and acting.

inner obstacles to happiness: The five obstacles of clinging, aversion, restlessness, lethargy, and doubt.

intelligent mental actions (Wise effort): Synonymous with wise effort, the sixth fold in the Buddha's teachings in the Noble Eightfold Path. Intelligent mental actions include realizing that concepts precede choices and behaviors, hence arousing interest, determination, responsibility, and desire to prevent false notions and harmful thoughts, as well as developing a moral outlook for responsibility and interdependence.

interdependence: An unavoidable, unstoppable chain of connections and reliance among all things and beings.

investigative awareness: The third type of awareness described by Diana Winston in *The Little Book of Awareness*. It refers to observing a personal experience; identifying it; delineating its various parts; and seeing its impact on one's mood, body, or mind.

judgment: A harsh criticism that lacks compassion or the understanding that it's not easy to be human.

karma: Action undertaken with intention that results in consequences one cannot be separated from. It is based on a complex web of interwoven actions and intentions of the past, which makes it difficult to know the origin of a given consequence. But positive actions and intentions can positively affect the negative consequences from past harmful actions, so with wise intention and the rest of the Noble Eightfold Path, one can reduce or altogether eliminate one's suffering.

Mindful Life Optimization lessons (MLOLs): Individual lessons from each of the three domains of mindful life intelligence.

mind: The space for conscious computing, analyzing, imagining, seeing, creating, interpreting, concluding, or switching from one thought or image to another. A space where all our mental experiences, including our moods and attitudes, are cognized, understood, or storyized.

mindfulness: Both a quality of mind and a practice to develop this quality. It involves being aware of what goes on in one's mind, how the body feels, and how emotions change; seeing the truths of impermanence; and, most importantly, having an interest and will to consistently create harmony within oneself and the world.

mindful authentication: Stage 2 of the Human Software Optimization model—verifying a given life lesson through personal experience and validation.

mind viruses: Mental contaminants that are carried from person to person like memes, causing unhappiness, judgment, worry, anxiety, tension, clinging, and so on. Mind viruses culminate in deep personal and societal discontent and delusion.

natural awareness: Being at peace in a restful state. While the body may be in action, the mind is present, content, steady, and empty of any agenda that is not about the present moment.

Noble Eightfold Path: The path and guidance taught by the Buddha, comprising eight folds, or factors, for living harmonious, wise lives.

not-self: The Buddha's teaching that says whatever we think is the representation of ourselves is not. What we experience is either one or a combination of these five aggregates: body or form, feelings, perceptions, mental formations, and consciousness. They are not-self because they change all the time and dissolve, and by clinging to them, we suffer.

Novelty Bias: New and novel things tend to capture our brains, minds, and attention, regardless of their usefulness or truthfulness.

Optimization (fifth stage): Having transformed one's ways of thinking and lifestyle in the three domains of mindful life intelligence (natural laws and constructed systems; our planet and sustainable living; and human experience, conduct, and happiness), one enjoys optimized human software.

regenerative design: Design that utilizes energy wisely through whole-system thinking and resilient systems and products that consider the needs of society and the integrity of nature.

Self-awareness: Being present to one's inner experiences, needs, desires, feelings, thoughts, choices, beliefs, physical sensations, and external results.

self-love deficit disorder (SLDD): Ross Rosenberg's term for an inability to love ourselves sufficiently as the cause of relationship issues between codependents and narcissists.

social reality: Concepts, beliefs, agreements, and lifestyles that are constructed by humans and become widely accepted and shared through communication, memes, rules, and interactions with one another.

SMADE stuck model: The five stages of how one ends up stuck in unhappiness. Badly transferred, wrong, or missing information received through the senses becomes false meanings and faulty interpretations, which become an adaptation of strategies to life and ineffective habits, which become one's disposition, or default personality. The person then ends up engulfed or stuck in causing and suffering from problems and issues.

source intelligence: Nature's generosity and equanimity. Cultivating source intelligence helps us to see the limitations of our egoic viewpoints and the reality of not-self. Having successfully resolved the attachments to our fabricated sense of self, source intelligence will bond us to pure equanimity and oneness.

storyize: To make up perceived stories about an experience and believe them to be true.

stuck: Being trapped in feelings of dissatisfaction, agitation, fear, worry, or grief and in cycles of wrong decisions that create harmful conditions. We become stuck when we don't have a clear path to work toward freedom and fulfillment.

sympathetic joy: Feeling joy for the joy of another. Cultivating this HQ will amplify opportunities for experiencing joy.

Three Domains of Mindful Life Intelligence: A combination of knowledge and skills necessary for every human to understand

and develop, categorized under three domains: (1) natural and constructed systems; (2) our planet and sustainable living; and (3) human experience, conduct, and happiness.

transformation: Stage 4 of Human Software Optimization. To live life with new, effective, wise traits effortlessly but with a road map to return to the path of truth when we veer off.

Transdisciplinary: A research strategy that involves collaboration of nonacademic and nonscientific stakeholders with experts and scientists from various sectors to gain knowledge and insight from all sources.

Truth Bias: The brain's inherent mechanism to accept or believe anything as the truth without requiring validation. This is the issue behind all biases.

wise actions: Actions that are well thought out, embody wise understanding and wise intention, and have beneficial karmic outcomes.

wise concentration: The settling of the mind, body, heart, and soul through the application of all the folds in the Noble Eightfold Path. It consists of clarity, goodwill, compassion, and generosity at the highest level, leading to a complete sense of peace within.

wise effort: Being determined and passionate to protect the mind from agitation, clinging, and delusion; uprooting those harmful mental activities; engaging in goodwill and generosity; and nourishing a sense of well-being for oneself and the world.

wise intention: The intention to not harm; to have unconditional goodwill for all, regardless of whether they deserve it; and to release all that we cling to.

wise livelihood: Any means of work that is beneficial, is done with integrity, and harms no being.

wise mindfulness: The act of being present, aware, alert, and engaged in the goal to produce goodness and well-being for oneself and the world.

wise speech: The ability to communicate truthfully and peacefully with care and kindness. The intention is to avoid divisive speech, slander, idle chatter, and hurtful words.

wise view: Seeing the nature of things as they are and knowing the Four Noble Truths.

LIST OF MLOLs

*For extended explanations and added MLOLs check out Dr. Motaghy's newer publications.

BIBLIOGRAPHY AND RESOURCES

BOOKS REFERENCED HERE

Barrett, Lisa Feldman. *How Emotions Are Made: The Secret Life of the Brain*. Mariner Books, 2018.

Barrett, Lisa Feldman. *Seven and a Half Lessons About the Brain*. Mariner Books, 2021.

Bhikkhu, Thānissaro. *The Karma of Mindfulness*. Metta Forest Monastery, 2015.

Bhikkhu, Thānissaro. *The Noble Eightfold Path*. Metta Forest Monastery, 2015.

Bhikkhu, Thānissaro. *Right Mindfulness*. Metta Forest Monastery, 2012.

Brodie, Richard. *Virus of the Mind: The New Science of the Memes*. Hay House, 2009.

Campbell, Joseph. *The Hero with a Thousand Faces*. New World Library, 2008.

Campbell, Joseph. *The Hero's Journey*. Edited by Phil Cousineau. New World Library, 2014.

Clear, James. *Atomic Habits*. Avery, 2018.

Einstein, Albert. *The World as I See It*. Citadel, 2006.

Friedman, Milton. *Capitalism and Freedom*. University of Chicago Press, 2020.

Grant, Adam. *Hidden Potential*. Viking, 2023.

Hawkins, David R. *Power vs. Force*. Hay House, 2014.

Hedrick, Larry, ed. *Xenophon's Cyrus the Great: The Arts of Leadership and War*. St. Martin's Griffin, 2007.

Helminski, Camille. *Jewels of Remembrance: A Daybook of Spiritual Guidance Containing 365 Selections from the Wisdom of Rumi.* Shambhala, 2000.

Hougaard, Rasmus, and Jacqueline Carter. *The Mind of the Leader: How to Lead Yourself, Your People, and Your Organization for Extraordinary Results.* Harvard Business Review, 2018.

Jayasaro, Ajahn. *On Love.* Panyaprateep Foundation, 2010

Louv, Richard. *The Nature Principle: Human Restoration and the End of Nature-Deficit Disorder.* Algonquin Books, 2012.

Maté, Gabor. *When the Body Says No: Understanding the Stress-Disease Connection.* Wiley, 2003.

Moffitt, Phillip. *Dancing with Life: Buddhist Insights for Finding Meaning and Joy in the Face of Suffering.* Rodale Books, 2012.

Pasanno, Ajahn, and Ajahn Amaro. *The Island: An Anthology of the Buddha's Teachings on Nibbana.* Abhayagiri Buddhist Monastery, 2022.

Payutto, P. A. Buddhadhamma: *The Laws of Nature and Their Benefits to Life.* 4th ed. Translated by Robin Moore. Buddhadhamma Foundation, 2021.

Rath, Tom. *Strengths Finder 2.0.* Gallup, 2007.

Rosenberg, Ross. *The Human Magnet Syndrome: The Codependent Narcissist Trap.* Create Space, 2018.

Schmidt, Amy. Dipa Ma: *The Life and Legacy of a Buddhist Master.* Blue Bridge, 2005.

Sucitto, Ajahn. *Buddha-Nature, Human Nature.* Amaravati, 2019.

Sucitto, Ajahn. *Kamma and the End of Kamma.* 2nd ed. Amaravati, 2021.

Sumedho, Ajahn. *The Four Noble Truths.* Amaravati, 2014.

Thaler, Richard, and Cass Sunstein. *Nudge: Improving Decisions About Money, Health, and the Environment.* Penguin, 2009.

Winston, Diana. *The Little Book of Being; Practices and Guidance for Uncovering Your Natural Awareness.* Sounds True, 2019.

ADDITIONAL BOOKS RECOMMENDED

Bhikkhu, Thānissaro. *Buddhist Romanticism*. Metta Forest Monastery, 2015.

Mc Garey, Gladys. *The Well-Lived Life: A 102-Year-Old Doctor's Six Secrets to Health and Happiness at Any Age*. Atria Books, 2023.

Samuel, Mark, and Sophie Chiche. *The Power of Personal Accountability*. Xephor, 2004.

DOCUMENTARIES

Clay, Jon, dir. *Breaking Boundaries: The Science of Our Planet*. Netflix, 2021.

Efron, Zac, and Darin Olien. *Down to Earth with Zac Efron*. Netflix, 2020.

Nixon, Robert, and Fisher Stevens, dirs. *Mission Blue*. Netflix, 2014. Psihoyos, Louie, dir. *You Are What You Eat*. Netflix, 2024. Solomon, Patrick Takaya, dir. *Finding Joe*. Pat & Pat, 2011.

EDUCATIONAL INSTITUTIONS

California State University of Channel Islands (CSUCI)

Mindfulness Awareness Research Center (MARC), UCLA Mindful, University of California, Los Angeles

Mindful NYU, New York University

Phillips Graduate University (PGU), Los Angeles Education Center of Campbellsville University

ENVIRONMENTAL INFORMATION

Bhargava, Ruma, and Megha Bhargava. "The Climate Crisis Disproportionately Hits the Poor. How Can We Protect Them?"

World Economic Forum, January 13, 2023. https://weforum.org/stories/2023/01/climate-crisis-poor-davos2023/

Biomimicry Institute. "What Is Biomimicry?" https://biomimicry.org/what-is-biomimicry.

Breau, Amy. "Are Cockroaches Actually Useful?" *Moment of Science*, Indiana Public Media, March 14, 2013. https://indianapublicmedia.org/amomentofscience/cockroaches_useful.php.

CLEAR (Clarity and Leadership for Environmental Awareness and Research) Center. "Why Methane from Cattle Warms the Climate Differently from CO2 from Fossil Fuels." University of California, Davis, July 7, 2020. https://clear.ucdavis.edu/explainers/ why-methane-cattle-warms-climate-differently-co2-fossil-fuels.

Farquhar, Brodie. "Wolf Reintroduction Changes Ecosystem in Yellowstone." Yellowstone Park. Updated June 22, 2023. https://yellowstonepark.com/things-to-do/wildlife/wolf-reintroduction-changes-ecosystem.

Law, Matthew A. "Mindful Leadership and Climate Action." *Mindfulness Studies Theses 90* (2024). https://core.ac.uk/download/596381807.pdf. Los Angeles County Department of Consumer and Business Affairs. "False Advertising." Updated April 14, 2011. https://dcba.lacounty.gov/portfolio/false-advertising.

McVeigh, Karen. "Small Island Nations Take High-Emitting Countries to Court to Protect the Ocean." *Guardian*, September 10, 2023. https://theguardian.com/environment/2023/sep/10/small-island-nations-take-high-emitting-countries-to-court-to-protect-the-ocean

NASA. "Our Sun: Facts." https://solarsystem.nasa.gov/solar-system/sun/in-depth.

National Geographic Society. "The Role of Scavengers: Carcass Crunching." *National Geographic*. Updated October 19, 2023. https://education.nationalgeographic.org/resource/role-scavengers-carcass-crunching.

Nature Conservancy. "Eight Ways to Reduce Waste." Updated August 22, 2022. https://nature.org/en-us/about-us/where-we-work/united-states/delaware/stories-in-delaware/delaware-eight-ways-to-reduce-waste.

Our Children's Trust. *"Juliana v. United States."* https://ourchildrenstrust.org/juliana-v-us.

Planet Positive 2030. *Strong Sustainability by Design: Global Methodologies.* IEEE Standards Association, 2023. https://sagroups. Ieee.org/planetpositive2030/wp-content/uploads/sites/541/2023/07/04 Methodologies_SSBD_v1_07.11.23-final.pdf.

Prete, Giovanni. "Tuvalu's Sinking Reality: How Climate Change Is Threatening the Small Island Nation." Earth.org, January 29, 2024. https://earth.org/tuvalus-sinking-reality-how-climate-change-is- threatening-a-small-island-nation/.

Schumpeter. "Generative AI Has a Clean-Energy Problem." *Economist,* April 11, 2024. https://economist.com/business/2024/04/11/ generative-ai-has-a-clean-energy-problem.

Stockholm Resilience Center. "Planetary Boundaries — An Update." Stockholm University. https://stockholmresilience.org/ research/planetary-boundaries.html.

Toyota Environmental Sustainability. "Contributions to the UN Sustainable Development Goals." https://toyota.com/usa/ environmentalsustainability/contributions-to-the-un-sdgs.

Toyota Environmental Sustainability. "Our Goal of Battery Ecosystem Circularity." https://toyota.com/usa/environmentalsustainability/ materials/our-goal-of-battery-ecosystem-circularity.

Toyota Europe. "Circularity: Building a Circular Economy." https://toyota-europe.com/sustainability/circularity.

US Climate Resilience Toolkit. "Ecosystems." Updated April 17, 2024. https://toolkit.climate.gov/topics/ecosystems.

USDA Economic Research Service. "Cattle and Beef: Sector at a Glance." Updated August 30, 2023. https://ers.usda.gov/ topics/animal-products/cattle-beef/sector-at-a-glance/.

Web MD. "What to Know About Cockroaches and Your Health." January 17, 2024. https://webmd.com/a-to-z-guides/what-to-know- cockroaches-health

Wikimedia Foundation. "Regenerative Design." *Wikipedia.* https:// en.wikipedia.org/wiki/Regenerative design.

Wikimedia Foundation. "Transdisciplinarity." *Wikipedia.*
https:// en.wikipedia.org/wiki/Transdisciplinarity.

Yau, Kam. "The Rollie-Pollie." *Earth Matter,* Summer–Fall 2016.
https://earthmatter.org/summer-fall-2016-the-rollie-pollie.

HUMAN LIFE

American Psychological Association. "Resilience." https://apa.org/
topics/resilience.

Browning, Elizabeth Barrett. "How Do I Love Thee? (Sonnet 43)." 1850.
https://poets.org/poem/how-do-i-love-thee-sonnet-43.

Dean, Ben. "Wisdom." *Authentic Happiness Coaching Newsletters.*
https://authentichappiness.sas.upenn.edu/newsletters/authentic
happinesscoaching/wisdom.

Dodson, William. "Secrets of Your ADHD Brain." *ADDitude.* Updated
November 1, 2024. https://additudemag.com/secrets-of-the-
adhd-brain. Ford, Donna Y. *Intelligence Testing and Cultural
Diversity: Concerns, Cautions, and Considerations.* National Research
Center on the Gifted and Talented, 2004.
https://nrcgt.uconn.edu/wp-content/
uploads/sites/953/2015/04/rm04204.pdf.

Grant, Adam. "11 Little Habits of Successful People." CNBC, November
3, 2023. https://cnbc.com/2023/11/03/highly-successful-people-
practice-these-11-little-life-changes-every-day-says-psychology-
expert.

Heart Math Institute. "Heart Intelligence." August 7, 2012. https://
heartmath.org/articles-of-the-heart/the-math-of-heartmath/
heart-intelligence/.

Hollington-Sawyer, Stephanie. "Are You Too Liberal or Conservative
with Your Anger?"

Dr. Gabor Maté (blog), June 15, 2005.
https://drgabormate.com/liberal-conservative-anger/.

IDG Foundation. "Framework." Inner Development Goals. https://
innerdevelopmentgoals.org/framework.

Ingenia. "The Earliest Declaration of Human Rights." September 29,
2022. https://Ingeniahistory.com/post/cyrus-cylinder.

Jayasaro, Ajahn. *On Love.* Aksron Sampan, 2010. https://perfectlyhere.
org/wp-content/uploads/2024/07/On-Love-Ajahn-Jayasaro.pdf.

Jha, Amishi. "How Your Brain Falls for the Wrong Ideas." *Mindful*, July 8, 2021. https://mindful.org/what-brain-science-tells-us-about-how-to-win-the-battle-against-false-narratives-and-divisiveness-2/.

Maté, Gabor, and Jay Shetty. "The Root Cause of Trauma & Why You Feel Lost in Life." *Jay Shetty Podcast*. YouTube, October 24, 2022. https://youtube.com/watch?v=OTQ Jmk XC2EI.

McIntosh, Peggy. "White Privilege: Unpacking the Invisible Knapsack." *Peace and Freedom Magazine*, July–August 1989. https://pcc.edu/illumination/wp-content/uploads/sites/54/2018/05/white-privilege-essay-mcintosh.pdf.

Pappas, Stephanie. "More Than 20% of Teens Have Seriously Considered Suicide. Psychologists and Communities Can Help Tackle the Problem. "*Monitor on Psychology* 54, no. 5 (July 1, 2023). https://apa.org/monitor/2023/07/psychologists-preventing-teen-suicide.

Psychology Today. "Bias." https://psychologytoday.com/us/basics/bias.

Raszek, M. "Genetics of Love." *Merogenomics Blog*, September 2, 2020. https://merogenomics.ca/blog/en/100/Genetics_of_love.

Sternberg, Robert J. "A Triangular Theory of Love. "*Psychological Review* 93, no. 2 (1986): 119–35. https://psycnet.apa.org/record/1986-21992-001.

Weinstein, Jack Russell. "Adam Smith (1723 – 1790)." *Internet Encyclopedia of Philosophy.* https://iep.utm.edu/smith/#SH2a.

Wikimedia Foundation. "2500-Year Celebration of the Persian Empire." *Wikipedia.* https://en.wikipedia.org/wiki/2,500-year_celebration_of_the_Persian_Empire.

Wikimedia Foundation. "Alfred Binet." *Wikipedia.* https://en.wikipedia.org/wiki/Alfred_Binet.

Wikimedia Foundation. "Virus of the Mind." *Wikipedia.* https://en.wikipedia.org/wiki/Virus_of_the_Mind.

Wikimedia Foundation. "White Revolution." *Wikipedia.* https://en.wikipedia.org/wiki/White Revolution.

Wikimedia Foundation. "Zoroastrianism." *Wikipedia.* https://en.wikipedia.org/wiki/Zoroastrianism.

ORGANIZATIONS

B Lab: Make Business a Force for Good: https://bcorporation.net/en-us For Humanity (works on issues of AI, finding solutions and regulations): https://forhumanity.center/

Imperative 21 (works globally toward economic justice): https://imperative21.co

Institute of Electrical and Electronics Engineers (IEEE) — Planet Positive 2030 study:
https://sagroups.ieee.org/2023/11/14/climate-change-planetpositive2030/and-human-algorithms-the-role-of-mindfulness-in- planet-positive-2030

Morality and Knowledge of Artificial Intelligence (MKAI): https:// MKAI.org

Patagonia as a B Corporation: https://bcorporation.net/en-us/find-a-b-corp/company/patagonia-inc/

Stockholm Resilience Centre: https://stockholmresilience.org

United Nations' 17 Sustainable Development Goals:
https://un.org/en/exhibits/page/sdgs-17-goals-transform-world

Learning for Nature (courses and workshops): https://learning fornature.org/en

TEACHERS

Thānissaro Bhikkhu, teachings: https://forestsangha.org

Allan Booker, regenerative design:
https://globalearthrepairfoundation. org/alan-booker-holistic-design-and-permaculture

Ajahn Chah, Forest Tradition teachings and biography: https://ajahnchah.org

Ajahn Pasanno, teachings, biography, service, and recognition: https://en.wikipedia.org/wiki/Ajahn Pasanno

Diana Winston, Mindfulness author, speaker, educator: https://dianawinston.com/

Jeffrey Rutstein, psychologist: Https://drjeffreyrutstein.com

Kevin Volkin, PhD: https://ciapps.csuci.edu/Faculty Bios/ Faculty Biography/kevin.volkan

ACKNOWLEDGMENTS

I have acknowledged many people on the dedication page and throughout the book and have likely forgotten someone important to me and my journey. Please know that every single person who has crossed my path has had a role in the culmination of this book. Thank you for that.

I'd like to go back and thank my first-grade teacher, Mrs. Ahmadi; my first English-as-a-second-language teacher, Mrs. Rosario; my first psychology professor, Dr. Baker; and Dr. Volkin, my Asian Thoughts professor, and Daniel Davis who set me on a path to awakening. Other Buddhist teachers: ajahns Amaro, Yatiko, Sanyamo, Karuṇadhammo, Kusalo, Nyaniko, Cunda, and Sucitto, as well as many associated ajahns and Debbie Stamp, who have all had a profound, positive impact on my life and sense of well-being. To Diana Winston for guiding us to transfer the invaluable skills of awakening in a secular language. Many thanks to all the other instructors, mentors, colleagues (Monika Manolova, Marisa Zalabak, Matthew Law, Elizabeth Rothman, Diane Baxter, Markus Krebsz, Richard Foster-Fletcher, Eric Hansel, John C. Havens, Mila Aliana, Maike Luiken, Vincent McNeeley), and others who have had a deep influence on my understanding of life.

Many thanks to Richard Havenick who has enriched my knowledge and curiosity about the necessity of policies and the immense efforts that go into making any kind of change a norm for the betterment of humanity and our planet.

Lastly, I must give credit to my dear friend, Lou Maurer, who insisted on the name of this book. Thank you.

www.ingramcontent.com/pod-product-compliance
Lightning Source LLC
Chambersburg PA
CBHW030908120626
46554CB00001B/51